This book is dedicated to Peter Hamley,
who loved the sea so much and
taught me that Scuba diving should be fun.

◆ **FIELD GUIDE FOR MEDICAL TREATMENT** ◆

DANGEROUS
Marine Creatures

CARL EDMONDS, M.D.

BEST PUBLISHING COMPANY

Disclaimer

Although I have collected a great deal of information on injuries from marine animals, I am not responsible for their actions. Sometimes they are as unpredictable as humans.

Nor am I responsible for the errors of omission or commission in this book. Inaccuracies in grammar are due to my typiste and wife, Cynthia. Enid, my other secretary, added some spelling errors to this latest edition, and their persistence is an indictment of the computer spell-check. Errors of taxonomy are attributable to my old diving buddy, Clarrie Lawler, and his wife Fay. Proof reading inaccuracies are the responsibility of both this couple and my other diving buddy, Dr. Chris Lowry. Inadequacies in design and layout are due to the publishers, and problems with the quality of the print and the binding are contributed by the printers. Incorrect medical descriptions and treatments are the joint responsibility of my colleagues and my patients.

The jokes are mine alone, and I retain fully copyright on them.

Carl Edmonds

Second Edition - 1995

ISBN: 0-941332-39-X
Library of Congress Catalog Card Number: 93-079539

Composed, printed and bound in the United States of America.

Best Publishing Company
2355 North Steves Boulevard
P.O. Box 30100
Flagstaff, AZ 86003-0100 USA

Contents

Preface

This book will introduce the reader to many of the dangers of the marine environment—only one aspect of a mysterious and enticing ocean world. The attractions are many, and they vary from love of natural beauty through excitement and fear, to an obsession with destruction. The most dangerous marine animal is a diver with a spear gun. His accomplices include the fishing trawlers, the industrial polluters and to a lesser extent, the line fishermen. Together these soldiers of destruction have decimated large areas of our harbours and our reefs.

This text describes the injuries that can be inflicted on humans by marine animals. It needs to be balanced by an appreciation of the damage that humans do to marine animals. For every shark attack on man, humans consume 32,000 ton of shark and ray.

The desolation of our national undersea environment has been the corollary of civilisation, but this need not be so. Underwater national parklands, where divers and snorkellers may visit, photograph, admire and return, are obstructed by commercial and political interests. Most countries have not learnt from the experiences of southern California, where their Scripps Canyon is retained as a national heritage, nor from Florida where many reefs have been destroyed. The small Hanauma Bay Reserve in Oahu, Hawaii, is an appetising relic of the beauty that once existed around much of the island. The author remembers diving in the Port Jackson, Port Hacking and Pittwater areas of Sydney admiring marine life and scenery that are denied his children. Oases have become deserts, and most governments have every reason to be humble.

Adlai Stevenson, a few days before his death in 1965, introduced the concept of "Spaceship Earth." This was meant to depict our small planet as a very limited reservoir of both resources and space. It also implied that what we destroy may be lost forever, but our contamination must remain with us. On this planet, oceans make up 70% of the surface area, and until recently it had been presumed that this extensive reservoir could be used to buffer and absorb the land pollutants.

Over the last two decades there has been an awareness of the danger of polluting the waterways and seas with industrial wastes and chemicals, pesticides, radioactive materials, mercury and other toxic substances. These must bring, in their wake, a reprehensible and diverse array of dangers to those populations reliant on the seas for their existence. It is estimated, for example, that 20,000 tonnes of DDT is present in marine life, although it is not known whether this is likely to produce clinical manifestations in humans who consume the affected fish. PCB and dioxins are detected in the fresh water rivers and lakes—as well as the Baltic and Mediterranean seas.

The outpouring of inadequately treated sewage and solvents from industrialised societies is a cause of concern to marine ecologists and public health authorities alike. Most proposals made by government departments seem designed to allay apprehension and divert blame, more than to remedy a tragic situation. Nor is this limited to one country. In Eastern Germany 42% of the water in the rivers and 24% in the lakes is totally unfit for drinking. The Minamata disease of Japan (1953-60), the French atomic tests in the Pacific (1970-88), the ditching of radioactive atomic waste of the U.S.A. (1970-1), the ditching of many Soviet nuclear submarines up until the 1992 revolution, and the sewerage and solvent pollution of most civilised cities and seashores, indicates that this attitude has no national boundaries.

Biopersistence is a factor often not as obvious in the land sciences. Not only do toxins become concentrated in many marine creatures, they remain and may become concentrated as they pass up the food change.

Most waste products added to the ocean will sink to the bottom, but solid wastes, oil and garbage, can contain many materials that will float, to be carried great distances by currents and winds. Dredge spoils constitute the largest single ocean pollutant, followed by industrial wastes. Many of the more highly toxic wastes are packed in drums, which seems a very temporary expedient to avoid leakage and detection. Pollution kills marine life both by its direct toxic effect and by interfering with the ecosystem, through oxygen depletion, biostimulation and physical changes.

In March 1967 the Torrey Canyon ran aground on the Seven Stones Reef off the southern tip of England. The 120,000 tonnes of oil that poured onto the holiday beaches of Brittany and Cornwall, decimated the marine ecology and bird life of over 300 km of coastline. The detergents used to break up the oil did even more damage to the marine life and the world waited in horror and anticipation for the final tally of marine destruction. Thor Heyerdahl, on his trip across the Atlantic on a papyrus raft, observed that the sea had become "a common sewer for oil slush and chemical waste."

Twenty five years later we are witnessing the construction of 800,000 tonne oil tankers. A single spill from one of these could add 20% to the amount of petroleum entering the oceans in a single year. Large scale accidents and spillage from these craft in ecologically sensitive waterways (the Exxon Valdez in Alaska, and the many tankers running inside the Great Barrier Reef) make the Torrey Canyon disaster relatively insignificant.

The sea, which holds both the past and the future of mankind, deserves respect and thought by those who would exploit it. The mineral, food and energy potential may be enormous, and the judicious extraction of these valued materials can be performed without the catastrophic effects that are now being perpetrated under the guise of industrialisation. To despoil the oceans with solvents, plastics and other non-biodegradable materials is tantamount to building a sewerage pit for our children to swim in. We must avoid fouling the beauty of the undersea world, slaughtering its inhabitants, and destroying our heritage.

There is now a new breed of divers who appear to be more caring and careful creatures than their predecessors. They are often armed with a camera, and can be seen admiring the flora and fauna of their undersea home. They are gentle divers, well read and with only a moderate belief in their own invulnerability. They respect the sea and its inhabitants. Instead of fabricating a James Bond shark hunter image, they are more likely to introduce their children to a world of beauty—a world they want to preserve and to share. With this attitude, they are becoming more demanding of national and state governments to ensure that the same safety requirements and facilities are available to them and their families when they enter the sea, as when they holiday elsewhere.

Our knowledge of marine biotoxicity is rudimentary. Most of the available information has both protagonists and antagonists, and the simple minded doctor and patient find themselves in the middle of complex biomedical discussions that contribute little to the relief of pain and disability.

In this text, an attempt has been made to describe the clinical "state of the art" at this time. Other texts are available which give much more detailed and authoritative information on marine biology. They are to be recommended to any reader wishing to further his or her knowledge on specific aspects of this subject.

Carl Edmonds
Sydney, Australia

Introduction

It is the intention in this book to describe and illustrate the most common dangerous marine animals likely to be encountered by fishermen, yachtsmen, divers, swimmers, coastline dwellers and dawdlers. It is also intended to present in a concise yet comprehensive manner the clinical features of the injuries sustained, the first aid procedures to be employed by onlookers or paramedical personnel, and an abbreviated description of the medical management.

It is not intended to mention all the marine animals known to be dangerous to mankind. There are over 1000 types of marine vertebrates alone which are believed to be either venomous or poisonous. The invertebrates are even more numerous and less well documented. Only the more common and interesting species are discussed.

When I completed my medical training in 1960, most of the formal information on dangerous sea creatures was restricted to shark attacks. I cannot remember one lecture on the subject, and fish poisonings were considered too unimportant to intrude into the medical curriculum of my island continent of Australia. But information was available, even if hidden from academic eyes.

One natural resource which we have renounced and which is given no credence by our office-bound administrators, is the knowledge and experience of simple men and women of the sea—be they sailors, divers, doctors, fishermen or others. This book is an acknowledgment to those forgotten workers, who deserve the title Researchers and who are responsible for much of the recorded data on this subject.

Some international organisations have also contributed much to this subject and must be acknowledged. In the U.S.A., especially from Hawaii and Florida, there arose a plethora of university and academic units. The armed forces have led developments in the field, through such departments as the Naval Undersea Center and the Office of Naval Research, and by support of the Shark Attack File and the publishing of the Halstead volumes of Poisonous and Venomous Marine Animals of the World. Defence laboratories have also been obsessed with the marine toxins, although possibly for other than altruistic reasons.

The South Pacific Commission has sponsored the brilliant French work on fish poisonings, and research on shark attack has been extended to many laboratories as distant as the Natal Anti-Shark Measures Board of South Africa and the Mote Marine Laboratory in Sarasota.

This book is a collection of information obtained from the above contributors, also from relevant literature, scattered as it is through medical journals, symposia and museum articles, and supplemented with information from victims and divers exposed to these hazards.

In some cases the information required on a certain species is simply not available, and it has been necessary to extrapolate from closely related species. Treatments may have been used which have no merit, but because of a positive placebo response were thought to be of value by the doctor. In anecdotal reporting, this is an unavoidable complication. In other cases drugs have been used without clear indications. The degree of polypharmacy and the lack of accurate clinical observations render the assessment of drug administration difficult, and for this reason an attempt has been made to review and rationalise many of the drug therapies.

In some of the marine injuries described, personal experimentation under controlled conditions, with a comparison of the recommended treatments, has resulted in a reappraisal of the traditional concepts.

Information on each marine animal is divided into seven major sections:

Identification data. For ease of identification, and especially because this book will be used by non-experts in the field, the common names of the marine animals have been used and, whenever possible, colour plates are included. The sizes of the specimens photographed are sometimes approximations. Synonyms have been supplied, as there are considerable differences in nomenclature in different localities.

The common names tend to cause confusion when they are used to describe different fish in different areas. The alternative method of entitling each with its family, genus or species is of value to the marine biologist, but virtually useless to the first aid and medical personnel referring to the book in an emergency. One can easily be led into academic controversies regarding the naming, or even the existence, of different species—and this book is not intended as a forum for debate by marine biologists. Even though experts will disagree on nomenclature, patients are usually in full agreement on symptomatology.

Geographical distribution and seasonal incidence. These are also approximations and generalisations. It is quite likely that many of the marine animals are distributed over a much wider region than has been reported.

General. This section includes information of general interest and is used to highlight significant differences between species.

Clinical features. The symptoms and signs of injury are described in non-technical terms whenever possible. Simple phrases such as "a red ring" are used in preference to the correct medical terminology "an erythematous annulus." Apologies are extended to medical colleagues, as information is sometimes less precise than it would otherwise have been. The advantage of using colloquial terms is that they are more likely to be understood by interested (and injured) observers, and much less likely to be misunderstood by first aid attendants with an inexact knowledge of medical terminology. The corollary of this is:

> If you don't understand any phrase—ignore it. It is only intended for physicians—and put in a box like this.

Prevention. In this section I rely heavily on a mixture of observations, commonsense and folklore.

First aid. It is intended that this should be applied by any person, patient or bystander, until specialised medical assistance is obtained. Prompt first aid in many cases will obviate the need for complex medical attention and will sometimes be the major factor in saving the victim's life.

Medical treatment. This section is only applicable to registered medical practitioners. It is presumed that the personnel performing the medical management have little or no knowledge of marine biology, but that they do have a basic knowledge of therapeutics. Not to presume this would involve us in an extensive treatise on physiology and pharmacology quite beyond the scope of this book. There is thus no attempt here to use colloquial terms in preference to the correct medical terminology.

Technical data on the pharmacological properties of the **venom, toxin** or **anti-venom** are often relegated to the appendix. References are included in this and the recommended bibliography.

This book is intended for clinical reference, not for light reading. It has unfortunately been necessary to duplicate some of the information in some chapters to ensure that the reader does not continually have to refer to other sections. First aid treatments have changed dramatically over the past decade, and I have used my discretion and prerogative in presenting these.

It was a temptation, too great to resist, to include a little more general information on the marine animals to enable the reader to appreciate their beauty. Animals that have such a terrifying reputation when viewed from above the water (after having a fish hook torn through the mouth) are so often docile and friendly underwater, when treated with respect. Once I had a dream of writing a text on marine animal injuries from the animals' viewpoint. It was not to be, but to redress the bias inevitable in this text, I have included notes from Dee Scarr . Dee is a beautiful, sensitive diver who loves to touch sea creatures, and who shares her experiences with other divers on her safaris in Bonaire. Her book, *Touch the Sea,* is a must for all enthusiastic divers.

Survival of the species is a well understood concept and marine creatures have employed various survival techniques which may result in the infliction of harm to humans who encroach upon their marine habitat, or who seek to destroy and eat them.

The most common survival attribute is that of camouflage and concealment. This, of itself, causes no problems to humans, but it does allow for inadvertent close contact between the human and animal.

Other survival technique involves the infliction of pain or incapacity. Venomous marine animals possess a toxin injected by fangs, spines or stinging tentacles. Some animals hide the venom delivery system until threatened or attacked. Others highlight or display the lethal looking appendages, relying on prevention rather than counter attack. Some species deliver an electric shock instead of a venom.

As a final *piece de resistance,* which works well for species survival, but which sacrifices the individual, there is the poisonous fish. Here the predator succeeds in killing and ingesting the marine animal, but suffers or dies from the effects. Survivors of the predator species then learn to respect and avoid the poisonous species.

In the event of an injury from a marine animal, this book should accompany the patient, and be made available to the medical practitioner who is responsible for management.

PART I

Marine Animals
That Cause Trauma

NOTES

Sharks

Barracuda

Crocodiles, Alligators and Caimen

Eels

Electric Rays

Groper

Killer Whale

Miscellaneous Biting Fish

Octopus and Squid

Seals, Sea Lions and Walruses

Swordfish (Billfish) and Sawfish

Tridacna, Giant Clam

NOTES

SHARKS

> But when the tide rises and sharks are around,
> His voice has a timid and tremulous sound.
> Lewis Carroll, *Alice in Wonderland.*

Although typical species are mentioned here, one must appreciate that there is considerable diversity and controversy regarding the nomenclature and identification of many sharks.

Family	■ Lamnidae (Isuridae)
Dangerous species	■ *Carcharodon carcharias* (White Pointer, White Death, Great White, Great White Shark, Blue Pointer), *Lamna nasus, Lamna ditropis* (Atlantic and Pacific Mackerel or Porbeagle Shark), *Isurus oxyrinchus, Isurus paucus* (Shortfin & Longfin Mako Shark).
Family	■ Carcharhinidae.
Dangerous species	■ *Galeocerdo cuvieri* (Tiger Shark), *Prionace glauca* (Blue Shark, Great Blue, Blue Whaler Shark), *Carcharhinus albimarginatus* (Silvertip Shark), *C. brachyurus* (Bronze or N.Z. Whaler or Copper Shark), *C. amblyrhynchos* (Gray Reef Shark), *C. amboinensis* (Java Shark), *C. brevipinna* (Spinner Shark), *C. falciformis* (Silky Shark), *C. galapagensis* (Galapagos, Grey Reef Whaler Shark), *C. leucas* (Cub, Bull, Zambesi or Ground Shark), *C. limbatus* (Blacktip, Spotted, Grey Shark), *C. longimanus* (Oceanic Whitetip, White-tipped Shark), *C. melanopterus* (Black Whaler, Blacktip Reef Shark), *C. obscurus* (Dusky Shark, Black Whaler Shark), *C. perezi* (Caribbean Reef Shark), *C. wheeleri* (Blacktail Reef Shark), *Negaprion acutidens, N. brevirostris* (Lemon Sharks), *Triaenodon obesus* (Reef Whitetip Shark).
Family	■ Ginglymostomatidae.
Dangerous species	■ *Ginglymostoma cirratum* (Nurse Shark).
Family	■ Odontaspididae.
Dangerous species	■ *Eugomphodus taurus* (Grey Nurse, Sand, Raggedtooth Shark).
Family	■ Sphyrnidae.
Dangerous species	■ *Sphyrna lewini, S. zygaena, S. mokarran* (Hammerhead Sharks).

| **Family** | ■ | Alopiidae. |
| **Dangerous species** | ■ | *Alopias vulpinus* (Thresher Shark). |

| **Family** | ■ | Orectolobidae. |
| **Dangerous species** | ■ | *Orectolobus maculatus* (Spotted Wobbegong or Carpet Shark), *Eucrossorhinus dasypogon* (Tasselled Wobbegong). |

| **Family** | ■ | Hexanchidae. |
| **Dangerous species** | ■ | *Notorynchus cepedianus* (Broadnose Sevengill Shark). |

Although some are referred to as "dangerous species", this only implies that occasionally—rarely in many cases—the species has been recorded as attacking humans, or retaliating when humans attack them or trespass into their environment.

General Information

The majority of the 350 species of sharks are marine inhabitants, but many will enter estuaries, and some will travel far up rivers, while a few are fresh water

Great White Shark. Photo: R. Taylor

species. Most live in the relatively shallow waters off the major continents or around islands and inhabit the temperate or tropical zones.

The shark is perhaps the most successful of all predators. It has roamed the seas since the very dawn of our history, and islanders and seafaring people have incorporated this creature into their folklore. The shark is variously feared, respected, worshipped, idolised and exploited. Mariners, fishermen and skin divers, who are not renowned for their strict observance of factual reporting, have perpetuated these shark obsessions.

More important than all precautions against shark attack, is to not exaggerate the danger. Many more people die in Australia and the U.S.A. from bee stings than shark attacks. Drowning is 1000 times more likely in the U.S.A. (including Hawaii) than shark attacks. The following is a table of relative fatal incidences during the 1980—90 decade, for Australia, recorded by Stevens and Paxton.

Shark attack	1.
Crocodile attack	0.7
Lightning	1.7
Bee Sting	1.8
Scuba diving	8.0
Drowning	306.
Motor vehicle accident	2979.

Once a shark attack has occurred, most of those involved would consider the species identification as somewhat academic. This is not necessarily so. Different species have different characteristics, and currently only about 30 of the 350 species have been reported as attacking man, 12 are suspected of such an attack and another 28 have this capability. The list will continue to grow, but so will our understanding of the reasons for the attacks. Preventative measures are based on an understanding of shark behaviour. The three major shark families are as follows.

Lamnidae (Isuridae)

This is the most notorious of the shark families. They have a fusiform shape, tapered from the pointed snout, with an equally lobed muscular tail, and are capable of fast but stiff-bodied swimming, with short rapid strokes. The large dark eyes testify to the deep water habits of the porbeagle and the mako, with the great white being a more shallow inhabitant.

The Lamnidae are open ocean or pelagic species, and although they are cold blooded animals, they have adapted to reduce the effect of low ocean temperatures. Their heart and blood characteristics are more similar to the pelagic bony fish such as tuna, where the arterial and venous systems are very closely interrelated. Body heat produced by the metabolism, and carried with venous blood, warms the oxygenated blood passing from the heart to the tissues—effectively giving the shark some of the advantages of warm-blooded animals. Thus their body temperature, metabolism and consequently their activity can remain high despite the cold ocean temperature (5-20 degrees Centigrade). In other families, activity of the shark may be more related to the water temperature.

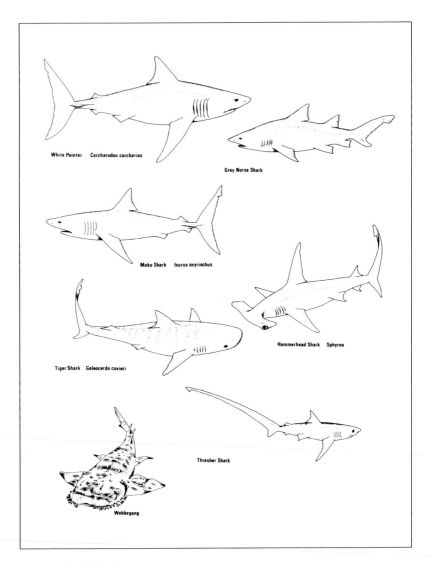

White Pointer   Carcharodon carcharias

Grey Nurse Shark

Mako Shark   Isurus oxyrinchus

Hammerhead Shark   Sphyrna

Tiger Shark   Galeocerdo cuvieri

Thresher Shark

Wobbegong

Diagrams by C. Lawler

The mako is famous for its leaps out of the water, allegedly up to 5 metres from the surface, and occasionally into boats. It is also much sought after in game fishing. It preys on large fish and there are many reports of its attacks on marlin and swordfish. It can reach over 590 kg weight and 4 metres long.

The great white is the epitome of the man eater, and the largest of the sharks. Some specimens (usually female) weigh between 1 and 2 tonnes, and measure up to 6.4 metres long. The teeth are triangular, serrated and disproportionately large—sometimes over 5 cm long. These sharks are especially found in the cold waters with large seal and sea lion population, and therefore in shallower areas than the other Lamnidae, which feed on deep sea fishes. The west and north eastern coasts of North America, southern Australia and South Africa are well documented areas of habitation, and also are favoured by some surfers and many abalone divers.

San Francisco with its 180 km of coast between Tomales Point at Bodega Bay in the north and Santa Cruz and Monterey Bay in the south, is known as the "White Shark Attack Capital of the World." The adult females give birth in late summer or early fall, in shallow waters south of Point Conception, with the pups remaining inshore and feeding on the prolific fish life. As they grow older, they travel north and offshore to the pinniped (seal and sea lion) breeding areas around islands.

There has been an increased number of shark attacks along the west coast of America, on both abalone divers and board riders, over the last few decades. Almost four out of every five such attacks are unequivocally due to the great white. It is believed that the attacks are of a feeding type (see page 14), with the surface swimmer or surf craft being mistaken as seal or sea lion prey.

Carcharhinidae

The requiem or gray sharks are large and aggressive, with a varied and confusing nomenclature. They range from 1-4 metres long, usually with the second dorsal fin much smaller than the first, and the upper lobe of the tail much longer than the lower. The eyes have a nictitating membrane.

Many of the attacks along the populated east coast of Australia were thought to be due to the "whalers" of this family, and the Natal coast of South Africa was similarly affected by the sluggish bull or Zambesi shark. The attraction of these sharks to estuary or fresh waterways may explain this incidence. Attacks seem to be more territorial than feeding, with repeated bites and slashings.

Cousteau described the oceanic whitetip as the most dangerous of all sharks. It is certainly one of the most abundant, and congregates rapidly at mid-ocean disasters such as ship wrecks and plane accidents.

Dr John Randall stated that the tiger shark may be responsible for more attacks than any other species. Others would claim that it is second to the great white. The tiger shark is so named because the young are born with stripes.

Sphyrnidae

The hammerheads are easily identified by their T-shaped head with eyes and nostrils widely separated, giving the shark a wide area of perusal as it slowly swings its head from side to side. It may grow to 6 metres length, and is often gregarious, being observed in packs of 10-20 in many areas and up to 200 in the gulf of Mexico and south eastern Australia.

Ecological perspective

The primary purpose of sharks is as a predator on other species, to ensure survival of the fittest and thereby promotion of ecosystem stability.

Sharks comprise a very efficient and successful evolutionary group of animals. Many of the present day sharks and rays are of the same genera as those which swam in the Cretaceous seas over 100 million years ago. Some species probably predated dinosaurs by a million years.

Certain species that were once considered "man eaters", such as the Grey Nurse sharks, are now visited regularly by divers and even protected by law in Australia. Spear fishermen have greatly reduced their numbers, so that they are now an endangered species. Even the Great White shark is endangered, and is therefore now protected, in South Africa. Over 34 000 Blue sharks are destroyed each year by the tuna long line and drift net fishing employed by the Japanese, off the coast of Tasmania

Shark fishing is an industry that experiences booms then busts. The latter, together with vulnerability to extinction, occurs due to the overfishing of an animal that matures late (10-12 years) and has few, but well nurtured, young.

There has been a detectable change in attitude since the advent of scuba diving. Initially, divers engaged in an orgy of destruction against sharks, using spears, power heads, and carbon dioxide darts. More recently, as divers have observed and then admired the beauty of these animals, attitudes have changed. As in other areas, the camera has replaced the gun. We now look on the sea and its inhabitants as an equally vulnerable and limited resource.

Sharks are still used as game fish and provide good quality food. The Japanese concoct dozens of various shark dishes. Up to 100 sharks are needed to produce 1 kg of shark fin, to be used for soups. Other nationalities are hypocritically moralistic about eating the flesh of scavengers, and rename it before consumer usage. It is also free of fish toxins, except for the liver (which is used as a lubricant and for cosmetics). Its cartilage is used for treatment of burns and for anti-cancer research. Corneas have been used in human transplant operations and shark skin for leather.

Shark Attacks in Perspective

Our knowledge of sharks has been based more on fashion than fact. Earlier this century they were regarded by the Europeans as scavengers and cowards, and it

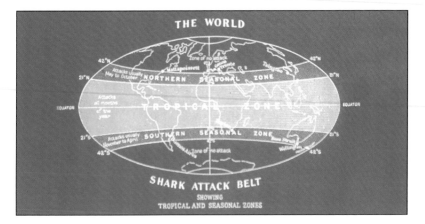

Shark attack belt. From V. Coppleson

was seriously doubted whether or not they did, in fact, attack man. The subsequent controversy resulted in a mass of accumulated data that left us in no doubt.

It has been said that the only parts of a shark that cannot be put to good use are its bite and its tail. Authors and film-makers, searching desperately for sensationalist themes which will shock and attract audiences, have even made use of these.

Some localities, especially in the U.S.A., were more likely to repress news of shark attack, to protect tourism and commercial interests. The film *Jaws* accurately depicted this attitude, and grossed more revenue than any movie in the history of Hollywood.

Rescue and first aid groups also have ulterior motives in sometimes exaggerating the risk of shark attack. Even Sir Winston Churchill, when Prime Minister of England, declared that "The British Government is entirely opposed to sharks"—presumably reflecting the attitude of the majority of voters. Other governments have become involved, as shown by attempts to protect beaches in Australia and South Africa, in funding of shark deterrents and sponsoring of the *Shark Attack File* in the U.S.A..

Shark attack remains a genuine but unlikely danger to seafaring people. Although rare, the attack is often terrifying in intensity, and the degree of mutilation produced has a strong emotive effect on civilised people. In this beautiful marine jungle, without the protection afforded by a superior civilisation, sophisticated technology, or terrestrial senses, humans are weak and vulnerable.

The value of sharks to the media is best exemplified by the popularity of *Jaws* and the many magazine and newspaper articles. In Australia, where millions of people enjoy the benefits of the Indian and Pacific Ocean beaches each year, many newspapers are sold in the week preceding the summer school holidays by headlining "shark sightings." In fact, even though Australia is renowned as one of the most dangerous areas in the world for shark attack, and has more recorded attacks than any other country, it now averages only one fatality per year.

In 1968, *Life* magazine published an article together with photographs of a stunt man, Jose Marco, who was attacked whilst filming *Shark,* a low cost thriller. The huge white shark apparently got through the netting protection. Marco was reported to have died in hospital two days later. In fact, the shark did not look like a great white. It was probably a drugged bull shark that was pulled through the water and tomato ketchup added. A detailed investigation subsequently revealed that there was no official record of such an attack, no stunt man called Jose Marco, and no hospital records or recollection of the

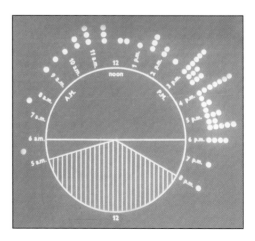

Time of attacks. From V. Coppleson

incident. Life magazine made no comment.

Information about shark attack comes from detailed observations from interested researchers such as Sir Victor Coppleson (Australia), Dr David Davies (South Africa) and Dr John Randall (U.S.A.). It is amply augmented by computer analyses of the *Shark Attack File*. The latter supplied us with many fascinating statistics, up until 1967 when the U.S. Navy suspended funding.

Of the recorded case histories in 25% there was no factual evidence that a shark attack actually happend; in over 50% the earliest documentation was made over a year after the attack; and less than 10% were reported by factual witnesses. The interpretations of this data thus have to be accepted with some caution.

The file included an analysis of 1165 cases. Divers underwater accounted for 25% of attacks, with 43% of these being free diving (not scuba). Males are attacked 13.5 times more than females, perhaps because they are more active, swim further from shore and in deeper water. More attacks take place when the water is warmer, during holidays and on weekends, and in the afternoons—reflecting the greater numbers at risk. About 20% of attacks were associated with line fishing and another 20% with spear fishing.

Anatomy and physiology

The size of sharks varies from 0.5—18 metres. The two giant sharks, the whale and the basking shark, feed on plankton. Sharks have no swim bladders, and if they stop moving through the water they tend to sink. Most species also need to swim continuously to prevent asphyxiation. They allegedly have a low intelligence, but this has not interfered with their ability to survive far longer than man in the evolutionary time scale. The shark's main natural enemy is other sharks.

They are well equipped to locate prey and their own species; they conduct seasonal migrations, and are able to identify specific localities. They react to multiple stimuli, with the sense of smell being a principal means of locating prey. They can detect some substances, such as blood, in minute quantities—less than one part per million. Fish blood does appear to attract sharks. This does not mean

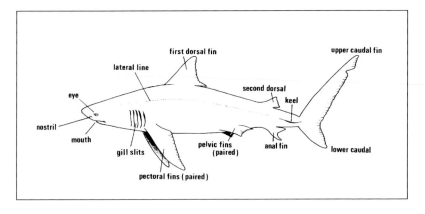

Anatomy of a shark

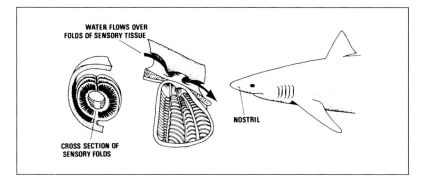

Olfactory (smell) sense

that the mammalian blood will necessarily provoke attack behaviour. On the contrary, some workers have questioned whether it attracts sharks at all.

Although their visual ability to differentiate form or colour may not be very selective, their ability to discriminate movements and minor contrast variations in low illumination conditions is extremely efficient. Their vision is thus very effective in detecting movement in murky water or at night. The eyelids are fixed, but some have a nictitating membrane which protects the eye against possible danger. Others rotate the eyes in the sockets for protection during an attack. Although in most species there is no consistent evidence of attraction to different colours , any material that is bright or highly reflective will attract them.

Their taste is not very well developed, but preferences for some foodstuffs have been suggested. A variety of objects have been detected in the stomach contents of sharks, including fish, turtles, sea birds, seals, dolphins, stingrays, terrestrial animals and, rarely, pieces of human tissue. Occasionally the shark will sample potential food, and reject that which it finds objectionable.

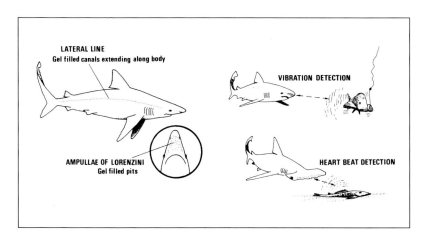

Other sensory systems

Smell is a highly developed sense, with 70% of the brain devoted to this function. The nostrils are situated at either side on the lower aspect of the snout, sensing the environment as it swims through the water.

The ampullae of Lorenzini are probably unique in the animal kingdom, being very sensitive electroreceptors, capable of detecting the electrical field surrounding their prey. They are distributed around the head and snout, and along the lateral line, and can even detect prey buried in sand.

The lateral line is a multi sensory system commencing at the head and passing along the body. This system receives a variety of information, including vibrations of low frequency, temperature, salinity, pressure and minute electrical fields such as those produced by other fish or humans in the vicinity. Vibration, such as the thrashing of a wounded fish, is rapidly detected and localised.

Hearing is especially sensitive to low frequency (10-640 Hz) sounds, and they have an extraordinary faculty for directional localisation of this sound. The attraction of sharks to marine accidents, such as plane crashes and ship wrecks, is probably related to the low frequency pressure pulses and sound, transmitted over great distances. The 900 or more survivors of the Japanese torpedoing of the U.S.S. *Indianapolis,* were reduced to 317 after 5 days of floating in the shark infested tropical waters of the Pacific. An estimated 1000 survivors of the S.S. *Nova Scotia* became shark attack victims after it sunk in the Indian Ocean. Even the hovering of helicopters above the water has been postulated as a possible attraction to sharks.

Attack patterns

There are different types of attack, and these may be identified by the behaviour of the animals and the subsequent nature of the injury. Three of these types represent different degrees of a feeding attack, and the fourth and fifth represent a territorial intrusion.

It seems the feeding response is related more to the presence of specific stimuli than to the nutritional requirements of the animal. The presence of physical and chemical stimuli, such as that released from freshly killed or injured animals, can cause considerable attraction to sharks and may result in a feeding response.

Sharks in a feeding pattern tend to circle the victim, gradually increasing their swimming speed. As the circles begin to tighten, the sharks may commence a cris-cross pattern (going across the circle). At this stage, they may produce the first type of injury by contact, when they bump or brush against the prey. The shark's very abrasive skin can cause extensive injuries and it is thought that the information obtained by the animal at this time may influence the likelihood of progression of the feeding pattern.

The shark bite is usually performed with the animal in a horizontal or slightly upward direction, with the head swung backward and the upper teeth projecting forward giving a great increase in mouth size and display of the razor sharp teeth. The physical force involved in an attack is often enough to eject the victim well clear of the water, and the bite force of some sharks is said to be about 1 tonne per square centimetre.

Once the animal has a grip on its prey, the mouthful will usually be either torn out sideways or the area will be totally severed. Other sharks in the vicinity,

Agonistic (territorial) attack patterns

may reflexly respond to the stimuli created by the attack and commence the third type of feeding pattern behaviour: a feeding frenzy.

It has often been noted that sharks may swim together in an orderly and smooth manner, but when vibrations are set up by one of the animals being shot or hooked, for example, then the abnormal activity of that animal may trigger feeding responses in the others. This may progressively increase into a feeding frenzy. The sharks are likely to attack both the original prey and the predator or any other moving object; cannibalism has been observed, and the subsequent carnage can be extensive.

This sequence may not always be followed, especially in the case of the great white, which has the size and strength to attack without warning behaviour. These attacks show five distinct head movements during the biting sequence. First the snout is lifted, probably obliterating vision, and the eyes roll back in the sockets—protecting them from damage by the struggling prey. The mouth is enlarged by a depression of the lower jaw. The upper jaw is then dislocated and rotated forward and downward, meeting the lower jaw as it moves upward. The snout then drops.

The first bite on a large animal may be to wound or kill, more than to eat. Thus the prey may be bitten and released, to die from blood loss. This "bite and spit" behaviour may avoid damage from still struggling pinniped prey (seals, sea lions). Wet-suited divers resemble pinnipeds, swimming near the surface and breathhold diving. Surfboard and paddle board silhouettes may also simulate these animals on the surface, where they are often attacked. The bite may be investigatory in nature, with the shark not necessarily continuing its feeding activity.

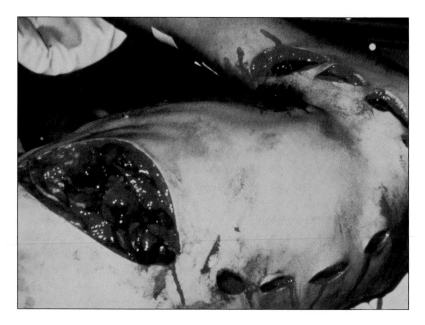

Great white attack on Rodney Fox, Port Lincoln, South Australia. Rodney Fox was an abalone diver engaged in a spear fishing contest, when attacked on December 8th, 1963. The thoracic cavity was opened, causing a haemopneumothorax, fractured ribs, exposure of abdominal contents and blood loss. Fortunately he was kept immobile, with his wetsuit on. Apparently Rodney heard the medical staff in the hospital query whether they should call a priest. He protested indignantly that he was a protestant, before the significance of the statement hit him. He subsequently ran one of the most famous seafood restaurants in Adelaide, and hosts trips for American tourists to see the great whites in the South Australian Gulf. It is hard to keep a good man down.

Once a subject separates from others, an attack appears more likely. Staying within a group offers some protection. Unlike lightning, sharks can and do strike twice in the same place. Four people have been attacked on more than one occasion, and one even had his artificial leg bitten.

The rescuers of shark attack victims are rarely injured themselves. There are, unfortunately, a few very dramatic cases where this was not so, and there are other instances in which there have been two or more people killed in the one episode. Nevertheless, in the 712 cases on the *Shark Attack File* where more than one person, including rescuers, were considered exposed to injury at the same time, by far the majority of the attacks (96%) led to injury only to a single victim. Where there have been instances of multiple deaths, these are mostly the result of major air and sea disasters.

The fourth type of attack is territorial or "agonistic." It is stimulated when an intruder (a swimmer or a diver) infringes a shark's territory. An agonistic attack may also happen if the shark is angry, frightened or engages in dominance behaviour. This type of attack is quite unlike the feeding pattern, and the shark tends to swim in a far more awkward manner, exaggerating a lateral motion with its head, snout upturned with mouth slightly opened, arching of the spine, and with its pectoral fins angled downwards. In this position, it appears to be more rigid and awkward in its movements than the feeding animal. It has been compared, both in appearance and motivation, to a cornered animal, adopting a defensive and snapping adversarial position. If the intruder vacates the area, confrontation will be avoided and an attack prevented. After all, the sharks were there first.

Probably most of the attacks from territorial sharks are of this type. If the intruder does not vacate the area the shark may snap or rake the victim with the teeth of its upper jaw. This may result in slashing wounds.

Another common type of territorial attack may be precipitated by a person falling, jumping or diving into the water, usually from a boat, either onto or near an unsuspecting shark . The shark responds by reflex snapping at the intruder. It is an automatic reaction to a presumed attack.

Clinical features

A great variety of damage is noted in different attacks. In some cases only abrasive lesions of the skin may be present, where the shark's skin has come into contact with the victim. These may be parallel shallow lacerations, and are quite distinct from teeth marks. Teeth marks are linear, concentric slashes where the teeth of the upper jaw have raked the victim. The sharpness of the teeth may result in profuse bleeding, but without the crushing and haemostatic (reduction of bleeding) effects seen in other causes of major physical injury.

Discreet teeth punctures from both jaws may encircle either the victim's body or neck—when the shark has had an appreciable amount of the victim within his mouth, but has still not proceeded with the attack. This is the "bite and spit" behaviour, described above. In the most extensive feeding attacks, tissue has been torn from the victim and the ragged wounds are often associated with damage to bone and viscera. Teeth fragments, clothing and other foreign bodies may be present in the depths of the wound. In most cases, there is a single bite, but occasionally a person may be the victim of multiple attacks and bites.

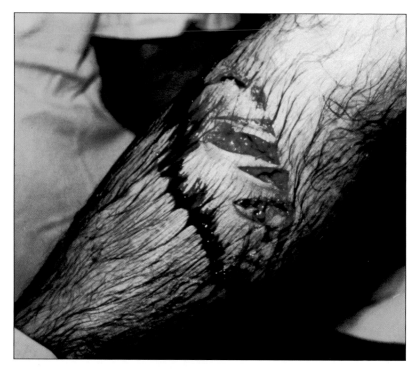

Typical teeth wounds

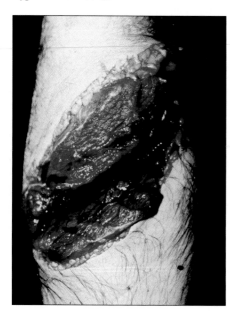

Amputations and extensive body wounds are common, and in those victims not killed immediately, the major problem will be massive haemorrhage and shock. Adjacent people are rarely attacked in such circumstances.

GENERALISED. Shock (cold, clammy appearance with a rapid pulse, fainting and hypotension) dominates the clinical picture. It is usually severe and is due to copious blood loss. Neurogenic

Destruction and tissue tearing effect of shark attack on the same victim. Photos courtesy of C. Barnes

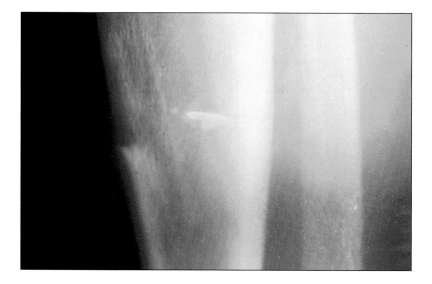

X-ray of leg of shark attack victim, showing bone damage and a shark's tooth. Courtesy M. Patkin

shock and exhaustion from the combat, add to the clinical picture. The death rate is proportional to the degree of haemorrhage and reduced by first aid measures taken to prevent further blood loss.

Extensive bacteriological contamination from marine organisms includes a paracolon bacillus resistant to penicillin. Other marine organisms are present. *Clostridium tetanus* and *Clostridium welchii* have also been isolated from shark wounds, but are usually from contamination after rescue from the sea.

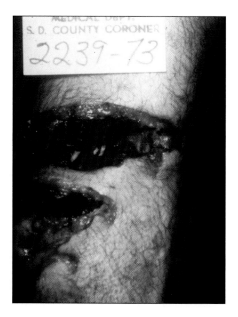

This abalone diver was attacked by a great white in southern California. The major wounds are shown, with three shark teeth obvious in the wound. Despite the needs of the diver a tourniquet was not employed— instead the Coast Guard was called. He died from shock and blood loss after being rescued from the water.

Prevention

Prevention of shark attack depends very much on the marine locality being considered. The following procedures will be relevant in different situations.

Preparation for shark attack has been most valuable in reducing mortality in both Australia and South Africa. Symposia in both countries, attended by those who had the most experience and knowledge of this problem, reached consensus on the principles of first aid management. In South Africa the surf lifesavers and other emergency groups were trained in first aid and were supplied with first aid packs which included the materials necessary (the Feinberg Pack was named after Dr S. Feinberg who treated many such emergencies around Port Shepstone). An emergency telephone number (usually 911 in the U.S.A., 000 in Australia) should be known to the public, giving advice and arranging for an intensive care ambulance with medical staff to attend the victim, on site.

A typical **Emergency Pack** should contain:
1. Sterile pressure pads and bandages.
2. Inflatable splints.
3. Simple tourniquet, rubber compression bandage or Esmarch tourniquet.
4. Disposable artery forceps.
5. Sterile pads for wound dressings.
6. Synthetic blood/plasma substitute and intravenous electrolyte fluids, 1 litre each, with at least 2 Intravenous sets and appropriate needles, catheters etc.
7. Sterile swabs, needles, syringes, and drugs if possible.
8. Space blanket for protection from sun, wind, rain, cold or cameramen.

Heavily Populated Beaches. The most effective method of reducing the incidence of shark attack is by netting enclosures or meshing. Total bay enclosures are effective in sheltered areas, if consistent surveillance is carried out to ensure the integrity of the net. Only small areas are suitable for this technique, and in one instance a shark attack occurred within the netted area.

Areas exposed to adverse weather or surf are best protected by meshing. It was introduced to the heavily populated beaches around Sydney, Australia, which had received an awesome reputation for shark attack. Commercial fishermen were aware that gill nets often caught sharks, without this intent, and so in 1937 intermittent meshing was introduced along the metropolitan beaches. Initially 1000 sharks were caught, reducing to 150 per year in recent times. No shark attacks have been recorded on meshed beaches since its introduction at Sydney or its surrounding cities. One such attack did occur on a meshed South African beach, although it was from a small shark and was not severe.

Meshing involves the intermittent use of a heavy-gauge net, 150 metres long. It is submerged from buoys on the seaward side of the breaking waves, often about 500 metres from shore and suspended between a float line on the surface and a lead line on the bottom and anchored at each end. Sharks can, in fact, swim around it or over it. Fortunately it produces few alerting stimuli to the sharks, and therefore, they are not aware of its presence. The mesh is approximately 25x25 cm, and the shark tends to swim into it. The net wraps around the animal and interferes with its gill function. As the shark is unable to retreat, it will struggle and attempt to push itself forward through the mesh. This results in the shark being further entangled, and thus produces death by suffocation.

Accurate records are kept of the type, number, and size of the catch. Most of the sharks are dead by the time the mesh is retrieved after 24 hours or so, and the others are killed at the time of retrieval. Not only does the resident shark population decrease, shark sightings also decrease, and shark attacks are virtually eliminated. The local population develops much more confidence in the safety of their surfing area, and tourism will often adequately compensate the local authorities for the cost of the shark meshing contract. Environmentalists abhor the action, as the mesh may also collect rays, turtles, dugong and dolphin.

Politicians vacillate in their approach to the cost-efficiency of meshing (expense vs votes). For the Sydney beaches, the cost is $600 000 a year; it probably prevents 1-2 attacks per year, and the environmental vote competes with the tourist dollar.

The South Africans extended the Australian experience, both by increasing the extent of meshing and conducting high quality research into shark morphology and behaviour. The Natal Anti-Shark Measures Board, under the able leadership of Mrs Beulah Davis, is an impressive monument to the importance of this work.

Survival Situation. The crash of a plane into the water, and sometimes the noises associated with a ship sinking, are themselves very effective in attracting sharks to that area and putting the survivors at risk. Survivors should move into life rafts as quickly as possible, or make use of the Johnson Shark Screen. This is a bag of thin, tough plastic with a collar consisting of three inflatable rings. The survivor partially inflates one of the rings, by mouth, gets into the bag and fills it with water by dipping the edges under the surface so that it becomes full. The other rings can be inflated later. This appears to the shark as a large, solid-looking black object. The bag retains fluid and excreta which may otherwise stimulate shark attack, and attenuates the bioelectric and galvanic fields surrounding the survivor.

Swimmers. Swimmers are advised not to urinate in the water or swim with abrasions or bleeding wounds. They are also advised to move gently and not thrash around on the surface. They should stay with a group, or at least with a partner. This is cynically claimed to reduce the chance of shark attack by 50% but, in fact, it probably reduces it far more. Swimmers are also advised not to swim in water with low visibility, near drop-offs or deep channels, or toward late afternoon or night when sharks tend to be involved in feeding.

It is sometimes claimed that women should not dive or swim while menstruating. There is no evidence to support the belief that decomposing blood will attract sharks; in fact the experimental and statistical evidence is in the opposite direction.

Divers. The incidence of shark attacks on scuba divers appears to be progressively increasing and now comprises one-third of all shark attacks. Wetsuits do not aid in prevention, and may well increase the likelihood of shark attack—despite popular theories to the contrary. Divers are advised in the same way as swimmers, but with added precautions. Underwater explosives tend to attract

swimmers, but with added precautions. Underwater explosives tend to attract sharks. Shark attacks are more likely with increased depth and can be provoked by playing with or killing sharks. It is preferable to dive in areas where spear fishing is not practised.

Powerheads, carbon dioxide darts and the drogue dart (this has a small parachute attached which disrupts the shark's orientation and swimming efficiency) are all specialised pieces of equipment which may be appropriate in certain diving situations. Nevertheless, they have disadvantages. Powerheads tend to misfire with wet cartridges, and the danger from them far exceeds the danger from shark attack.

Divers are also advised not to tether fish or abalone near their body. If sharks are encountered, it is best to descend to the seabed or to retreat to the protection of rocks, a cliff face, or some other obstacle so as to disrupt the normal feeding attack pattern described earlier. If the diver recognises an agonistic attack pattern from the shark, the area should be vacated by backing away.

Experimentation was performed on the use of Kevlar incorporated into wetsuits as a shark-bite-resistant material. It is currently being used as bulletproof vest material and is able to stop a .45 calibre bullet, although it does not stop penetration of teeth from a relatively mild dusky shark.

Steel meshed diving suits definitely discourage an attack, but are dangerous unless extra precautions are taken to ensure buoyancy. The striped wetsuit, designed by Dr Walter Starck has broad, high contrasting bands of white painted over the black wet suit at right angles to the axis of motion. This is said to deter some of the potentially aggressive reef sharks of the Pacific, but not all.

If one is diving in shark-infested waters, the use of a shark billy can be effective in pushing away any curious or interested shark. The shark billy is a sturdy stick with a nail stuck in, and is of great value to experienced divers who often encounter sharks.

In many areas of the world, shark feeding is an attraction for scuba divers, and the thrill of seeing the reef sharks remove fish from the guide's mouth in the Maldives, was recently brought into perspective when a female guide had both the fish and her hand taken.

Action to Take if a Shark Attack is Threatened. Although the shark may do the unexpected, more often the behaviour is predictable.

If the shark is involved in feeding behaviour, separate yourself from the probable source of the stimulus. Abandon any caught fish, no matter the sacrifice. Sometimes divers defend their catch, or even hold it out of the water, so that stimuli are prevented from reaching the shark. If the stimulus is your own behaviour, such as overhand swimming, kicking, prising abalone off rocks, then stop it. As calmly as possible, and without heading into open water, leave the area. Continue to face the shark.

If scuba diving, it is often worthwhile moving to have a wall at your back and to avoid the surface. If the shark returns, then slowly move along the shelter, or head for the beach or boat when the shark is furthest away. Always stay in a group, both below and on the surface.

If the attack is an agonistic type, with the typical posturing described above, remain motionless for a few seconds while you appraise your situation. Face the shark, be prepared to fend it off with anything at your disposal and quietly vacate the area.

If the shark comes within a metre or two, any action may disrupt the feeding or agonistic pattern, so that yelling, blowing bubbles, sudden body actions may be of value. Striking the shark in a sensitive area—eyes, snout, gills—with a knife, snorkel or whatever, or kicking it, may terminate the attack.

Shark Repellants. A vast number of experiments have been carried out to demonstrate ways of preventing shark attack. During the Second World War, the Naval Research Laboratory in Washington, D.C., gave high priority to developing shark deterrents for their sailors, and deduced that everything that could conceivably be expected to work, did not. Potent fish poisons, dyes, vibrations and poison gas were all tried.

Chemical deterrents had an unsavoury history against shark attacks. Nevertheless, because of the incidence of shark attack on sailors, every life jacket in the U.S. Navy came with packet of Shark Chaser. Despite naval backing, it was of value only to the manufacturer. It consisted of 80% nigrosine dye and 20% copper acetate; the black dye was meant to work by confusing the shark's vision, while the copper acetate was thought to be similar to a deterrent chemical, produced in decaying shark tissue. Shark Chaser was subsequently shown to be valueless except for its psychological effect on the sailors. Over 200 chemicals have been tested, without success.

Attempts have been made to repel sharks by injecting them with poisons before they bite. The presumption is that the victim sees the shark before the attack and is technically competent to administer the injection. Enough strychnine nitrate to kill several horses may have an effect after a minute or so. What is the shark doing all this time?

Another chemical, a whitish secretion produced by the Moses Sole, *Pardachirus marmoratus,* and similar to the chemical structure of many commercial detergents, is still being investigated, after being observed by Dr Eugenie Clark to deter one species of shark.

Many methods of repelling sharks will, given different conditions and different sized animals, result in an alerting or an attraction response in the very animals that they are meant to deter. Such is certainly the case with some electrical and explosive devices.

Electrical repellents have been repeatedly introduced as a new concept over the last decade. If an electrical field is produced around a fish, there is an initial convulsive movement followed by an alerting pattern. With the increase in electrical field intensity, electrotaxis results, with the fish orientating itself to face the positive electrode and swimming in that direction. If the field intensity is raised further the fish is anaesthetised by a process known as electronarcosis and will suffocate. The practical application of this knowledge is doubtful. Power consumption is excessive due to the high electrical conductivity of sea water, and the voltages required to produce electrotaxis and electronarcosis are totally unsafe for nearby swimmers. Also, the larger the shark the less the effect produced by the same electric voltage. The principle works best with the smaller and less dangerous species. The only effect able to be produced with portable repellent units suited for use by a diver, is that of the convulsive/alerting response — and whether this prevents attacks more than it provokes them has still to be clarified.

Bubble curtains were proposed with great enthusiasm, but only 1 of 12 tiger sharks was deterred. Sound and ultrasonic waves have been tried by a number of workers, with unimpressive results. The ability of different sharks to respond differently to these various stimuli is equalled only by their ability to adapt to them. None of these physical forces have the same excellent record as the enclosure or meshing techniques.

First Aid

1. Remove the patient from the water, as further attacks are possible.
2. Begin treatment immediately on the spot, do not rush the patient to hospital. Move the patient only as far up the beach as is necessary, to prevent drowning.
3. Stop the bleeding immediately. This is done by applying direct pressure above or on the bleeding artery. On a limb, this may be superseded by a tourniquet (page 239). Pressure, by hand or bandages, may be applied if blood loss from the area cannot be controlled by tourniquet. Ensure that the bandages actually stop the bleeding—and do not merely conceal it. Air splints are sometimes effective, when available.
4. Reassure the patient.
5. Position the patient on the sand with the head lowermost, and only lightly cover him with clothing or a towel. If a wetsuit is being worn, leave it on. Removal may result in too much movement and further haemorrhage. It may also be of value in reducing shock or retaining organs and tissues in place.
6. Do not move the victim further. Send for ambulance and medical personnel.
7. Give nothing by mouth. An anaesthetic may be required.

MEDICAL TREATMENT

If medically trained personnel are present during first aid treatment, haemostasis is achieved by any means available—such as pressure to the site of bleeding or proximal to this site, tourniquets, air splints, pressure bandages, tying of blood vessels, etc. One should use any material available. The mortality rate is such that there need be no apprehension regarding either the use of tourniquets or the contamination of wounds.

Medical treatment is best commenced prior to transfer of the patient to the hospital. Infusion of blood, plasma, or other intravenous replacement fluid should be given top priority until the state of shock has been adequately controlled. This can be ascertained by the clinical state of the patient, including pulse rate, blood pressure and central venous pressure. The use of morphine intravenously is likely to produce considerable benefit, despite its mild respiratory depressant effect.

Recording and assessing the vital signs then becomes an integral part of the management; they should be monitored throughout the transfer of the patient to the hospital. At all stages, the first aid resuscitation takes priority over the need for hospitalisation. Transport to hospital should be performed in as gentle and orderly manner as possible. Excess activity aggravates the shock state in these patients. Case reports abound with statements that the victims died in transit. They could more accurately state that:

Victims died *because* they were transported.

After stabilisation of the clinical state, the patient is transferred by the least traumatic means available. The areas are swabbed, and bacteriological culture and sensitivities are subsequently obtained. Bacterial growth may depend on using culture media that are compatible with the marine environment, such as 4N hypertonic saline as well as the conventional techniques.

Broad spectrum antibiotics are required, and it should be remembered that the bacteriological contamination is sometimes extensive, both with marine and terrestrial organisms (*Pseudomonas, Aeromones,* etc.). Most of the marine organisms respond to flucloxacillin, ceftazidime, doxycycline, erythromycin and other broad spectrum antibiotics. *Clostridium tetanus* and *Clostridium welchii* have both been isolated from shark wounds, although the contamination almost certainly would have occurred after the initial injury. Tetanus prophylaxis is therefore required, and gas gangrene prevented by appropriate antisepsis and surgery.

X-rays should be taken, both to show bone damage and to detect foreign bodies. Ultrasound may also be used.

Once the greater liability to haemorrhage has been appreciated, surgical procedures are not significantly different from those used for a motor vehicle accident case. Surgical excision of the obviously necrotic material is required. The surgical techniques should otherwise be of a conservative nature, especially if the blood supply is still intact. Tendon suture should not be attempted, unless the wound is very clean. Skin grafting is performed to preserve nerves, tendons, vessels, joints, and even muscles.

BARRACUDA

Family	■	Sphyraenidae.
Dangerous species	■	*Sphyraena barracuda* and others.
Common names	■	Giant Sea Pike, Snooke, Striped Barracuda, Dingo-fish, Oda.
Distribution	■	The larger and more aggressive specimens are encountered throughout most tropical and subtropical waters. American texts refer to the ferocious Australian species whereas Australian texts tend to stress that the ferocious species are found in the West Indies.

Barracuda are carnivorous, fast swimming fish, greatly feared in some parts of the world. They often travel in schools, however very large ones are sometimes seen alone. Many grow to a length of 2 metres, and weigh up to 40 kg. They are known to herd fish into areas, and then decimate their prey with razor sharp teeth, slashing from side to side. After they have killed sufficient fish, they then devour them at leisure.

There are long canine-like teeth in both jaws which are able to spear and hold prey. The teeth are particularly sharp on both edges, and produce a smooth cutting wound which may not cause much pain at the time, but bleeds copiously.

Barracuda, length 1.5 m. Photo by W.A. Starck

Occasionally a barracuda will stalk a diver, often at a distance of only a few metres, and sometimes into water no more than knee deep. This does not necessarily result in an attack, and the barracuda can be chased away by an aggressive or forward movement of the diver. The fish, however, may only travel a short distance before it turns and continues the stalking behaviour. This intimidation is aggravated by the adverse psychological effect the dental structure of the barracuda has on the diver.

In the Hawaiian and Australian areas barracuda are considered to be rarely dangerous to humans. Most barracuda bites are usually on victims who were themselves the predator—having speared barracuda, or hauled them inboard on a fishing line. Although divers have been attacked in the Pacific—one spearfisherman having his kneecap bitten off—they are few in number and without evidence of fatalities.

Many more serious attacks have been reported from the Atlantic species, with occasional deaths. One such fatality off Key West in Florida, involved an airline pilot who wore fluorescent swimming trunks. The barracuda slashed his groin and buttocks and then hovered around the area as rescuers tried to protect him and then transport him to hospital. He bled profusely and died en route.

The danger of attack from barracuda is greatest when diving at night with a light. This is thought to blind the fish and cause it to panic, resulting in possible injury to any diver in its path. The barracuda may also act reflexively by slashing with its teeth at any fast moving or brightly coloured object near it. It is also attracted to the abnormal movements of a speared fish.

Prevention

1. Do not swim or dive in areas where barracuda are prevalent.
2. Avoid colourful clothing, bright shining objects and lights whilst swimming.
3. Do not spear barracuda.
4. Do not handle or carry speared fish.

First aid and **medical treatment.** See shark attack (pages 24-25).

CROCODILES, ALLIGATORS AND CAIMEN

Order	■	Crocodilia.
Dangerous species	■	*Crocodylus porosus* (Salt water crocodile), *C. niloti-cus* (Nile Crocodile), *C. acutus* (American crocodile), *C.pelastris* (Indian Mugger), *Alligator mississippiensis* (American alligator).
Distribution	■	The tropics and subtropics of the Americas, Australia, Indo-Pacific islands, Asia and Africa.

These reptiles (crocodilians) are the last remaining link with the age of dinosaurs. They feed and swim in water, but bask and mate on the river banks. They are prized for their skins and as a target for shooters. Over this century, they have been decimated, but recently there has been a tendency to protect adult crocodiles from their only real enemy, the human hunter. Eggs and baby crocodilians are considered a delicacy by other animals and some humans.

Crocodilians, despite their unlovable appearance, live a highly developed social life. They are very territorial and communicate underwater by a variety of deep throated sounds and higher pitched oral noises. They display emotions by specific body postures, and become more aggressive during breeding times. The young are hatched from eggs and are protected by both parents.

The species considered as man eaters are the salt water crocodile and the Nile crocodile which grow to 8 metres; and the American crocodile and American alligator, which grow to 3.5 metres. South American caimans are of the same family as alligators. Even the Indian mugger crocodile may attack humans if provoked while nesting. All crocodilians are carnivorous. They range in size from 1-10 metres long, and the larger specimens are the ones potentially dangerous to humans. The largest grow up to a tonne in weight.

South American caimans can grow up to 5.5 metres long, although most are much less. As one moves north to the Gulf of Mexico, southern U.S.A. and the Caribbean, crocodiles become more frequent. The crocodilians of Florida were nearly wiped out by hunting in the Everglades and land development of the Keys. Conservation attempts over the last decade has resulted in a rise of some crocodilian populations, but this also has consequences that are difficult to reconcile. As the animals grow older and larger, conflicts with humans re-emerge. They are often believed to compete with fishermen, damaging nets, and may prey on both domestic animals and humans.

Alligators are slower moving, and generally less dangerous to man. Crocodiles have narrower snouts than alligators, and the 4th tooth in each side of the lower jaw is usually visible when the mouth is closed. If you can observe the fourth tooth, then you are too close.

As alligators are only found in China and southeastern U.S.A., if you see one in South Pacific, you may find it necessary to renegotiate with your travel agent. The salt water or estuarine crocodiles are usually bigger than the freshwater types, which are usually harmless in the Australian region.

Salt water crocodilians may be found in fresh water. They may have swum inland from an estuary or travelled many kilometres overland. Freshwater croco-

Crocodile, length 4 m

dilian are also found in lakes and rivers that have no connection with the sea, and in some countries they may be both large and dangerous.

As a general rule, any animal—salt water or fresh water, alligator or crocodile—over a metre long is likely to be dangerous.

Crocodilians are important predators in the food chain, eating water beetles, water spiders, dragon flies etc in their earlier life, and reptiles, amphibians, crustaceans, molluscs and fish as they become older. Only 2% of the eggs are likely to survive their many predators, and sexual maturity takes 12-15 years.

The animals are usually territorial, with dominant males prepared to fight for this territory. Any passing male must elevate his head and exposes his neck, in submission, to gain passage through another's territory. If humans or other animals intrude into the territory the crocodilian sometimes give warning by exhaling loudly or even growling at the intruder. Mating, nesting and rearing is formalised in a complex and sophisticated behaviour pattern.

They have very complex brains for reptiles, and are intelligent enough to stalk a human, strong enough to destroy a water buffalo, and gentle enough to release its own young from the eggs with their teeth. They even carry the newly hatched babies in their massive jaws. Stones are swallowed to increase the animal's specific gravity to achieve neutral buoyancy in the water.

Crocodilians tear their food from the carcass, twisting and turning in the water to achieve this. They then swallow it whole. Once an attack pattern has been instigated, the crocodilian will attack repeatedly until the prey is captured, and it may follow the victim from the water if necessary. If the animal captures large prey, it may hide the carcase underwater, entangled in submerged trees or under ledges, until it is ready to resume feeding.

Crocodilians often lie along the banks of rivers, with the nostrils intermittently protruding above water to breathe. The prey, especially land animals such as horse, cattle, giraffe, rhinoceros, kangaroo and wallaby, come to the river bank to drink and may be suddenly grabbed in the immensely strong jaws of the crocodilian, and twisted off their feet. This movement will sometimes break the neck of the victim. Once the prey is in the water it is vulnerable to panic and drowning. Although this is the classical attack pattern, crocodilians can move fast on land and in water, and recent attacks have included attacks with the victim in boats, on dry land and free swimming in deep water.

On land the attacks are especially at night when the animal commonly stalks for food. They can move suprisingly fast, faster than most humans, making a hissing sound, and they sometimes attack by sweeping the victim with the powerful tail.

In the U.S.A., and other countries where the animals have been protected for more than a decade, and allowed to grow longer and larger, the danger of attack is becoming greater. There is also an increase of tourism into remote crocodilian territories.

In Australia, crocodiles and sharks have about the same number of attacks on humans (two per year) and cause the same number of deaths (one per year). This was not always so, but while there is a diminishing number of shark attacks due to meshing, there is an increased crocodile attack frequency due to increased crocodile numbers. Controlled culling is now employed.

Prevention

1. Do not wade, swim, stand or canoe in tropical waterways and estuaries.
2. Do not walk along, camp or fish from the banks of tropical waterways and estuaries.
3. Take notice of local advice.
4. An attack may be thwarted by throwing objects at the crocodilian or hitting its snout or gouging its eyes.

First aid and **medical treatment.** See shark attack, pages 24-25.

These wounds are often ragged and traumatised. Occasionally a tooth fragment will be found by X-ray of the wound. Sometimes large portions of the human body may be found in the animal's gastrointestinal tract for weeks after the attack.

Media exploitation of crocodile attack.

EELS

Family	■ Murenidae.
Dangerous species	■ *Gymnothorax melaegris* (Tropical Moray Eel) and others.

Family	■ Leptocephalidae.
Dangerous species	■ *Conger labiatus* (Conger Eel) and others.
Distribution	■ Tropical, subtropical, and temperate waters.

The moray eel's fearsome reputation is due more to its appearance than habits. Their bead-like eyes seem to transfix the potential victim, and their open mouth seems ready to bite. In fact, the mouth is open to allow water to pass through its gills to extract oxygen.

There are many instances of morays being tamed and fed by divers, using cut urchins, sausages or pieces of fish. Some dive resorts have their own pet moray, which can be handled and fed if the diver moves slowly. The eel then learns to equate divers with food, and may become aggressive when this does not eventuate. Attacks are sometimes seen when divers wave their hands near the eel, when the eel is speared, or if surfers dangle feet or hands over their boards. The eel may attack in open water—behaviour that I have not witnessed in the past, but which now happens frequently where eels are fed. Skinny dippers, especially males, should take note.

Freshwater eels have also been known to attack and bite humans.

Sea snakes are sometimes mistaken for eels, but snakes can be readily identified by the presence of a flat paddle-shaped tail, occasional scales, no fins or gills, not feeling slippery to the touch and having to surface regularly to breath.

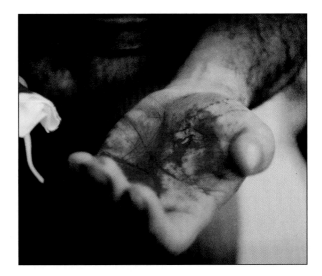

Moray eel bite on hand. The Scuba diver swiped at the moray, which was nibbling his ear. Bonaire, 1984. Photo by W. Lissauer.

Eels grow up to 3 metres in length, and 30 cm in diameter. They rarely attack without provocation but can be provoked by intrusion into their territory or on being injured or caught. They are night-feeders and bottom-dwellers, and in the daytime are commonly found in holes and crevices, under rocks or corals.

The upper teeth are hinged from the roof of the mouth, and when not in use they may lie flat, pointing backwards. The muscular jaws can clamp with great power, and the eel tears the flesh off its prey by winding its tail into a knot and slipping the knot down its body until it reaches the head. The eel then uses this solid support to prise off the meat. If they do attack, they are very awkward to grasp and difficult to dislodge, and even then may resume the attack.

Sharp, slashing lacerations may occur, and are probably defensive rather than feeding in behaviour. The presence of any significant venom apparatus is questionable or unlikely.

The eating of moray eels may result in severe poisoning (see Part IV). Gymnothorax toxin is absorbed after ingestion of eels and the result is identical to ciguatera poisoning or similar to paralytic shellfish poisoning from eating affected shellfish (Russell). The "ciguatoxin" isolated from eels is very unstable. Moray eels are also incriminated as having ichthyohaemotoxic poisons, but this has not yet been reported in most of the regions which harbour moray eels. The eel form of ciguatera poisoning may result in prolonged paralysis, lasting over one week in duration.

Conger eels are deemed to have a vicious disposition. Exceptional ones may grow up to 3 metres in length and 40 kg in weight, but frequently they are found in the 1 metre/10 kg. range. Their colour varies from black to brownish yellow, with a purple tinge and a pale underside.

Clinical features

LOCAL. The wounds are usually of a torn and ragged type. Initially there may be profuse bleeding. Secondary infection in the area is particularly common. It has also been claimed that the area may be affected by a venomous substance, resulting in local paralysis, although this is not well documented.

GENERALISED. The major complication of this injury is that of blood loss, with shock. The clinical features include a sweaty (cold and clammy) appearance, rapid pulse, hypotension and syncope on standing (fainting).

First aid and **medical treatment.** See shark attack, pages 24-25.

Prevention

1. Do not spear eels.
2. Do not intrude into their domain.
3. Do not feed eels. They can be befriended without this.
4. Wear heavy protective clothing (boots, gloves) when contact is possible.

Dee Scarr's Scuba Diary   Spooky

Usually, a spotted moray eel (Gymnothoras moringa) which hasn't been fed is quite shy. Such an eel has no interest in unnatural food such as hot dog and retreats into its crevice when it is offered. When fish is offered, these eels generally approach it warily at first, then grab it speedily and retreat into their dens to swallow it. They emerge a bit less warily than before, and with each piece of fish—as long as they are hungry—they become less shy. Only when they are very hungry (or very small, young spotted morays are often more aggressive than large ones) will an eel not used to being fed, emerge far from its crevice, no matter how enticing the food is.

The first day I approached Spooky I expected him to behave according to the rules. I offered him a piece of fish, which he gobbled down in the way of a hungry eel.

But then, much to my surprise, he completely emerged from the tire that was his home and began actively swimming around me, eagerly searching me

Dee Scarr playing with Spooky the Spotted Moray. Bonaire, 1984. Photo by K. Hansell.

for more fish. When an eel is that eager, it usually goes after exhaust bubbles (I suspect because, to an animal with weak eyesight, those fast-moving shiny things seem the source of the fishy smell), and Spooky was no exception. As I faced upward to keep my exhaust bubbles away from my face, I felt Spooky "taste" my ear lobe by placing his teeth on it. Luckily, the unfamiliar feel of my earring discouraged him. He then tasted the nose pocket of my low-volume silicon mask, perhaps attracted by the light colour. Although his movements were frenetic, his teeth didn't pierce the mask. Lastly, moving his head between that low-volume mask and my small Tekna second stage, he placed his teeth on my upper lip.

My usual behaviour in such a situation is simply to hold still, so as not to frighten the eel into biting. Theoretically, it will soon learn that nothing it tastes is worth eating and go away.

But when Spooky tasted my lip I decided that passive resistance might not be the best alternative, and VERY gently I pushed him away. He allowed me to do this. I retreated, decided to name him "Spooky," and also decided to avoid him in the future.

I did this successfully for a couple of weeks. Then one day I saw a snake eel about 3 metres from Spooky's tire. I didn't see Spooky's head, so I decided to offer the snake eel a small piece of fish. Before the snake eel even realised the fish was there Spooky had emerged from his tire and begun to swim toward me. Hastily, I put the fish back into the can and took out a whole hot dog. I didn't merely hold out the hot dog to Spooky, I pretty much shoved it into his mouth. I figured the relatively large hot dog might slow him down a bit, and his reaction to it would help me decide if I should try to work with him again or to leave.

As he ate the hot dog his movements were slow and appeared calm. I held out my hand, clad in a brightly-coloured glove (I almost always wear gloves when I work with morays; fingers look a lot like hot dogs and fish, and I think the gloves give the eels a colour and texture message that "this is not food"), and Spooky lowered his external nostrils to the glove. I began to stroke him under his "chin." He swam over my hand toward my face, but calmly, not in the frenetic way he had the one other time I worked with him.

In all my other experiences with free-swimming spotted morays, they always swim continuously; around my neck, under my tank, between my legs—but they never stop swimming. Spooky stopped. I supported his body with one hand as I stroked him under the chin with the other. He allowed me to support and stroke him in that way for what seemed a long time. He was clearly not looking for food. He was not behaving aggressively, and it was as if he wanted to learn more about this strange creature that was me.

I felt he had crossed a barrier and I was eager to respond with a barrier-crossing behaviour of my own, but I could think of nothing more to do than continue stroking him gently. Eventually, because my buddies were low on air, I swam with Spooky still in my arms to his tire and lowered him down to it. He swam in and extended his head for a last stroke before we left.

That second interaction with Spooky was very special, made even more so by the fact that we didn't have a long series of interactions building up to his trusting behaviour, and also by the difference in his behaviour from one interaction to the other.

I was eager to continue working with Spooky, but I never saw him again.

ELECTRIC RAYS

Family	■ Torpedinidae
Dangerous species	■ *Hypnos monopterygium, Torpedo macneilli, Narcine tasmaniensis* and others
Common names	■ Numb Ray, Numbfish.
Distribution	■ Temperate coastlines between the Tropics of Capricorn and Cancer.

Electric rays are slow and ineffective swimmers, and usually lie submerged in mud or sand at shallow depths, where they are found throughout the year.

The electric discharge varies from 8 to 220 volts, and is passed between the electrically negative under side of the ray to the electrically positive top side. The thick electric organs are usually discernible on each side of the fish, alongside the spinal column. They discharge an electric current automatically if the fish is touched. The ray can deliver a successive series of discharges, but these are of lessening intensity. There is then a latent period in which the fish regains its electric potential. It is not necessary to have direct contact with the body of the ray for a shock to be felt.

Clinical features. The receipt of an electric shock may rarely cause a serious temporary disabling of the victim, leading to possible drowning. There are usually no local manifestations visible on the skin affected.

First aid and **medical treatment.** Recovery is uneventful, and treatment is not usually required. In the rare event of cardio-pulmonary resuscitation being required, see Appendix I .

Electric ray. Photo by J. Joiner

DEE SCARR'S SCUBA DIARY   **A Shocking Tale**

In almost 4000 dives, most of them in the Bahamas and Caribbean, I've only seen one electric ray.

It was on San Salvador. I saw the ray and thought it was one of the little yellow spotted stingrays that are fairly common there, but since it didn't look quite right, I approached it more closely. It remained in place, facing away from me under a ledge in the coral. I reached out and gently stroked one of its "wings"; it stayed still.

So that I could reach it better, I stuck my hand under the ledge in front of it and tickled it, hoping it would turn around and come closer to the opening of the ledge. It did. I began to stroke its wing again, this time a bit closer to the center of the ray's body. That's when it shocked me.

It was a very mild shock (though strong enough that I didn't touch that ray again), almost as if the ray wanted to help me identify it. I called a bunch of divers over, pointing excitedly to the ray and, taking my regulator out, shouting "It's an electric ray. It shocked me." No one understood what I was saying; the ray remained my own private experience.

GROPER

Family	■	Serranidae
Dangerous species	■	*Promicrops itaiara, Plectropomus* spp, *Epinephelus* spp, *Polyprionum* spp and others.
Common names	■	Grouper, Jewfish (U.S.A.) Giant Cod, Rock Cod, Spotted Cod, Hapuku, Sea Basses, Cod, and others.
Distribution	■	Tropical, subtropical and temperate waters.

Gropers are the heavyweights of the sea. In the Persian Gulf they have been recorded at lengths of over 4 metres, and weighing over 450 kg. Most of the larger specimens of the Great Barrier Reef and the Caribbean would not, however, reach half this size.

Many species prefer to remain in shallow water during the summer months, travelling deeper during autumn and winter, where they can spawn. They tend to stay near rocks, and this perhaps explains the many scars on the jaws and the underside of the body, probably due to trenching on the ocean floor, to establish egg beds. It is a slow growing fish and growth is often more related to the vitamin A content in the liver than actual years of life. With increased age, there tends to be an increased vitamin A, and therefore an increase in size (see page 229).

Gropers have become probably the most friendly of all fish to divers. They live in wrecks, caves, coral caverns and are protected by overhangs. They are often photographed, being very curious and appear to make very good friends. Once they appreciate that divers can supply food, in the form of fish offerings as opposed to a human sacrifice, the groper will often remain in the area and approach other divers later. There is a slight danger when hands and feet are

Blue groper. Photo by D. Boyall

waved around, simulating perhaps the activity of fish, and may certainly attract the attention of the myopic groper. This is responsible for most of the minor injuries that have occurred, although the appendage will usually be spat out when it is unable to be swallowed (whilst still attached to an arm or a leg).

Groper usually eat octopus, squid, swimming crabs, other fish and anything else that happens to be passing by. Despite their size, gropers can move very fast and have even been known to devour the deep diving birds. Most of the food is swallowed whole despite the jaws which are capable of ripping most prey apart.

Unprovoked attacks on swimmers divers have been reported, and in some areas such as the Torres Straits, gropers are feared more than sharks. They have been known to grab hands, feet and even the whole body of divers and surfers, verifying their potential to cause injury. Occasional fatalities have been described, although not well documented. The only case known to this author involved a small female child.

Clinical features

LOCAL. The wounds may be ragged, with extensive maceration of tissue. Bleeding may be profuse. Secondary infection is to be anticipated.

GENERALISED. The clinical features are those of shock: a pale, sweaty (cold, clammy) patient with a rapid pulse and hypotension. Syncope on standing (fainting) may be due to blood loss.

Prevention

1. Do not dispute the territorial rights of a groper.
2. Ensure that there is no contact with injured fish. Do not handle or carry speared fish.
3. Some claim that traces of grease or perspiration will attract this animal.
4. Most scare techniques used by divers against sharks (blowing bubbles, making a noise, moving toward the fish, etc.) are of little avail with gropers.

First aid and **medical treatment.** As for shark attack, pages 24-25 .

KILLER WHALE

Dangerous species ■ *Orcinus orca, Grampus orca*
Common name ■ Orca
Distribution ■ All oceans of the world, but more frequent in the polar regions.

Said by some to be one of the largest and most dangerous creatures (a mammal) to be found in the sea, the killer whale grows up to 9 metres in length, and has a blunt, rounded snout. It is shiny black in colour with white over the eyes and on the belly, giving it a spotted appearance.

The killer whale is strictly carnivorous and is exceptional in being ferocious without provocation. Attacks are not related to environmental temperature and the whale, which is really a dolphin, has been known to leap out of the water to attack and destroy boats and to up end ice floes to reach its victim (usually a seal).

The bite is achieved with 10-14 interlocking conical teeth on each jaw. They hunt in packs of up to 40, preying on other marine animals, including whales, seals and penguins. The name is derived from the fact that it is a killer of whales.

It is particularly difficult to ascertain the source of the killer whale's reputation for aggression against humans. Attempts by divers to approach these animals in the wild are usually unsuccessful, with the whales retreating rapidly, which is not consistent with their horrendous reputation.

Killer whale, length 7 m. Photo by F. Fay

Perusal of the *Journal of Scott of the Antarctic,* which is often quoted as evidence of a killer whale attacking a human, leaves great doubt as to the closeness of the killer whale to the alleged victim. There is one case history of a young lady who, about 2 decades ago, had her leg injured, between a killer whale and the side of an aquarium when she was trying to ride the animal. Neither of these two sources produce a great deal of credence on which to base any further Hollywood marine monster epics.

Recently a sole case history was supportive of the reputation. In 1991, at the Victorian Aquarium in Canada, a female university student, an assistant trainer, slipped into a holding area for killer whales. She was towed into the centre of the area by the animals, and pulled underwater on a number of occasions, until she finally drowned. This is predictable killer whale behaviour towards other prey. For over an hour, attempts to throw ropes to her or rescue her were unsuccessful. At autopsy there was no significant physical trauma.

There is ample evidence for the high intelligence, learning ability and the potential for sophisticated behaviour of these animals. Whalers at Twofold Bay, near Eden in N.S.W., Australia, were surprised by a group of killer whales which learnt, probably because of their observation of the whalers, that when other whales were caught considerable amounts of meat (including the tongues) were jettisoned. As a result, packs of killer whales continually shepherded other larger whales into the whaling area and station at Twofold Bay. There the whalers made their catch and fed the whale tongues to the killer whales. This continued for many years, and was a great tourist attraction in the area until the whale population declined and the station closed.

Clinical features. As for shark attack, pages 17-19.

First aid and **medical treatment.** As for shark attack, pages 24-25.

MISCELLANEOUS BITING FISH

Piranha

The piranha (**Serrasalmus** spp) probably have the worst reputation of all small fish, and although they are carnivorous, and can be very ferocious and voracious, they certainly do not deserve their terrifying reputation. Abundant in the rivers of South America, most of the 20 or more species of piranha are harmless. The largest grow up to 45 cm long, while others grow only a few centimetres. Only towards the black piranha and its relatives, need there be any cause for concern. If they are in sufficient numbers, they are believed to be able to remove all the flesh from a large sized animal within a few minutes.

Piranha have a very deep body, blunt head and strong jaws with triangular razor-sharp teeth that inter digitate during the severing bite. They are thought to be attracted by blood, even though the usual source of food is other fish. When they do attack larger prey, each bite will take a chunk of flesh, cut cleanly with the razor sharp teeth.

Human attacks are rare, although there was a report of a bus tumbling into the piranha infested waters of the Urubu river, 200 km east of Manaus, in the Amazon region of Brazil. When rescuers arrived nine hours later, most of the 38 passengers were apparently reduced to skeletons.

Because of their reputation, tight government controls are imposed on the importation of these fish, which have been popular with home aquarium owners. Unfortunately, there is always the humourist who introduces the animal to waterways by flushing them down toilets, and throwing them into streams.

Piranha, length 30 cm

Taylor or Blue Fish

Taylor or blue fish (*Pomatomous saltatrix*) do not have the same reputation as the piranha, although they certainly work in large schools and have caused occasional injury to bathers. When caught on fishing lines they can react violently and there have been reports of fingers being amputated. They commonly travel in large numbers along the east coast of the United States, and on August 12, 1974, the beaches near Bakers Haulover, Miami, Florida, had to be closed when swimmers were driven from the water by large numbers of blue fish which, although probably attracted by schools of mullet hugging the coastline at that stage, attacked many swimmers. A number of fingers and toes were badly injured, and many people needed sutures.

Others

Spanish mackerel (*Scomberomorus maculatus*) have also occasionally attacked and injured swimmers en masse.

Some fish not usually known to bite humans may do so under certain circumstances. The very beautiful and famous **bat fish** (*Platax* spp) around Heron Island in the Great Barrier Reef, an area that has for long been a marine reserve, are used to being fed by divers and are likely to move in large numbers and nip at divers' exposed skin.

Most of the **tetrodotoxic** fish (see pages 203-207) have four strong biting teeth and are slow swimming. They are encountered frequently by divers and fishermen. As the jaws are designed to crunch through crustaceans, the tip of a human finger is not beyond a nibble.

CASE REPORT   **Toadfish bite**

Occasionally, one fish will become a bit of a rogue, and be prepared to attack without the security of numbers. Thomas the Terrible Toadfish, was one such example. Toadfish, of the order Tetraodontiformes, have four large fused teeth, very effective in breaking the shells of crabs, which they eat. Thomas became famous, and then infamous, because of the campaign of terror he conducted through the Whitsunday Islands, again, near the Barrier Reef.

During the Easter weekend of 1979, six-year-old Margaret Lewis had two toes bitten off, while wading barefoot in Shute Harbour. Later on, Thomas removed a large chunk from the leg of a boy wading in Shute Harbour. In October of the same year, Richard Timberley was standing in water half a metre deep, near the Shute Harbour ramp, when the 65 cm toadfish zoomed on his sneakered feet. Despite jabbing from the fishing rod, the toadfish pursued Richard, chomping at the sneakers, until he was almost beached. Timberley then made up a large "wanted" poster, to warn locals about this terror, which he named "Thomas the Terrible Toadfish." It seemed to me that the villain was misnamed. He should have been called "Thomas the Terrible Toefish".

One of my surgeon colleagues, who was bemused by the story of Thomas the Terrible Toadfish, had nevertheless learnt to feed fish by hand in one of the "Touch

the sea" guided experiences in the Maldives. Again, a relatively small puffer fish decided to accept not only the morsel of meat being proffered, but also the index finger. The crushing injury was fairly extensive, and certainly put the surgeon off the operating table for a short while.

Toad Fish, length 25 cm

OCTOPUS AND SQUID

OCTOPUSES

Class	■	Cephalopoda.
Order	■	Octopoda.
Dangerous species	■	*Octopus hongkonensis, O. vulgaris* and others.
Distribution	■	All oceans.

It is not easy to unravel the literature on this subject. Homer in 700 B.C. in the Odyssey, wrote about the octopus . He was almost certainly recounting a legend based on actual sightings. Victor Hugo in *The Toilers of the Sea,* in 1886, related with vivid terminology the problems encountered in the life of a diver, Gilliatt, during a life and death struggle with a giant octopus. It is hard to believe that the event did not happen exactly as Hugo described it, such was his literary skill.

From that time, everyone seems to have had a go at outdoing their predecessors, either in gullibility or scepticism. It is a great tragedy that almost all the reports are written in the third person: "I once knew a man who said that...."

The following account is my assessment of the middle ground.

Anatomy and physiology. The octopus is an eight-armed Cephalopod of the order Octopoda. They inhabit all oceans from the Arctic to the Antarctic, from the surface waters to depths of 5000 metres. The largest is the Pacific *Octopus hongkongensis,* which has an arm span of up to 9.5 metres. The common octopus, *O. vulgaris* lives in tropical and temperate waters, and can have an arm span of 3 metres and weigh 22.5 kg.

During the octopus massacres by scuba divers of previous decades, octopuses with a span of 5 metres and over 50 kg were commonly caught in the Puget Sound, Washington State.

The octopus is the underwater chameleon. It changes colour to match the slightest variation in the environment (a cloud overhead, a swimmer nearby), to suit its own moods (feeding, sexual activity, fear, alertness) and to conform with the surrounding terrain. It can remain immobile for hours before capturing prey such as crabs and shrimp, or can make sudden spurts of speed to capture its victim, or remove itself from predators. It often attacks oyster beds and fishermen's pots for lobsters.

The octopus has many enemies including sharks, whales, seals, large fish, eels and people. The life and death struggles between octopus and moray eels have often been observed. The octopus has great difficulty obtaining suction on the slippery skin of the eel, as the eel has a very good technique for removing the tentacle, by using its knot and slip technique.

The octopus can move by crawling or dragging itself along on one or two arms, trailing its body and the other arms behind. It can glide in a delicate ballet style motion, with the tip of each arm lightly touching the bottom, and the web undulating gently. It can also transport itself by jetting a stream of water through the siphon, pushing its body at a rapid speeds over a very short distance, or up to 5 km per hour over longer periods.

Behind the head, in the globular sac or mantle, are the major organs and extending from the mantle are the eight arms. Expansion of the mantle causes water to be drawn into the aperture, and when the mantle contracts, it forces the water through a narrow muscular tube, called the siphon, producing a jet propelled swimming style. Ink can be ejected along with the water.

The octopus has the ability to regenerate lost parts of its body and can voluntarily sacrifice one of its tentacles if the need arises. This is not dissimilar to the lizard or ghekko which jettisons its tail in order to escape. It can even regenerate eyes which have been lost. The eyes of the octopus are highly developed sensory organs similar to those of mammals.

The octopus has a larger brain than those of other invertebrates and is supposed to be one of the most intelligent forms of invertebrate life. The brain has two distinct memory storage areas, with an ability to learn and remember information from previous behaviour. The octopus can therefore can be taught and conditioned.

The reproductive techniques vary with different species. In many, the male inserts the tip of his third right tentacle into the female's mantle, near the funnel. Spermatophores then travel along a longitudinal groove, the whole process taking many hours to complete. The female carries these in her mantle cavity, until she returns to her den, where she will then spawn. Over 100,000 eggs may be laid within a period of two weeks. During this period, the female will eat very little, if at all, and after the eggs hatch, she will usually die, presumably from exhaustion. There is also a reduction or cessation of the venom production in her salivary glands.

The octopus has a beak capable of piercing shellfish, suction pads which are strong enough to prize open bivalves and oysters, and defensive sepia or ink which can be used as a "smoke screen," as a false aggressive threat, as a decoy to distract large predators and to confuse predators with a scent similar to that of the octopus. A moray, shark or grouper could waste valuable time attacking the ink cloud left behind the disappearing octopus. It can discharge this ink a number of times in rapid succession.

Colour changes produced by the chromatophores of the octopus are also likely to interrupt the stimulus response of the predator, again giving time for the octopus to depart or conceal itself.

Venom in the salivary glands can be injected directly into a bite, or into the sea water surrounding a small victim. This venom contains enzymes (such as hyaluronidase, serotonin and octopamine) and cephalotoxin, a substance which is toxic to crabs and which varies from one octopus species to another.

Human injury. The bite from an octopus can cause various symptoms in humans, sometimes causing pain very quickly. At other times a severe tissue reaction or inflammation occurs with gross swelling and numbness. It may take many days to resolve, and often produces itching.

Lane, in his text *Kingdom of the Octopus,* published in 1962, reviews the literature on octopus attacks against humans. A review published in 1971 could find only nine reports of octopus bites, other than those of the deadly blue-ringed octopus (see page 127).

One anecdotal report from Chile tells of a diver who received a direct hit with the ink of a large octopus, resulting in severe pain, blistering, swelling and discolouration of the area affected—the genitals. One's imagination runs rife in contemplating how this could have happened. Nevertheless, as I have seen a very nasty reaction from contact with the dye of a Hair-jelly (another cephalopod), I believe that the story could be factual.

By far the commonest conjecture regarding damage from octopus to divers, is the possibility of the octopus fixing itself to an undersea structure whilst holding onto a skindiver with the suckers on its other arms. It would be easy to write this off as Hollywood or poetic licence, had it not been for the experiences of some divers who would otherwise be classified as reasonably credible.

The eight arms of the common octopus have a double row of suckers, 240 on each arm. Thus there are 1920 sucker discs, the largest at the middle of each arm, and diminishing in size in each direction. Each disc, depending on the diameter, has an amazing holding power. The extreme difficulty encountered in trying to prise a very small octopus from rocks on which it has a grip is certainly consistent with the inability of a human to dislodge many of the larger animals. The octopus can use these arms and sucker discs to successfully fight and sometimes kill an aquatic animal as versatile and capable as a moray eel, and can even catch land animals along the seashore. There are many reports of an octopus sending out an arm to grasp the foot or hand of a diver, or even the foot of someone walking along the shoreline.

There have been reported cases in which an octopus has actually attacked a diver, originally "hard hat" or standard divers, but more recently breathhold and scuba divers. Occasionally they have been unprovoked, but more often the octopus is retaliating against a spear or knife.

One investigator, Thomas Helm, who seems to have more than his fair share of encounters with dangerous sea creatures, states that after he had severed part of a tentacle from an octopus in the Caribbean and then proceeded to try and spear it, the octopus obtained a good grip both on the sea bed and the diver, and Helm was released only after he drove a blade into the head of the octopus. Helm claims that it would be possible for an octopus with a span of

**Octopus,
length 1 m**

only 2 metres to trap a grown man. Even excellent swimmers can be restrained underwater by a weight far lighter than their own body weight. Unless the rocks or reef can be used to prise oneself away from the suction pads, it is difficult to envisage how a person could pull clear of a moderately sized octopus merely by swimming.

The advice given to most divers is to thrust a knife or spear into the animal's head, near the eye, and manoeuvre it from side to side to destroy the animal's brain. Another innovative way of killing an octopus is to grab it below the mantle and turn it inside out; another to bite it between the eyes. Both, however, seem overly dramatic.

Trying to sever the tentacles is not usually recommended for three reasons. One is that the octopus arm is tough and difficult to cut, which can be testified by calamari connoisseurs. The second is that the animal appears indifferent to pain, and the loss of an arm or two does not seem to immediately concern the animal. The third reason is the time factor, which is relevant to skindiving, perhaps more than scuba diving.

As most swimmers use beaches which have a sandy bottom, they are most unlikely to ever encounter octopus. This environment offers little or no shelter for these animals, whereas the skindiver and scuba diver is more likely to move into octopus territory of corals and reefs.

Lane, who canvassed the experience of many divers, noted that opinions ranged from "a large octopus is the most dangerous animal encountered by divers" to "a farmer in a cornfield is in more danger of being attacked by a pumpkin that a swimmer is of being attacked by an octopus." Perhaps the truth lies somewhere between the sceptics and the believers.

In fact, both statements could be correct. There seems no doubt that there have been injuries to swimmers and divers by the common octopods, that some have been rescued by the action of their companions, and that some others may have been killed. Nevertheless, each is a very rare event.

Poisoning from the ingestion of octopus and squid has been reported, especially from Japan where there has been some impressive but sporadic outbreaks. Symptoms develop within 10-20 hours, consist of gastrointestinal upset, abdominal pain, headache, weakness, paralysis and convulsions. About 10 deaths have been recorded, but most patients recover within 48 hours. Cooking did not destroy the poison.

DEE SCARR'S SCUBA DIARY   Octopus

The most unusual series of interactions I've ever had were with an octopus (Octopus vulgaris) *I named Olivia.*

I found Olivia's den in November 1984 and, as is my habit in such cases, I offered her a piece of fish. She took the fish and my hand—and pulled everything into her den. This happens to me more often than not on the first interaction I have with an O. vulgaris *in its den, and I'd always assumed that the octopus figured that relatively huge, noisy me could make a much better guardian for its doorway than a few old cans or shells.*

Usually by the second or third interaction, though, the octopus realises that I'm going to take my hand back. It stops trying to grab me and often greets my arrival with jets of water from its siphon (apparently in an attempt to blow away the Indian-giving intruder).

Olivia, however, continued to grab my hand. She'd hold on tenaciously, too. I'd have to lever myself against the pipe in which she lived to get my hand back, and would often have a collection of little sucker marks when I finally succeeded (the highest total was 52).

I was worried that she'd injure herself in our battle for my hand, and since I could not very well make her a gift of it, I decided to offer her the food in such a way that she could not easily get my hand. This worked once. The next time she reached out for the food with two arms—and snuck two arms around to the back of my hand at the same time. As soon as she got my hand she dropped the food and hauled me into the den.

As we got to know each other better, Olivia seemed to realise that I was stronger than she was (although I wondered about that a couple of times), and when I really pulled, she would release my hand.

I began positioning my hand so that it went across her doorway rather than into her house. She'd hold my hand braced there and would let my buddies (one at a time) stroke her arms. Sometimes she took food, sometimes not, but always my hand.

I tried offering my hand several centimetres from her doorway and she reached out to grab it; ultimately she'd come all the way out of her den to fetch my hand home for a visit.

One day in January as my buddy and I arrived at Olivia's pipe, I realised that there was another octopus scrunched up against the side of the pipe near Olivia's doorway. We settled down about 3 metres away to watch. I'd seen octopuses mating before but that day it looked as if we were just in time for the beginning of the show, voyeurs that we were. Olivia's suitor eased closer to her doorway, then extended one arm and began to stroke her body. In mating, the male octopus inserts a specialised arm beneath the mantle of the female and passes her his sperm sac. As Olivia's suitor moved his arm toward the bottom of her mantle I assumed that this was what he would do, but I never would have predicted what she did: She walked out of her den, grabbed my hand, and towed it (with the rest of me attached) the 3 metres to her den.

All I can figure is that the fish and hot dogs I'd been showering her with for the past months were preferable to a measly few caresses. Her jilted suitor, meanwhile, remained scrunched up at the side of the pipe, presumably wondering what was going on. Eventually he moved back along the pipe and swam off. I couldn't follow him because Olivia was still holding my hand.

Up until then she had never done more with my hand than hold it with her arms, but that day I could feel something more going on. When I finally extracted my hand there were three pairs of small scratches which I think she made with her beak. When it happened her movements felt exploratory and certainly not at all aggressive. There was no envenomation and the scratches healed quickly.

A few days later when I arrived at the pipe Olivia was not home, but there was an octopus in exactly the same position as her suitor had been. Again, we settled down 3 metres or so away from the pipe to watch. After less than two minutes the octopus, which I believe was Olivia's suitor, began moving off in the same direction he had when he left before. Staying at the limits of visibility so as not to *frighten him, we followed. He would swim for a while, than walk—almost as if he wanted to be sure we could keep up. About 50 metres away from the pipe he oozed into a crevice and I noticed another octopus under a crevice a couple of feet away. Embedded in the mantle of the second octopus was a fishhook with its barb all the way through the flesh. The hooked octopus was pulling at the shank of the hook (which would only have resulted in its pulling the barb back into its flesh).*

The hooked octopus allowed me to take hold of the hook, and I tried to pull it all the way through. The eye was big, though, and I must have been causing the octopus some pain because after I pulled the hook part way through, the octopus began pushing my hand away. All the time this was going on the octopus that had "led" us there stayed within 4 metres of me and seemed to be watching the operation.

A couple of days later when I next visited that den, the octopus wasn't there—but the fishhook was.

Soon after that I found an octopus living in a paint can very close to Olivia's pipe. I held out my hand and it immediately grabbed the hand and pulled it into its can. I noticed it had wounds in the places the hooked octopus had been hooked, so I concluded that the paint can octopus and the hooked octopus were the same. Its behaviour in regard to my hand told me it was Olivia.

One day as Olivia held my hand she began to drill me. I'd heard that the venom of a Caribbean octopus was not particularly potent, and I'd been wondering for a while exactly what it would be like to be envenomated, so I kept my hand still until the pain overcame my curiosity. When I pulled my hand from the can Olivia came along with it but almost immediately swam off.

The wound was a tiny hole smaller in diameter than a pencil lead, between the bases of my middle fingers. At first the surrounding area turned white but by the time the dive was over, about 30 minutes later, it was red. I was conscious of the wound but it wasn't terribly painful. I had a busy schedule that night and was not able to treat my hand in any way. It stopped hurting in a couple of hours and began to swell and itch.

The next morning my hand was quite swollen. It continued to swell for another day or so; then the swelling went down.

I had taken my ring off and applied some hydrocortisone ointment to my hand (it didn't do any good), and for the next couple of days Olivia refused to take my hand—because of the foreign taste of the ointment? Because the ring was gone?

But eventually, after the swelling and ointment were gone and the ring was back, her interest in my hand revived and our interactions were like old times. One day she tried to drill me again. Once was enough for me, though, so I withdrew my hand immediately. I offered it again on that same dive and she took it again, but she never again tried to drill me.

My biggest problem with Olivia was trying to think of ways to intrigue her. I wonder if she was having the same problem with me, and that the nibbling and drilling were two things she could do to see how I would react?

In April an overzealous diver who couldn't pry Olivia out of the paint can brought the can onto his boat, "played" with her a while on the boat, and dumped her and the can (separately) back into other water. I found the can and put it back where it had been. Two days later Olivia was back home but her behaviour was greatly altered. Understandably, she didn't trust divers any more. Less than a week later she disappeared.

SQUID

Class	■ Cephalopoda
Order	■ Decapoda.
Dangerous species	■ *Dorsidcus gigas, Architeuthis harveyi* and others.
Distribution	■ All oceans.

The squid has ten appendages, eight short arms and two extendable tentacles for snaring prey. At the end of the two tentacles, are four studded suckers, considerably more dangerous than the usual suckers. The body is elongated, with a fin at the posterior end. Not only is it larger, but is also far faster and more agile than the octopus.

Squid have been known to bite large chunks from the tough wooden handle of a gaffe used to pull them into a boat. They are also said to be able to cut through wire cables with their beaks. Squid fishermen claim that the savagery of a squid fight exceeds that of a shark feeding frenzy.

There are over 350 species of squid, some reaching up to a length of 18 metres, such as *Architeuthas*. There is evidence to suggest that some squid can reach a length of 18-30 metres. These can be very large animals, and even if one excludes the length of the extended tentacle, the body length can be between 5 and 6 metres. The larger squid tend to stay in the open ocean.

The Humboldt squid, *Dorsidcus gigas,* is found off the Peruvian coast, it weighs about 136 kg and has a length of 4 metres, excluding the extra length of the two tentacles.

The Protestant bishop, Eric Pontoppidan, in his *Natural History of Norway* published in 1755, is famous or infamous for his descriptions of the giant squid and its unprovoked attacks on seagoing craft.

In Newfoundland in the 1870's, a large number of giant squid were found washed up on the shore. The reason remains unknown, nevertheless, it was then clearly shown that the giant squid was not just a myth. The Rev. Moses Harvey documented many such animals, and one of the largest had a mantle of 5 metres long with 12 metre tentacles. The creature is now named after him, and is known as *Architeuthis harveyi*. There were said to have been animals much larger than this, and the largest of all was unfortunately used for fish bait by the local fishermen.

It is not clear why, when quoting from these reports, emphasis is always placed on the religious faith of the observers. Is this meant to convince or to caution us?

There are many reported attacks by the larger squid on fishing boats and other craft, and there is evidence of them attacking both whales and yellow fin tuna. By comparison to a floating or swimming human, tuna is exceedingly fast and powerful in the water, and any animal that could hold and destroy a yellow fin tuna, should have little difficulty with a swimmer or diver. They are also capable of cannibalism against an injured animal of the same species.

It has been claimed that there have been unprovoked attacks on humans, and Lieutenant Cox of the sunken troopship *Britannia,* in March 1941, witnessed the death of one of his shipmates, by a large squid that grabbed the man and pulled him below the surface. Cox was also attacked and held by the squid, but only briefly. He stated that the claw-studded suckers caused intense pain, and the circular scars on Cox's legs of 2.5 cm were still present years later.

SEALS, SEA LIONS AND WALRUSES

Suborder	■	Pinnipedia.
Dangerous species	■	*Zalophus californianus, Neophoca cinerea, Hydrurga leptonyx, Erignathus barbatus* and others.
Common name	■	Californian Sea Lion, Australian Sea Lion, Leopard Seal, Bearded Seal.
Distribution	■	Arctic, Antarctic and cool regions.

The suborder Pinnipedia have special adaptations for their marine activities. These mammals are fusiform-shaped because of the subcutaneous fat layer, reducing temperature loss and streamlining their underwater swimming. Their limbs are modified to look and perform like fins, with webbing between the digits. Some species can dive to depths of 200 metres for more than 30 minutes.

True seals lack ears, tend to use the hind limbs for propulsion, and form pairs during the breeding season. The eared seals (sea lions and fur seals) use

Leopard Seal, length 3 m

their forelimbs for underwater propulsion and gather in large herds and harems for breeding.

All pinnipeds are carnivorous, but are known more for their placid nature than aggressive acts. Even though they may grow up to 6.5 metres and weigh a tonne, most are considered friendly, intelligent animals that are able to be trained.

Walruses are found in arctic waters, often congregating on ice floes and have developed tusks which are of value in fighting and for pulling themselves onto the ice. Although generally peaceful and shy, walruses can be antagonised by hunters and stories abound of Eskimo hunters who have been speared with a tusk, dumped from a kayak or umiak, or crushed against the ice by a ton of angry walrus.

The Californian sea lion *Zalophus californianus,* and its cousins *Neophoca* spp from Australia and New Zealand, have been incriminated in minor attacks on humans, usually by intrusion of the latter into breeding harems. They are usually found in the cooler waters of the poles and less inhabited coastlines.

The more infamous leopard seal *Hydrurga leptonyx* is a solitary animal in the antarctic and cooler southern waters and will stalk penguins, seals and other warm blooded prey (rarely humans), swimming above them until finally the prey has to surface to breath. Then the leopard seal attacks. It is likely that divers are mistaken for seal prey. If a leopard seal is sighted, diving should be suspended. If underwater at the time of sighting, divers should not surface in mid water, but follow the seabed to the shore before leaving the water.

Clinical features. See shark attack, pages 17-19.

First aid and **medical treatment.** See shark attack, pages 24-25.

SWORDFISH (BILLFISH) AND SAWFISH

Dangerous species ■ *Xiphias* spp (Swordfish), *Istiophorus* spp (Sailfish),
                            Makaira spp (Marlin), *Hemirhamphus* spp (Garfish),
                            Pristis spp (Sawfish) and others.
Distribution   ■ Tropical, subtropical and temperate waters.

Although uncommon, there are enough documented cases of death and injury
from these fish to warrant mention. Injury can be caused by the large spear or
saw like extension of their jaw.

Billfish are renowned for their fighting abilities, and marlin are the epitome
of game fish. Other billfish include the swordfish and spearfish which can be of
a similar size and nature, and the usually smaller sailfish.

There are documented cases, together with the evidence in maritime museums, of these fish ramming ships and embedding their spear in the hull. They
have also been known to attack whales, other fish and humans. The attack is
usually precipitated by fear rather than a need for food.

Death to humans has usually occurred after the capture of a fish, usually by
a game fisherman, and during the attempt to bring the fish on board. Under such
conditions the fish fights to obtain its freedom and this results in the injury to
the fisherman.

Garfish. These fish are members of the order Beloniformes, and have also been
known to "spear" humans. They are smaller and include many species in temperate and tropical waters. They are known by various names including garfish,
needlefish, long tom, alligator, gar, aiguillie, flying fish and skipper (alluding to
the habit of jumping out of the water and skimming along the surface for short
distances). The slender spear-like beak consists of both narrow jaws with small
pointed teeth. Members of the family Hemiramphidae (half-beaks) have only an
elongated lower jaw.

Garfish can often be seen in schools, racing close to the surface of the sea
and leaping up, sometimes up to 2 metres above sea level. They frequently jump
out of the water at night time, and may leap into the canoes of fishermen. They
are sometimes attracted, or perhaps dazed, by bright lights used at night time by
fishermen, and some attack the light. These fish can impale themselves into humans as they skim over the surface. In one series of garfish injuries in Papua
New Guinea, of the ten accidents to humans; three died, three recovered after la-
parotomy, two were blinded and two had no sequelae.

Sawfish. These fish can grow up to 6 metres and weigh up to 450 kg. They are
sometimes captured by fishermen in nets, although they can usually chop
through most fishing nets, as they can through schools of fish (destroying many
and eating few). If, by accident, the saw penetrates a large fish, then the latter is
rubbed off on the sea bed, the sawfish scraping the victim off the saw before
consuming some of its remnants.

Sawfish belong to the order Rajiformes, which includes the rays and skates,
and are therefore relatives of the sharks. They give birth to live young whose

saw is covered with a protective membrane, allowing it to emerge without damaging the parent. This is soon lost, and the infantile specimens are very capable of using the saw as a weapon. The saw resembles a cross-cut saw with teeth on each side, and is an extension of the upper jaw. Sawfish frequent shallow coastal waters, and in theory they could be a threat to swimmers and wading fishermen. In practice this is not likely because they tend to move away quickly, and almost all the accidents can be attributed to attempting to extract a sawfish from a fishing net, or bringing it on board a boat after having caught it on a line.

Occasional unprovoked attacks have been reported. One was an attack on a fifteen year old boy who had been collecting shiny cans from the water. The cause of death was thought to be a combination of severe blood loss from the abdominal wound, and subsequent drowning.

Prevention

There are very few unprovoked attacks from these animals. Fishermen are advised not to use bright lights, which are likely to attract and panic the garfish and other flying fish. This was certainly the case referred to in the New Guinea series.

The capture of large billfish, including marlin and swordfish, may preface a dangerous situation, as they often apparently return to life, long after they have been proclaimed dead by their hopeful hunters. Removing either billfish of sawfish from lines and fishing nets needs care.

First aid and **medical treatment.** See shark attack, pages 24-25.

TRIDACNA-GIANT CLAM

Dangerous species ■ *Tridacna gigas.*
Common names ■ Great Clam, Killer Clam.
Distribution ■ Tropical waters.

The shells of these animals can grow over a metre across and weigh more than 100 kg. Ingestion may result in digestive and neurological manifestations, and death. An outbreak in Bora-Bora in 1964 affected some 30 persons and many domestic animals that ate the mantle or the viscera of the clam.

The giant clam poses a more difficult problem for inveterate theatre-goers than divers. It has been stated, based on anecdotal stories, that these clams have closed on an arm or leg, and pinned the unwary diver to the sea bed.

Tridacna need strong sunlight to grow and are usually found in very shallow water or on tidal rocks. The clams are certainly capable of exerting a considerable anchoring force, and are possibly a potential hazard to breathhold divers or to divers walking on the sea bed, but only under exceptional circumstances. The clam will usually close only about one quarter of its opening initially, but then takes minutes to complete the closure. The diver would thus have to be both provocative and procrastinating. Occasionally, however, they will close more rapidly.

Treatment

Insert a knife alongside the trapped limb and cut through the adductor muscles of the clam. This will allow the clam to be opened easily.

Because of this ever present possibility, with its inherent danger of accidental amputation, Clarrie Lawler, an old diving buddy, always dives with a surgeon.

PART II

Venomous Marine Animals (Stinging)

Venomous Fish
Venomous Coelenterates
Other Venomous Marine Animals

NOTES

Venomous Fish

STONEFISH

STINGRAYS

MISCELLANEOUS SCORPION FISH

CATFISH

OLD WIFE

RABBITFISH

RATFISH

STINGING SHARKS

STARGAZER

SURGEONFISH

TOADFISH

WEEVERFISH

<u>NOTES</u>

Venomous Fish

More than 1000 species of fishes are either poisonous to eat or venomous. The latter have spines and the venom apparatus is used more for protection, than incapacitation of prey. Spines may be concealed, only becoming obvious when in use (e.g., stonefish), or highlighted as an apparent warning to predators (e.g., butterfly cod or firefish).

Some fish envenomations have resulted in death, especially by the stonefish and stingray. These will be described separately. Others, such as the infamous scorpionfish and firefish (family Scorpaenidae), catfish (Plotosidae and Ariidae-), stargazers (Uranoscopidae) have also been responsible for occasional deaths in humans. Weeverfish (Trachinidae), toadfish (Batrachoididae), rabbit fish (Siganidae) and some species of leatherbacks (Carangidae) are also believed to have potentially dangerous venom. There appears to be a similarity between the venoms of different fishes, and envenomation can occur even from dead fish.

As a general rule, fish that have been damaged—such as those in fishing nets—cause less problems, probably because some of the envenomation system may have been previously triggered or damaged. Those wounds that bleed profusely are also less likely to have intense symptoms, probably due to the loss of venom with the blood. Some spines are not associated with venom sacs, and therefore produce few symptoms.

General manifestations of fish stings, such as shock, respiratory depression and death, are due to the venom entering and dispersing through the body. The victims body weight will be a major factor in the severity of the symptoms. Thus children are at greater risk than adults for the same amount of venom. The physical health of the victim is also relevant, and such diseases as asthma and coronary artery disease may adversely influence the outcome and mortality rate.

Other fish may produce cutting injuries with knife-like spines which may or may not result in envenomation, e.g., old wife (family Enoplosidae), surgeon and unicorn fish (Acanthuridae), ratfish (Chimaeridae). In many cases the slime that exists on the spines may contribute to the symptoms and subsequent infections, as much as the possible venom.

It is not always possible to obtain identification of the species of fish which is responsible. Fortunately there is often little variety in the type of symptom, although the severity may vary greatly between and within species.

Clinical features

The first symptom is usually an immediate local pain which increases in intensity over the next few minutes. It may become excruciating, but usually lessens after a few hours for an average sting, more rapidly with a minor sting and longer with a major sting. The old mariners' attempted reassurance to the patient is that the pain will lessen "with the turn of the tide."

The puncture wound or wounds become numb, but the surrounding area hypersensitive. Pain and tenderness in the lymph glands of the armpit or groin from the upper or lower limbs respectively, may extend even more centrally. Paralysis of the surrounding muscles is common.

Locally the appearance is that of one or more puncture wounds, with a blanched rim. Around this there is a red inflamed and sometimes bluish zone. Surrounding this is an area which is pale and swollen, developing within half an hour. The swelling is made worse by activity and lessened by elevation of the injured area.

Generalised symptoms are sometimes severe. The patient is often very distressed by the degree of pain, and this distress can merge into a delirious state.

Generalised weakness may develop into paralysis and even involve the cranial nerves, affecting facial muscles, vision, and speech. Malaise, nausea, vomiting and sweating may be associated with high temperature and changes in the blood. Respiratory distress may develop in severe cases. Occasionally a cardiovascular shock state may occur and can result in death.

After recovery from the acute phase of a serious fish sting, neuropsychological symptoms are not uncommon, and may last between days and months. Symptoms include anxiety, apathy, weakness, impaired concentration, insomnia and depression.

Other delayed complications (see later) include a recurrence of the inflammation, usually about 1-3 weeks after envenomation. Neuropathies are rare complications.

First aid

1. The patient should be laid down and reassured. If the spine or integument is still present, it should be gently extracted. A little bleeding may help remove some venom. Surface venom is removed by washing the area with water. The patient's state may become far more serious than it first appears. Copious bleeding (rare) should be stopped.

2. The affected area should be rested in an elevated position. Arrangements can then be made to immerse the wound in hot (up to 45°C, 113°F) water for 30-90 minutes—or until the pain no longer recurs. Unaffected skin should be immersed, as well as the wound, to avoid scalding. If the area cannot be immersed, as on the head or body, hot packs may be applied. The duration of the hot water immersion depends on the symptoms. If the site of injury is removed from the water and the pain recurs, it should be re-immersed. In a series of fish stingings, 84% had good results merely by the application of hot water.

    Local variations are often promoted by different groups. Some claim that other fluids are more beneficial than water, including vinegar, oils and gasoline. Water is more readily available, effective and less explosive. Hot water may be obtained from the radiators of engines, diluting the coffee from thermos flasks etc. Sea water can be used.

3. The wound should be washed and cleaned, after the heat treatment is no longer required. Following pain relief the limb should be immobilised in an elevated position, and covered with a clean dressing, e.g., an unused newspaper.

WARNING: Read the above very carefully. One unfortunate Australian fisher-man lost the top of his finger because of the treatment. His injured finger was first anaesthetised by local anaesthetic and THEN immersed in very hot water. The anaesthetic worked well—he did not feel his finger cooking.

Alternative therapies

A small incision can be made across the wound and parallel to the long axis of the limb, to encourage mild bleeding, and relieve pain if other methods are not available, and if the therapist is prepared to risk legal repercussions. Although a 1 cm cut made with a razor blade may give relief if instituted early, most authorities do not approve of it. Fishermen, being more sensible and courageous, use any treatment that works.

Other applications were proposed in the past, including oxidising agents, such as a 5% solution of Condy's crystals, alkalies such as cloudy ammonia or sodium bicarbonate (a desert spoonful in a cup of water), acidic substances (emetine or vinegar), meat tenderisers (by cannibals?) etc. These may have been of value, but are now superseded by hot water immersion.

Ligature, tourniquet and pressure bandages are not indicated. Further injury can be caused by restricting circulation with these.

MEDICAL TREATMENT

ACUTE. This includes first aid, as above. Local anaesthetic, e.g., 5-10 mg Lignocaine 2% without adrenalin (epinephrine), if injected through the puncture wound, will give considerable relief. Often it will only last for an hour or less before being required again. Bupivacaine is longer lasting, probably for some hours, and may be the local anaesthetic of choice. Local or regional anaesthetic blocks may also be of value.

Local anaesthetic not only works against the local pain, but is also absorbed by the lymphatic system and results in relief of the pain in the regional lymph glands and more centrally.

Emetine HCl, 0.5-1.0 ml at a concentration of 50 mg/ml, injected into wound site is of great value, but hard to obtain. The effect is probable due to the low pH, 4.2.

Symptomatic treatment may be needed for generalised symptoms of cardiogenic shock or respiratory depression. Systemic analgesics or narcotics are rarely needed, however they may be of value in severe cases.

Local cleansing of the wound, with removal of any broken spines or their integuments, is best followed by the application of a local antibiotic such as neomycin or bacitracin. Tetanus prophylaxis may be indicated if there is necrotic tissue or if the wound has been contaminated.

If the stings are severe they can mimic the lesions described under the headings of stonefish or stingray. The treatment sections of these injuries should be referred to, as the principles (other than the use of antivenom) have general application to all fish stings.

continued

DELAYED. Often, whenever early or adequate cleaning of the local wound has not been carried out or when antibiotics have not been used, redevelopment, exacerbation or persistence of symptoms may be observed. These can continue for many weeks or months. A mucoid discharge may develop.

Symptoms which continue for weeks or months after the injury, usually include hypersensitivity of the area, recurrent swelling, breakdown of wound, or continued signs of inflammation. The abnormal sensations (tingling, prickling etc) are initially made worse by pressure or dependency (putting weight on an injured foot), but later are worse in the morning and clear with mobility. The same sequence is seen with swelling.

Soft tissue radiology and/or ultrasound is advised to exclude foreign bodies such as the tip of the animals spine, as is the trial of broad spectrum antibiotic therapy for a possible residual infection. Often the foreign body may be the covering (skin) over the spine, or perhaps even venom or organisms introduced at the time of the injury.

In such cases, the following procedure is usually successful: Soft tissue X-ray and/or ultrasound to demonstrate spines or foreign bodies. Broad spectrum antibiotics, such as cotrimoxazole or doxycycline. Cone biopsy and removal of all necrotic tissue around the spine's pathway. Bacteriological examination and culture in hypertonic saline medium. Local antibiotics, as above.

Usually the surgical excision of the abnormal tissue is easier to do in a bloodless field, under anaesthesia, and histologically the appearance is of a granuloma, sometimes with giant cells and even acid-fast bacilli.

Usually the symptoms will abate rapidly after the surgery. It is likely that small pieces of the animal's spine or integument have perpetuated the venom-like effect.

Elevation of the wound is recommended for a few days, and symptoms rarely recur.

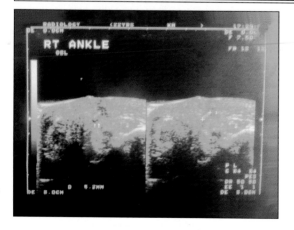

Ultrasound demonstration of fish spine persisting in wound— despite a negative soft tissue X-ray.

STONEFISH

Family	■	Scorpaenidae
Dangerous species	■	*Synanceja verrucosa, S.trachynis, S. horrida*
Common names	■	Dornorn, Rockfish, Goblinfish, "Nofu" (The Waiting one), Devil Fish, Warty-ghoul, Deadly Stonefish.
Distribution	■	Indian and Pacific oceans. Many similar species are found in other tropical areas, such as the spotted scorpionfish of the Caribbean, and may have similar toxicity.

Probably the most venomous fish known. Apart from the tip of the spines, it is covered by loose skin.

This fish grows to about 30 cm (12 inches) in length, but can be larger and is perfectly camouflaged for its surroundings. It lies in shallow waters and can survive many hours out of water (on the reef.), especially if the skin is kept wet. At greater depths it is easier to recognise because of its bulky floppy swimming style. It can burrow under sand and mud with its large pectoral fins and catch small passing fish by sucking them into its gaping mouth, or it can produce a suprising burst of speed over a short distance to capture its prey.

The thirteen spines on its back, capable of piercing a sandshoe and then skin, become erect when the fish is disturbed. When pressure is applied (e.g., by standing on the fish), two glands on each spine will discharge venom into the penetrating wound. Each spine has 5-10 mg of venom (see Appendix VI, page 255) associated with it, and is said to be neutralised by 1 ml of Commonwealth

Stonefish, to show spines. Photo by R. Taylor

Serum Laboratories antivenom, made in Australia. Occasionally a stonefish spine may have no venom associated with it. It is thought this is because venom is regenerated very slowly, if at all.

Clinical features. See also Antivenoms and Advice, page 249, pages 59-60.

The effects of such an injury seem to depend on many factors, including the geographical locality, the victim's size, the number of spines involved, the depth the spine penetrated, protective covering, previous stings, and first aid treatment.

LOCAL. Immediate intense pain is noted. This may increase in severity over the next 10 minutes or so. Sometimes the pain comes in waves, a few minutes apart. The pain, which is excruciating, may be such in some cases as to cause delirium or unconsciousness, and thus result in drowning.

The blood supply to the area becomes restricted, causing a blanched or bluish appearance. It becomes swollen, often hot, with numbness in the centre and extreme tenderness around the edge of the swelling. The swelling may become quite gross, extending up the limb. Paralysis of the surrounding muscles may immobilise the limb, as may pain. Twitching and jerking of the limb is sometimes seen.

The pain is likely to spread to the nearest lymph glands, i.e. in the armpit or groin from the upper or lower limbs respectively. Both the pain and the other signs of inflammation may last for many days. Delayed healing and ulceration

**Stonefish,
length 30 cm**

can persist for many months. Swelling can likewise continue, although gradually lessening over the next few months. Those patients who get treated correctly in the first few days with antivenom, cleansing, local antiseptics and surgical removal of dead tissue, do not usually suffer long term complications.

GENERAL. The general symptoms depend on the degree of venom injected and the body weight of the victim. Signs of mild heart failure are not uncommon. The victim's face becomes pale. Sweating, low blood pressure and fainting may be noted. Problems with breathing may be due to the accumulation of fluid in the lungs, heart failure and/or paralysis of the chest muscles. Slowing of the heart rate, irregular heart rate and even an absence of the heart action are also possible.

Exhaustion, fever and shivering may progress to delirium, incoordination, generalised paralysis, convulsions and death. Convalescence may take many months, and may be characterised by periods of general debility and vomiting.

Prevention

Wear tough thick sole shoes when in danger areas. Be particularly careful on coral reefs and while entering or leaving boats. A stonefish sting is said, by some fishermen, to produce some degree of immunity for future episodes.

First aid. See page 60.

In cases of loss of consciousness, apply external heart massage and mouth to mouth respiration as indicated (see page 233). Resuscitation may be required for many hours. Do not cease until death is confirmed.

MEDICAL TREATMENT. See page 61.

Good results have been achieved in stonefish stings with traditional treatments—a local injection into the site with hyoscine butylbromide (Buscopan), or emetine hydrochloride (pH of 3.4)—if given early.

Occasionally the swelling is so great that decompression of the tissue with fasciotomy may be needed to reduce the ischaemia.

Stonefish antivenom (page 249) may be administered with 1 ml neutralising 10 mg of venom (i.e. the venom from one spine). Initially, 2 ml of antivenom is given intramuscularly, although in severe cases the intravenous route can be used. Further doses can be given if required, but it should never be given to people with horse serum allergy. It should be stored between 0 and 5 degrees Centigrade, but not frozen, and protected from light. It should be used immediately on opening.

Appropriate cardiopulmonary resuscitation techniques may have to be applied (Appendix I).

CASE REPORT   Stonefish Sting

Dr. J.L.B. Smith was one of the world's greats in marine biology, and specifically in the identification and treatment of marine animal injuries. Dr. Smith was collecting fish along the Portuguese East African coast, when he got stung by the Sherovea (the local name for the stonefish), with two spines, not penetrating very deeply, from a 12 cm specimen (moderately small). He applied a venous ligature and sucked the wound vigorously. Within 5 minutes, before reaching the beach, the pain had spread from his finger to his hand, and was of an intensity never before experienced. As he had previously been stung by both stingrays and catfish, it must be presumed that the pain was very severe. He travelled half a mile overland with little recollection of the journey other than the extreme agony of pain. By the time he reached his camp, the hand was numb and swelling fast.

"I managed to sterilise a syringe, but while trying to withdraw some novocaine (local anaesthetic)from the bottle, it fell and broke on the concrete floor. As I stood stupidly, my wife burst in and soon injected novocaine. For a short time this had some effect, but the pain had by now become a searing agony, mostly across the back of the hand, with spasms reaching the head, neck and shoulder. The perspiration was such that my wife on arrival thought someone had splashed me with water, for it dripped to the floor. According to her account, during the next two hours, of which I have little recollection, I was close to collapsing several times, but managed to keep on my feet. At about two and a half hours after the stab, my wife injected 1/3 grain morphine sulphate subcutaneously. After about 20 minutes, I felt drowsy, but the drug had no apparent effect upon the pain. At about three and a half hours after the stab, the pain was undiminished, and the perspiration was still profuse.

"My wife decided to try immersion of the wound in hot water. The effect was dramatic. The agony diminished rapidly to bearable proportions, and I returned to normal consciousness with an unquenchable thirst. We continued this immersion in hot water and I drank innumerable cups of tea for the next four hours, by which time the intense agony no longer recurred on removal from hot water. In the morning, the thumb was greatly enlarged, and had turned black all around the area of the stabs, and was without sensation. The hand was greatly swollen, also the lower forearm, and was intensely painful to touch. 24 hours after the stab, large yellow blisters started to form, and spread rapidly over the thumb, becoming exceedingly painful, and when punctured, released a watery fluid, which dripped steadily thereafter for six days. The swelling gradually increased, reaching a maximum after three days, extending to above the elbow. In this time, joints and weak spots such as old wounds, ached intensely all over the body. On the sixth day inflammation and pain in the thumb increased alarmingly, and pus appeared. The injection of 1 million units of penicillin in 5 doses over 16 hours had a rapid and marked beneficial effect on the local condition, with retraction of the inflamed and blistered area."

On the ninth day, some degree of sensation returned to the thumb. The blisters were subsiding and the swelling was much less, but the hand was still swollen and painful. After 14 days the hand and thumb only were still swollen and painful and unusable. After 30 days the black portion started to fall away leaving pink scars. The site of the cut opened to a discharging cavity, and did not heal finally until 50 days after the stab. After 80 days, the hand was still weak and the thumb barely movable at the joints, being slightly swollen and painful when moved. The injury had a marked adverse effect on his general health.

CASE REPORT   Stonefish Sting

J.H. was a 42 year old female, holidaying at Club Med, Moorea, Tahiti. She was walking in waist deep water when she stood on the fish. She immediately summoned attention because of the extreme pain. There was very little bleeding, but 2 punctures were seen. The patient was yelling and screaming with pain, the worst she had ever experienced (compared to child-bearing without anaesthesia, extensive dental repairs and a fractured arm). The foot became very swollen, within 2 minutes, and was reddish in colour with a white circle round the puncture wounds. On admission to the local hospital she was given analgesics including pethidine, but without any significant effect. She was said to have been hysterical or delirious, and has little memory of the next few hours. There was some difficulty with breathing, and she lost sensation and power in both arms. She was unable to move the affected limb.

Repeated injections were given for the pain, together with steroids and antihistamines. The area was packed in ice and her foot was elevated.

After about 10 hours the pain lessened in intensity but it had extended to include the groin. This cleared within 24 hours. The swelling remained for the first five or six days during which time she was kept in hospital. It was aggravated by movement and lowering of the leg. The foot and toes remained numb to any sense of touch, for approximately 2 weeks, before sensation started returning to the outer part of the foot.

There was no attempt to treat the injury by immersion in hot water. No stonefish antivenom given, no surgical exploration and cleansing of the wound, and no soft tissue X-ray performed (to identify pieces of spine broken off in the wound).

Antibiotics were being given throughout. She complained of nausea and depression, very disruptive sleep, forgetfulness, tiredness, feeling muddled and a difficulty in concentration after the incident.

I examined this lady approximately 2 months after her injury, when she had still a severely swollen foot, was unable to touch the ground with the foot because of extreme hypersensitivity, and induction of pain. There were 2 large black areas on the heel, with a great deal of scaling of the skin.

In general she felt that she had some good days, and others in which she was exhausted and tired. She was still waking in the early hours of the morning, very agitated and distressed. She also continued to complain of crying and moderate depression.

Surgical excision of the major puncture and damaged tissue was performed. Excision of the major area, which was the most sensitive, was

Stonefish spine and sac containing venom

performed in mid April. There was an immediate improvement in the patient's state and the swelling reduced. Sensation returned to the foot and toes within two weeks, but there was still a hypersensitivity of the heel, and she had less difficulty in placing it on the ground. A small piece of spine was noted in the specimen and the histology showed extensive scarring with dead tissue.

A month later, the patient still had a very slight swelling of the ankle, and the area near the minor wound was still hypersensitive. The swelling only developed if she walked a great deal, the numbness continued to a minor degree but would tend to diminish with the weight bearing as the day progressed, whereas the swelling would be likely to increase. The patient was not really back to her normal self, even some three months after the incident. In retrospect, the surgeon considered that it was not wise to have left one of the puncture wounds unexplored, and the patient expressed the same feeling. By this time there was no evidence of a confusional state, and the patient was emotionally back to her normal self.

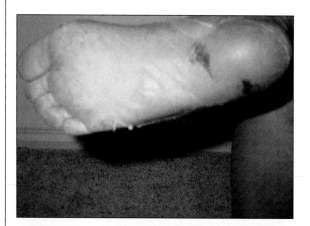

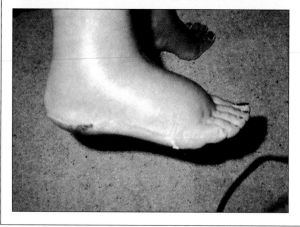

Stonefish injury to wader in Tahiti. Two discoloured spine puncture wounds and swollen foot, two weeks after injury.

STINGRAYS

Families	■ Dasyatidae (Sting or Whipray, Giant Stingray), Gymnuridae (Butterfly or Rat-tailed Ray), Myliobatidae (Eagle Ray or Bat Ray), Urolophidae (Round Stingray), Rhinopteridae (Cow-nose Ray), Mobulidae (Devil Rays or Mantas), Potamotrygonidae (Freshwater Stringray, River Rays)
Distribution	■ Tropics to the temperate regions.

Stingrays are bottom dwellers, so that their flat body is often submerged in sand and only detectable by an eye or two, a piece of tail or the spiracles showing above the elevated disc of sand or mud. Suddenly, there is a swirl of sand and the ray elegantly flies away, sometimes very fast, with wings gently flapping. Although said to be shallow water creatures, I have often encountered the large specimens (2 metres across, 4 metres long) in the tropical Pacific at depths of 30-60 metres. Many have lost their long tails, probably to sharks. They appear interested in divers and will sometimes swim with them.

Manta rays are usually welcomed as exciting companions on which divers hitch hike rides. The more likely damage to divers is when they tumble off the giant manta, or ascend too rapidly, or are injured by the momentum of a 2 ton animal. Manta often jump out of the water and occasionally have damaged fishermen's boats. There are also a number of stories of anchor lines being caught by the "arms" of the manta and the fish heading off into the wide blue yonder at an unacceptable pace dragging a boat behind it, with the fisherman clinging to the gunwales and wondering how he got into this predicament. Unfortunately these

Stingray, with tail and spine being thrust forward. Photo by R. Thomas

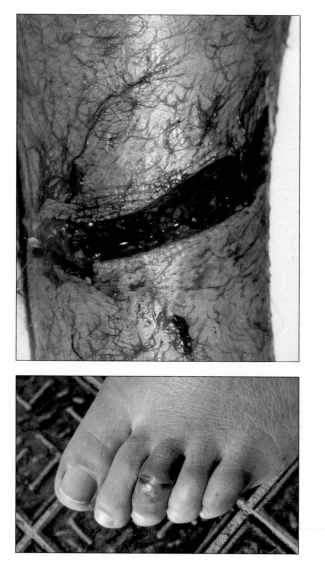

Top: Stingray injury of the slashing type. Photo by C. Acott.
Bottom: Stingray injury with puncture on top of third toe.
Photo by R. Thomas

magnificent creatures are sometimes the object of ego trips with fishermen's
harpoons and divers' spearguns.

Many divers develop relationships with these animals, feeding them and allowing the ray to glide over them. The ray is a very gentle delicate animal, reminiscent of a pet cat as it rubs against the skin.

Rays feed on a variety of shell fish, molluscs, crustaceans and worms, and the one or more spines are used for protection. Although described as fresh or salt water species, many enter brackish river inlets for many miles upstream, whereas the freshwater species of the Amazon and elsewhere have no connection with the sea.

Ulysses was said to have died from a spear tipped with a stingray spine. Captain John Smith, explorer and founder of the first English settlement at Jamestown in North America, was severely injured by a stingray in Chesapeake Bay in 1608, but survived to eat the ray. The American Indians should have taken note of this philosophy.

The stingray is non-aggressive, but is capable of protecting itself against intruders. It buries itself in the sea or river bed and the unwary wading victim may tread on its dorsal surface or the diver may descend over it. The stingray swings its tail upward and forward in a reflex action, either producing sword like lacerations or driving the spine into the limb (especially the ankle) or body of the victim. A skin-like integument over the serrated spine is ruptured. Venom escapes and passes along grooves in the spine, into the perforated wound. Extraction of the saw shaped spine results in further tissue damage due to the serrations and retropointed barbs, and may leave spine or sheath within the wound.

The local injury causes damaged tissue, with haemorrhage and death of fat and muscle within the hour, which can extend an inch or more around severe injuries. This condition, together with the resulting symptoms, may take many months to resolve.

Damage from the spine may cause death from either physical trauma, such as the penetration of the body cavities (pleural, pericardial or peritoneal) or from the venom of the spine, or both. In Australia the deaths tend to be from the penetration of body cavities, whereas in the U.S.A. the deaths are more likely from the venom effects. There are said to be 1500 injuries per year from stingrays in the U.S.A.

Venom. See Appendix VI, page 255 .

Fishermen who handle these fish in nets are less seriously affected as the integumentary sheath is probably already damaged.

Clinical features. See pages 59-60.

LOCAL. Pain is usually immediate and is the predominant symptom, increasing over 1-2 hours and easing after 6-10, but may persist for some days. Aggravation of pain within days may be due to secondary infection. The pain may be constant, pulsating or lancinating. Bleeding may be profuse, and may relieve the pain. A mucoid secretion may follow and may imply contamination or a foreign body. Integument from the spine may be visible in the wound, which may gape and extend for a few centimetres in length. The area is swollen and pale, with a bluish rim, centimetres in width, spreading around the wound after an hour or two. Local necrosis, ulceration and/or secondary infection are common and if unchecked may cause incapacity for many months, and even amputation resulted in earlier years. Osteomyelitis in the underlying bone has been reported.

GENERAL. The following manifestations have been noted: anorexia, nausea, vomiting, diarrhoea, frequent urination and salivation. There is extension of pain to the area of lymphatic drainage. Muscular cramps, tremors and paralysis may occur in the affected limb and surrounding areas. Fainting, palpitations, hypotension, heart rate irregularities and cessation of heart activities are possible. Difficulty in breathing, cough and pain on inspiration may occur. Other symptoms include fever during the night with copious sweating, nervousness, confusion or delirium.

Symptoms may persist for weeks or months after the injury, even though the wound may have closed over. These include a dull ache over the area, and a swelling that may develop under the influence of gravity. Thus, ankle injury may become painful and swollen after standing or walking, but may reduce after resting with the foot elevated. X-ray and/or ultrasound should be performed to exclude a foreign body (stingray spine) in the soft tissues of the body. Usually a fibrotic nodule is found if the area is surgically explored and cleaned, and rapid recovery follows this minor surgery. It may be due to a tissue reaction from a piece of spine or sheath. Antibiotics do not help at this stage.

Fatalities may occur immediately or within 2 weeks if the spine perforates the pericardial, peritoneal or pleural (e.g., heart, stomach or lung) cavities.

First Aid.   See page 60. Occasionally the injury is less a penetration than a slashing type, and then attention has to be paid to reducing blood loss and treatment of shock (Appendix I, II).

Prevention

1.   Waders are advised to shuffle the feet when walking in the water. This gives the ray time to remove himself—which he cannot do with a foot on his dorsum. Divers swim well above the sea bed.
2.   Wearing protective clothing decreases the severity of the sting, although the spine will penetrate most protective material.

---

3.   Exercise care when handling fishing nets.
MEDICAL TREATMENT.   See page 61

ACUTE. Local anaesthetic without adrenalin (epinephrine), infiltrated into and around the wound, or by regional block, will relieve the pain. Systemic analgesia may be required, e.g., pethidine. Treatment for cardiac arrhythmias may be required. A pressure bandage is only indicated if the medical practitioner is seriously worried about generalised symptoms, with care taken to avoid aggravating the already ischaemic tissues.

X-ray and/or ultrasound may demonstrate foreign bodies, such as a broken spine, and bone injury. The basic physiological signs (TPR, BP, CVP, urine output etc.), serum electrolytes, electroencephalogram, electrocardiogram are monitored as indicated. Debridement, cleansing and suturing, if required, are performed as early as permitted by the patient's general state. Broad spectrum antibiotics, together with local application of neomycin, are used at an early stage. Symptomatic treatment is given for the clinical features present. Cardiopulmonary resuscitation (Appendix I) may be required. DELAYED TREATMENT. See page 62.

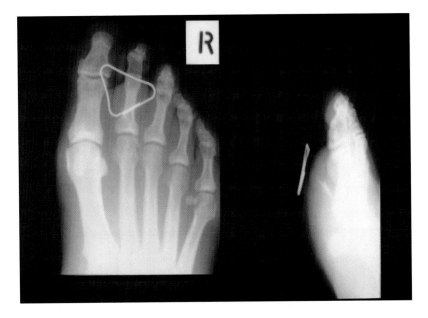

Stingray spine submerged in the ball of the foot, shown by soft tissue X-ray. The triangular marker is for localisation. Ultrasound may be used (see page 62).

CASE REPORT   **Stingray Attack**
[Dr. DAVID NOTT, as quoted by Sutherland.]

A clinician, who was taking part in sailing activities 200 km south of Sydney, jumped off his sailing dinghy, into an area with a large number of stingrays—in approximately 60 cm of water. Most of the stingrays swam away, but one was caught, and apparently struck the physician who sustained a severe impact on the dorsum of his right foot causing him to lose his balance and producing a severe boiling hot pain. He first thought it was a shark attack, and this was supported by the large amount of blood in the water. There was an extensive ragged laceration on the dorsum of the foot with excessive haemorrhage.

He was assisted ashore and the blood flow was stemmed by the firm application of a towel. The pain was severe, burning in type, and rapidly extended to involve the whole foot, and within 20 minutes had reached the hip. Within half an hour, the whole extremity from foot to buttock were enveloped in a burning searing pain of severe intensity. It was aggravated by movement. He was pale and had a bradycardia, felt anxious and remote. No first aid or emergency procedures were instituted. He was then taken to a hospital, feeling more comfortable when the limb was elevated. He was examined and in consultation with a colleague, decided that exploration was not indicated, and a dry dressing was applied.

On examination of the wound, there was an extensive laceration on the dorsum of the right foot, together with one ragged puncture mark from the spine. The laceration revealed a clear view of several extensor tendons. The skin surrounding the laceration was discoloured and bruising extended to the lateral malleolus. The x-ray revealed no abnormalities. *continued*

The wound bled freely throughout the night, and every time the dressings were changed, it bled again. There was gross swelling of the foot, and extravasation of blood, for the first 7 days. Walking was possible during the second week, although the swelling remained for over three months. The wound itself was not completely healed until seven months after the event, and was then still tender. The skin was thin and bluish and had altered sensation.

Even 18 months later, while normal activities had been regained, at the end of most days, the foot was slightly swollen, and following tennis or squash, the foot became extremely swollen.

Editor's Note: It seems unusual that the natural history of the disease would be witnessed by a clinician who had the knowledge, as well as the literature available, to have carried out both first aid and delayed treatment to prevent the symptoms and signs described above.

DEE SCARR'S SCUBA DIARY   Southern Stingray

Discussions of dangerous marine animals always include stingrays, often with photos showing the ray's spine and text covering how difficult the spine is to remove.

I found a stingray spine once, and I discovered first hand that they're difficult to remove: that spine entangled itself with the lining of my pocket and I thought I'd NEVER get it out.

But that's the only problem I've ever had with the spine of a stingray.

Southern stingrays frequently rest on sandy bottoms with only their spiracles (water intakes) and eyes exposed. It's a challenge for me to touch them; their skin feels wonderful, like wet velvet. On those occasions that the ray wants no part of the game, by the way, I've never been threatened; it simply swims away and settles down somewhere else.

Once on Grand Turk I crept up to a resting stingray and began to gently stroke its "wing." It didn't seem at all disturbed at my touch. As I stroked it I noticed something protruding from the top of its wing. I waved the sand away and exposed a homemade snag hook: four fishhooks tied back-to-back with fishing line, one of them embedded in the top of the ray's wing. Gently, I probed the ventral side of the wing to see if the hook went all the way through, and found it did not.

Well, I couldn't just leave that poor ray like that, could I? I zipped back to the boat and unearthed a set of rusty wire clippers. I realised what poor condition those clippers were in as soon as I fastened them around the hook. I squeezed as hard as I could and absolutely nothing happened. I tried using BOTH hands on the clippers and accidentally twisted them a bit. Thus disturbed, the ray began to swim. As it left the bottom all I could think about was that I had better leverage on the clippers, and I continued squeezing as hard as I could.

The ray was in a perfect position to zap me with its spine but it never tried. After a few seconds of the ray trying to swim and me staying put and holding onto the clippers which were gripping the hook, the ray broke free and swam off leaving me holding the hook.

The ray calmly settled back down in the sand about twenty feet away.

MISCELLANEOUS SCORPIONFISH

Family   ■ Scorpaenidae
Dangerous species   ■ *Apistus carinatus, Centropogon australis, Notesthes robusta, Scorpaena guttata, S. plumieri, Scorpaenopsis diabolus,* etc.
Common names   ■ Bullrout, Cobbler, Devilfish, False Stonefish, Firefish, Fortesque, Goblinfish, Kroki, Jacopever, Lionfish, Redfish, Red Rock Cod, Rock Cod, Rockfish, Roguefish, Saddlehead, Scorpioncod, Sulky, Waspfish
Distribution: ■ This large family is widespread throughout the tropical, subtropical and temperate regions. Some species even occur in the polar regions.

There are at least 330 members in this family, which includes the most venomous fish known. They are perch like with large scraggy heads and spines on

Butterfly cod, length 30 cm. Photo by K. Gillett

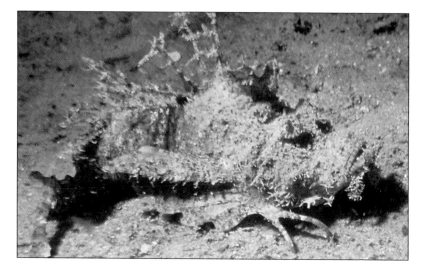

Devil fish. Photo by J. Hall

their fins. As a general rule they take upon themselves the colouration of their
environment. Thus in clear tropical waters with coral, the fish tend to be colourful, often with reds, blues and yellows. In murky estuaries and harbours they are
dull and brown. Sizes vary from a few centimetres to half a metre long.

The spines will become erect if the animal is alerted, threatened, or
touched. The single dorsal fin may contain 11-17 spines. The spines are covered
by an integumentary sheath, which is pierced and displaced when contact is
made with the victim's skin. There are also spines on the pectoral and anal fins.

Red rock cod, length 18 cm. Photo by R. Thomas

Fortescue, length 10 cm. Photo by S. Parrish

Venom (see Appendix VI, page 255) then passes along the spine, which may be grooved or hollow, into the wound. The intensity of the sting depends on the size of the fish (usually 5-30 cm), the number of spines penetrating the skin and other factors. There is a variable number of spines, depending on the species involved. These fish are less venomous after being damaged, e.g., in fishing nets.

BUTTERFLY COD (*Pterois volitans, P. antennata, P. russeli, P. zebra* and others) Also known as red fire fish, lionfish, zebrafish, coral cod, fire cod, turkeyfish and

Bullrout, length 30 cm

tigerfish, these attractive, brightly coloured fish grow up to 30 cm in length and are found especially in shallow water over coral reefs, around rocks. Large specimens are found in the tropics and subtropics, with juvenile specimens sometimes found in temperate regions. They frequently swim in pairs, show little fear and may orientate their body so that their 13 dorsal spines project forward. They also have anal and pelvic spines.

DEVIL FISH (*Inimicus barbatus, I. didactylus, I. japonicus*) Also known as demon stinger, and bearded ghoul, this grotesque looking fish commonly grows up to 30 cm in length and is usually found in deep water offshore, but occasionally inhabits rivers and estuaries. It has been known to attack underwater photographers and is a menace to trawler fishermen.

RED ROCK COD (*Ruboralga cardinalis, S. jacksoniensis* and others). Also known as red scorpion cod and mouth almighty, this fish grows up to 35 cm in length, is coloured a deep sunset red, and resembles in form and colouring the rocks and weeds among which it lives. There are normally twelve dorsal spines. The grotesque head is associated with a funnel-like mouth, earning its owner the name of "Mouth Almighty." There are many short, sharp, broad-based spines on the head.

Clinical features, first aid and **medical treatment.**   See pages 59-62.

DEE SCARR'S SCUBA DIARY   **Scorpionfish**

Scorpionfish make a living pretending to be rocks, which is really handy for people like me who like to touch marine critters. After all, rocks can't swim, and a well-educated scorpionfish knows that. So, when a diver approaches, scorpionfish often stay put and quite often I'm able to stroke them.

I follow a couple of rules, though; I always make sure the scorpionfish sees me before I touch it, and I always make sure that it knows it has a clear path if it wants to swim away.

The venomous spines of these fish are purely for defence, and in my experience they're not even the first line of defence. If the scorpionfish feels threatened, its preference is to swim away. Only if trapped or stepped on will the venomous spines come into play.

I've learned to approach scorpionfish low to the bottom and from the side, and I initially stroke them just next to the base of the first dorsal spines. One day I concluded that the scorpionfish's spines probably can't envenomate unless they're erected, and I HAVE stroked very calm scorpionfish right on top of the spines on occasion, and emerged unscathed.

One day I was feeding a mob of small grunts and noticed a scorpionfish nearby. Since the grunts were the right size for it to eat, I moved the food closer. The grunts followed. The scorpionfish wriggled a bit, much like a cat does before it strikes, and suddenly lunged up into the mob of grunts. I didn't see it actually get one of the grunts—the movement was really fast—but later it turned its mouth out (a burp?) and a bunch of fish scales floated out, so I suppose it was successful.

For the past few months I've concentrated on trying to get scorpionfish to eat, sometimes by attracting small fish close to them, sometimes by offering the bait directly. Of the seven resident scorpionfish there, two consistently refuse my help. Two will occasionally take fish when I brush their mouths with it.

Ah, but the other three. Once in a while I'd notice a scorpionfish nearby after I'd been feeding other fish for a while, but I thought it had been there all alone and I hadn't noticed it at first. Then one day, as I rested on my stomach on the sand offering fish to Godzilla, a mantis shrimp friend, my buddy pointed under my chest. I looked down, and there, cuddled in the six inches of space between me and the bottom, was a scorpionfish. Now I know that scorpionfish wasn't there when I began to feed Godzilla, so therefore it must have arrived after I did, right?

After Godzilla returned to his burrow I offered some fish to the scorpionfish. It gulped the fish down with no hesitation at all. I took a second piece of fish and held it several inches away from the scorpionfish, who "walked" up to my hand on its pectoral fins and gobbled down the offering. My buddy dubbed that scorpionfish the "Cookie Monster."

Tentatively, I concluded that the scorpionfish had been attracted to us that day by the scent of the fish I'd given Godzilla, but I began to keep a sharper watch for scorpionfish. Soon I realised that it was not only scent that attracted them (it turned out that three scorpionfish were behaving this way), since sometimes they'd arrive even if I was using hot dog for food. I decided maybe they were attracted by the crowd of wrasses, damselfish, and other small fish munching on my hot dog. I marvelled at that, because scorpionfish seem to be more passive than active predators—yet here they were "walking" twenty feet or more to get within range of the little fish around me. The behaviour seemed even more unusual considering that I stand upright when I feed, so the little fish are about a four feet off the bottom, a long distance for a scorpionfish to lunge.

I'd always offered them food when they got close to me, and they always took it immediately.

Then one day one of my buddies called me back to show me a scorpionfish. The fish was resting on a rock when he pointed it out to me, but it looked as if it had moved recently. It took food eagerly, and was even willing to lunge for the food when I held it 12 inches or so off the bottom. After the dive the man who'd shown me the scorpionfish told me what had happened. He'd been following me and was about 15 feet behind me. I swam over the rock, and the scorpionfish hopped off the sand and onto the rock "as if", my buddy said, "he was disappointed that you hadn't seen him." I hadn't been feeding at the time, and my fish food was in a sealed can. That scorpionfish had clearly made the connection between me (or divers, anyway) and food.

I have dived that reef over 400 times in the last three years. Most of the French angelfish zoom over for a snack as soon as they see me (or divers). The grunts actually do know me as an individual; if my buddies and I all take exactly the same posture in the water, the grunts will ignore my buddies and hover around me.

Scorpionfish, on the other hand, are ambush predators rather than foragers. They rest quietly on the bottom waiting for their food to come to them, and their natural food is whole live fish, not pieces of fish and certainly not hot dog. The unusual behaviour of the Cookie Monsters is emphasised by the behaviour of their four cohorts who haven't figured out that, at least when I'm around, there is such a thing as a free lunch.

CATFISH

Family	■ Plotosidae and Ariidae
Dangerous species	■ *Cnidoglanis* spp, *Plotosus* spp, *Tachysurus* spp, *Netuma* spp and others
Common names	■ Sea Barbel, Eeltailed Catfish, Cobbler, Cattie
Distribution	■ Tropic, subtropic and temperate waters.

The name "catfish" comes from the "whiskers" (sensory barbels) protruding from around the mouth. These are harmless and are used for detecting food un-

Catfish, length 55 cm. Photo by R. Thomas

Catfish, length: 22 cm. Photo by E. Friese

der the sand. The fish are often encountered in mud flats, rivers, estuaries, lakes and on beaches, and are often trapped in fishing nets. Sea catfish vary in size from 5 cm in length to 1 metre.

Both fresh and salt water catfish are dangerous to handle. The fish has three spines in its stinging apparatus. The retropointed serrated spines are attached to the dorsal and two lateral (pectoral) fins. They are usually covered by a skin-like integument which is pierced and displaced when contact is made between it and the victim's skin. Venom passes from glands at the base along the spine, into the wound. The venom can be readily destroyed by heat, is a water soluble protein, to which an immunity may be developed. It is a vasoconstrictor (i.e. constricts the walls of blood vessels).

Catfish do not attack. Many injuries occur when the fish is being removed from a fishing line or net. Often the spines will remain erect after a fish has been thrown away, making it a hazard to unsuspecting victims when they stand on a damaged or dead fish.

Removal of the spine, if it breaks in the wound, will often cause more tissue damage, so is often best done by elective surgery.

Clinical features, first aid and **medical treatment.** See pages 59-62 .

OLD WIFE

Family	■	Enoplosidae
Dangerous species	■	*Enoplosus armatu*
Common names	■	Zebrafish, Bastard Dory
Distribution	■	Tropical, subtropical and temperate waters.

This fish is abundant in harbours and sheltered foreshores, around wharves, pylons and jetties. It is well known to divers because of its zebra-like markings, which may be brown or black, and grows up to 20 cm. The name is said to be due to the fish's habit of grinding its teeth and "grumbling". They often swim in pairs or groups, but when disturbed they separate. Although it has been described as venomous, this apparently is of a variable nature as many lacerations from the knife-like dorsal spines have been known by this author to be relatively painless. It appears as if the severity of pain and bleeding may be related, perhaps due to venom being washed out by the blood. Handle old wives with care.

Clinical features, first aid and **medical treatment.** See pages 59-62.

Old wife, length 10 cm. Photo by W. Deas

RABBITFISH

Family	■	Siganidae
Dangerous species	■	*Siganus lineatus, S. rivulatus* and others.
Common names	■	Golden-lines Spinefoot, Black Trevally, Mi Mi, "Happy Moments," Black Spinefoot, Spinefoot, Stinging Bream.
Distribution	■	Throughout the tropical, subtropical and temperate waters of the Indian and Pacific oceans, and the Red Sea.

Rabbitfish closely resembles the surgeonfish. The common name "Happy Moments" is an ironic tribute to the pain this fish can inflict. They travel in schools and feed on seaweed. The fish has 13 dorsal, four pelvic and seven anal spines all of which have associated venom glands. The first dorsal spine is the one usually involved in stinging, sudden movement of the fish driving this spine forward and into the victim.

Clinical features, first aid and **medical treatment.** See pages 59-62.

Rabbitfish, length 20 cm. Photo by R. Thomas

RATFISH

Family	■ Chimaeridae
Dangerous Species	■ *Chimaera monstrosa, Hydrolagus colliei* and others
Common names	■ Chimaeroids, Elephantfish
Distribution	■ Found in most oceans.

Ratfish are more commonly found in cooler waters at great depths. It is a slow swimmer and sometimes encountered by trawler and deep sea fishermen. The single spine is situated along the front of the first dorsal fin, and is associated with a venom apparatus. Only one authenticated case of a ratfish sting is known to this author, and may reflect the rarity of contact between this fish and humans. It is also capable of inflicting an unpleasant bite with its well developed jaws, and is said to be poisonous to eat. All in all, it has a formidable defence system.

Clinical features, first aid and **medical treatment.** See pages 59-62.

Ratfish, length 50 cm. Photo by E. Friese

STINGING SHARKS

Orders	■ Heterodontiformes (Bullhead Sharks) and Squaliformes (Dogfish Sharks)
Dangerous species	■ *Heterodontus portusjacksoni, H. mexicanus, H. francisci, Squalus acanthias*
Common names	■ Doggie, Oyster Crusher, Pigs, Bullhead, Dogshark
Distribution	■ Throughout tropical and temperate waters.

The most studied of these is the Port Jackson shark, a piebald coloured animal which grows to 1 metre in length, and was initially sighted in Port Jackson by Captain Phillip's first fleet, sailing from England to Australia. It has a spine in front of each of its two dorsal fins, and these are thought to have an associated venom mechanism. The shark will usually wriggle away from humans diving or wading near it—but occasionally it takes bait from anglers, or is caught by divers. Young animals (found during late winter months) have particularly sharp spines, but these become blunted by abrasions as the shark grows. The handling of this usually docile animal may result in it twisting so that the spine (a few centimetres long) penetrates the victim's skin. His jaws are very powerful and can crunch through oyster shells, or fingers if they are offered. Puncture by the spine results in pain, redness, swelling, numbness and local weakness. It usually lasts only a couple of hours.

The "doggie" is attractive, easily befriended and able to be trained for aquariums—a venerable exhibit as his ancestry extends for over 200 million years.

Clinical features, first aid and **medical treatment.** See pages 59-62.

Port Jackson shark, length 30 cm. Juvenile with white spines on each dorsal fin.

STARGAZER

Family	■ Uranoscopidae
Dangerous species	■ *Uranoscopus duvali, Kathetostoma laeve, K. nigrofasciatum Ichthyscopus barbatus*
Common names	■ Deepwater or Fringed Stargazer, Stonelifter
Distribution	■ Tropical and subtropical Indian and Pacific oceans, the eastern Atlantic and Mediterranean Sea.

The stargazers are bottom dwelling animals having a square head and a vertical mouth with fringed lips. The eyes are on the flat upper surface of the head. These fish spend a large part of their time buried in the mud or lie with only their eyes and a portion of their mouth protruding. The venom apparatus consists of two shoulder spines one on either side, each of which protrudes through a sheath of skin. The venom glands deliver the venom along double grooves on each spine. Some stargazers are also capable of inflicting an electric discharge similar to the electric rays and eels. Deaths have occurred in the Mediterranean from similar species.

Clinical features, first aid and **medical treatment.** See pages 59-62.

Stargazer, length 22 cm. Photo by S. Parrish

SURGEONFISH

Family	■	Acanthuridae
Dangerous species	■	*Acanthurus dussumieri, A. Triostegus* and several others
Common names	■	Tang, Doctorfish, Spinetail, Five-banded Surgeonfish.
Distribution	■	The tropics and subtropics of the Indian and Pacific Oceans, extending into the Red Sea. Also in the tropical Atlantic.

Surgeonfish are reef dwellers. They are more commonly caught by skin-divers than anglers, although they are also found in fishing nets, and may even attack if a person wades through a confined area. They have movable blade-like spines on their sides, near the tail, and these normally point forward. When the fish becomes excited, and thrashes its tail, the spine may cause a deep laceration. This spine may also be venomous, although details of the chemistry or toxicology are not available. Naso spp (unicornfish) are related but have more than one spine on each side. These are also found in tropical and subtropical reefs, and have similar harmful effects. (page 197)

The surgeonfish can also cause ciguatera poisoning (page 194) if eaten.

Clinical features, first aid and **medical treatment.** See pages 59-62.

Surgeonfish. Photos by E. Friese

Surgeonfish, showing the coloured scalpel emerging from the junction of body and tail.

TOADFISH

Family	■ Batrachoididae
Dangerous species	■ *Halophryne diemensis, Batrachoides cirrhosus, Opsanus tau* and many others
Common names	■ Frogfish, Bastard Stonefish, Munda, Sapo, Oysterfish.
Distribution	■ Mainly in tropical and subtropical, but also in temperate waters, worldwide.

Toadfish are scaleless bottom dwelling fish with frilly side fins. They grow to approximately 25 cm in length, and are found among stones and coral. It sometimes creeps out over mud and can survive long periods out of water. The strong jaws can inflict an unpleasant, but not dangerous bite. The spines are on the first dorsal fin and the gill covers and allow venom to pass up the hollow shaft.

Because of its remarkable camouflage, most of the injuries occur when waders tread on it or divers touch it accidentally. At other times fishermen can be stung when removing it from a hook or net.

Clinical features, first aid and **medical treatment.** See pages 59-62.

WEEVERFISH

Family	■ Trachinidae
Dangerous species	■ *Trachinus draco, T. vipera*
Common names	■ Dragonfish, Aragno, Sea-cat, Lesser and Greater Weever.
Distribution	■ Mainly in the North Atlantic, North and Mediterranean Seas.

The weeverfish are confined to the eastern Atlantic and Mediterranean coastlines, and possibly along the Chilean coastline. The lesser weever is less than 25 cm long, usually found in shallow bays, buried in sand or mud with only its head visible. It can be aggressive and may suddenly dart forward and strike at its victim, not unlike a snake strike (thus its name, derived from the Anglo-Saxon word "wivre", meaning viper) with one of its opercular (at the rear of the gills) spines. They can remain alive for hours out of water. The greater weever, which can grow to a maximum of 50 cm., swim in deeper waters, and are therefore of more danger to fishermen.

There are five to seven venom-containing dorsal spines and one spine on the operculum (gills) on each side. The operculum spines are used to attack intruders or larger animals that move into the weeverfish's territory, but the dorsal spines are of use in discouraging an animal treading on the fish. Humans do both. Deaths have been reported from the envenomation, which appears to be comparable in severity to that of the stonefish. The venom has a haemotoxin (harmful to blood cells) as well as the neurotoxin (harmful to nerve cells).

Destruction of muscle tissue and secondary infections can result in serious long term damage.

Clinical features, first aid and **medical treatment.** See pages 59-62.

NOTES

Venomous Coelenterates

PORTUGUESE MAN O'WAR, PHYSALIA

CHIRONEX, SEA WASP, BOX JELLYFISH

SEA WASP VARIANTS

BLUBBER JELLYFISH

CYANEA

IRUKANDJI

JIMBLE

MAUVE STINGER

MISCELLANEOUS JELLYFISH, NETTLES & LICE

FIRE CORAL

SEA ANEMONE

STINGING HYDROID

NOTES

Venomous Coelenterates (Jellyfish)

Classification of the various coelenterates is difficult. The most practical way is to differentiate the free swimming jellyfish from the stationary or attached coelenterates. There are 9,000 species which contain, amongst others, jellyfish, sea anemones, fire coral and stinging hydroids. Although many appear flower-like, all are carnivorous animals.

The common factor amongst the coelenterates is the development of **nematocysts** (stinging capsules). There are of two types of nematocyst:

1. either it adheres to the prey by either sticky mucus or a hook, or
2. it acts like a needle, penetrating the prey and discharging venom into it.

The force of penetration is 20-33 kPa (2-5 psi). This needle may be just visible (0.5 mm). The discharge of venom from the nematocyst is triggered by many factors, including trauma and the absorption of fresh water.

The function of the nematocyst is to immobilise the prey, which may then be eaten. Nematocysts of different types of coelenterate may be identifiable, and therefore are of value in identifying the marine stinger. Characteristic patterns of nematocysts may be found, depending on the structure and appearance of the tentacles.

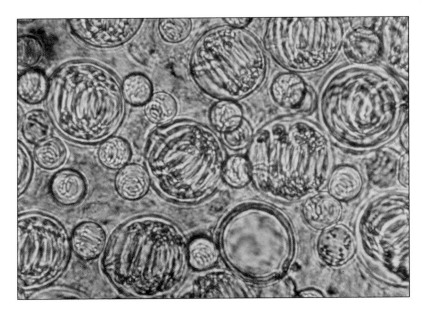

Nematocysts, one discharged (empty) and others undischarged. Photomicrographs from K. Gillett

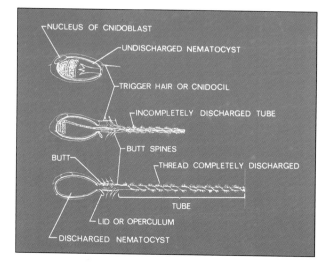

Diagram to show action of nematocyst or stinging capsule. From Cleland and Southcott.

Free swimming jellyfish inhabit all oceans, but are especially in the equatorial band between latitudes 45 degrees north and 30 degrees south. They extend into areas of warm waters, such as the Gulf Stream. Occasionally some species extend into the Arctic and Antarctic waters.

The injury they cause depends on the length and number of tentacles. Thus the **Portuguese man o'war** usually produces a single long strap with small blisters along the skin, whereas the **jimble** produces 2-4 short red lines. The **box jellyfish** produces multiple, long red lines, and if the patient is seen early there may still be tentacles present—due to a thick, sticky substance.

The attached coelenterates—**fire coral, sea anemone** and **stinging hydroid**—being non-mobile, sting only where touched. They spend most of their adult life attached to rocks, reefs, wrecks and gold bullion, especially in the shallow (less than 30 metres) warm waters of the tropics and sub-tropics. They are thus found in the Caribbean, Mediterranean and Red seas, Indian and Pacific oceans. Like other coelenterates, the injury is caused by nematocysts.

The venom consists of a variety of inflammatory chemicals and enzymes that destroy cell membranes, causing injury to the skin, muscles, heart, brain and nerves.

Clinical features

These may vary from a mild itch locally to severe systemic reactions, affecting the whole body.

The skin reactions may be local, a mild prickly sensation developing immediately on contact, a sever burning or throbbing pain, local sweating, keloids, atrophy of underlying fat tissue, with delayed (5-30 days), recurrent, generalised or satellite (distal) lesions.

For the more common immediate stings, intensity increases over 10 minutes or so, and the red, inflamed area may develop blisters or, in severe cases, ulcers. The pain may spread to involve the lymph glands, and can cause abdominal and chest pain.

Generalised symptoms include fever, sweating, gastrointestinal disorders, heart failure, difficulty in breathing and with the victim becoming confused or delirious.

Neuropsychological symptoms, such as anxiety, depression, insomnia, weakness and apathy, may follow. Sub-acute or chronic complications, such as peripheral nerve lesions or thrombophlebitis, have been described.

The intensity of the symptoms varies according to the species involved (the box jellyfish is often lethal, whereas the blubber jellyfish can often be handled with impunity); the extent of the contact area ; the thickness of the skin at the point of contact; the maturity of the animal; the body weight of the victim (being more severe in children than adults); and individual factors such as allergic reactions and pre-existing cardiac or respiratory disease.

Variations of the mode of injury can occur in the following circumstances:

1. CORAL CUTS are often experienced in the tropics. In these cases there is a laceration of skin, which allows the nematocysts to discharge directly into the wound tissues. This is aggravated by a foreign body reaction to the injury, coral pieces or other marine organisms. See page 171.

2. NUDIBRANCHS, especially the *Glaucus,* eat certain coelenterates and then use the nematocysts for their own Machiavellian purposes. This means that humans may sustain an injury from contact with the nudibranch.

3. ALLERGIES and Anaphylaxis (see pages 245-248) can develop from contact with jellyfish or after jellyfish stings. Asthmatic re-

Tentacle with undischarged nematocysts. (top)

Nematocysts discharged by treatment with methylated spirits. (centre)

Nematocysts prevented from discharge by treatment first with vinegar and then methylated spirits. (bottom) Photomicrographs courtesy J. Williamson

Nematocysts ejecting and screwing spine from the nematocyst sac.
K. Gillett

sponses may develop in some patients who come into contact with either inhaled jellyfish material, or after jellyfish stings. There is usually a history of allergy in such patients. Allergic reactions may also involve the skin, joints, eyes, digestive tract and cardiovascular system.

4. INGESTION of cooked jellyfish is common in Asia and especially Japan, usually without problems. Jellyfish are gathered and prepared as food by boiling and preserving certain parts according to traditional recipes. Eaten raw, some anemones cause poisonings in the Gilbert Islands, New Guinea, Samoa and the Philippines. In Western Samoa an anemone eaten either raw or after cooking may cause of the gastointestinal (nausea, vomiting and abdominal pain) symptoms and/or neurological paralysis lasting 8-36 hours and possibly leading to death from respiratory failure. It is used as a method of suicide. In South America, the ingestion of dried or fresh *Physalia* has been used to kill rats, but a rabbit, horse and human have also succumbed.

5. WOUNDS. The "deadly seaweed of Hana" is an anemone which was used to smear on the blades of the spears of the Hawaiians to make the wounds fatal.

6. EYE injuries. See page 98.

As the most dangerous coelenterate is the *Chironex fleckeri,* called the sea wasp or box jellyfish, this is dealt with in detail (page 102). *Physalia physalis* or the Portuguese man o'war is so widespread that this also is dealt with in some detail (page 100).

First aid

1. The victim should be rescued from the water, laid down and reassured.
2. Resuscitation (see pages 233-238) may be needed. Enlist medical attention.
3. If tentacles or nematocysts are still adhering to the skin, such as with the very severe cases of *chironex* or box jellyfish, it should be doused liberally with vinegar and lifted off, with tweezers or glove preferably. It should be done as gently as possible, to avoid further damage from the firing of more nematocysts. See below.
4. Local applications may be of great value in relief of pain. But what ones?

Local Applications. The recommendations have varied greatly, and are still contentious. Just over a decade ago it was believed that alcohol was of great value in dehydrating the nematocysts and thereby reducing the likelihood of further damage—although it was not claimed to reduce the existing degree of pain. Surveys both at the James Cook University at Townsville, and the Royal Australian Navy School of Underwater Medicine, suggest that alcohol is of value in neither prevention nor treatment. It may actively trigger the discharge of more nematocysts. Stale wine or Coca-cola may help.

Fashionable remedies such as "rb-Instant Aid Man O'War Stings," "Stop Itch," "Stingose," are of little value except to their commercial promoters. The theories on which they are based (enzymatic denaturation of protein, papain or trypsin effects, black magic) are not supported by field studies or objective assessments.

Many preparations may relieve the pain of the milder stings. Any treatment that works for superficial burns (such as sunburn sprays) will also work to some degree against coelenterate injuries. Local anaesthetic ointment is often effective in reducing pain, and steroid ointment may be used later if itching becomes a problem. Ice packs are said to give some relief, and any preparation which cools by evaporation may help. With the major severe stings, all these remedies are inadequate.

As a first aid measure, the currently fashionable treatment is vinegar (mild acetic acid) which does reduce the number of nematocyst discharges from some of the more severe jellyfish stings (*Chironex*). Vinegar does not give relief of pain, it merely stops or reduces further potential nematocyst discharge. Local anaesthetic sprays, ointments and creams can do both. Vinegar may cause other jellyfish species, including *cyanea* and the Portuguese man o' war, to discharge more nematocysts. Baking soda has been recommended for *Chrysaora* stings.

Calamine lotion has been recommended in the past. Others, such as washing blue, lime juice, ammonia, have lost most of their proponents, but have not really been disproved in good clinical trials. Baking soda and meat tenderiser were fashionable for a time. Tannic acid sprays are in vogue, now.

MEDICAL TREATMENT

1. Administer first aid.
2. Local anaesthetic ointment (Appendix III) is effective as a pain reliever, and is usually superior to other applications mentioned above. In a series of stingings performed on volunteers, both immediately and following a 10 minute delay, the following results were obtained. Lignocaine 5% ointment was superior to Ultralan 0.5% and lignocaine gel, and both of these were far better than Benadryl cream. Methylated spirits was the least effective of all. Commercial preparations were effective only for a short time.
3. Despite the absence of verified deaths from many species, it would be wise to monitor severely affected cases as one does with box jellyfish stings (see pages 105-106) and to give cardiovascular and respiratory assistance if needed (Appendix I). A number of jellyfish stings can result in a syndrome similar to the Irukandji syndrome (page 111).
4. Tranquillisers and muscle relaxants, such as diazepam 10 mg, i.v., may be indicated in distressed patients.
5. It is possible that allergy-prone patients are more susceptible to injury from coelenterates. The use of hydrocortisone may be indicated in these patients (100 mg i.v. and repeat p.r.n.).
6. Severe itching may develop within a few days, and this responds to steroid ointments, hydrocortisone for example.
7. Specific IgG serum titres, greater than 1 in 50, allow serological identification within a few days.

Jellyfish stings to the eye

If the eye is affected, corneal jellyfish stings usually produce a brief and self limited reaction but they do have the potential for long-term sequelae. Pain or a burning sensation develops rapidly. Vision is often blurred and there may be considerable watering from the eye and sensitivity to light

Topical administration of household chemicals (see above) that may prevent nematocyst firing in skin injuries are not recommended for ocular stings because of the risk of further tissue damage when applied to the eye.

Previous advice was to apply a non-aqueous local anaesthetic solution, e.g., cocaine eye drops or ointment, followed by a steroid ointment. Aqueous drops may result in further nematocyst discharge, but this may have to be accepted in order to treat the pathology. Homatropine 1% and cocaine drops may be instilled later and a steroid-antibiotic eye ointment combination, such as Hydrophenicol or Sofradex is also a reasonable addition to reduce inflammation and protect against infection.

Rapoza and his colleagues examined 90 Chesapeake Bay watermen who gave a history of ocular jellyfish stings sometime in the past. The stings typically produced intense burning pain and tearing and were severely incapacitating. However, the injuries were self-limited, with spontaneous resolution in 24 to 48 hours.

Recently, excellent descriptions from Glasser and his colleagues of corneal stings from the sea nettle (*Chrysaora quinquecirrha*), which is indigenous to the Chesapeake Bay, have resulted in a greater understanding of the pathology and treatment (although total extrapolation from one jellyfish injury to all others must be made with some reservation). These workers describe the following:

Medical Treatment

It is usually a painful but self-limited injury, with resolution in 24 to 48 hours. Corneal jellyfish stings typically produce intense burning pain, tearing and photophobia. Reported ocular findings include conjunctival and limbal injection with or without chemosis, punctate epithelial keratitis, corneal stromal edema, endothelial cell swelling, and mild anterior chamber flare. Signs and symptoms usually resolve without sequelae within 24 to 48 hours.

However, five patients who developed unusually severe and prolonged iritis and intraocular pressure elevation after receiving corneal sea nettle stings were followed for 2 to 4 years. Decreased visual acuity, iritis, and increased intraocular pressure (32 to 48 mmHg) were noted in all cases. Iritis responded to topical corticosteroids and resolved within 8 weeks. Elevated intraocular pressure responded to topical beta blockers and oral carbonic anhydrase inhibitors. Mydriasis decreased accommodation (2 of 5 cases), peripheral anterior synechiae, and iris transillumination defects also were noted. Mydriasis and decreased accommodation persisted for 5 months in 1 case and for more than 2 years in another.

continued

One patient has chronic unilateral glaucoma. Visual acuity returned to normal in all cases.

Based on our clinical experience, we recommend topical corticosteroid therapy and cycloplegia for the initial treatment of corneal jelly fish stings. Unusually severe cases such as those presented above may require hourly topical corticosteroids. Topical beta blockers and systemic carbonic anhydrase inhibitors should be used to control intraocular pressure elevations.

from Glasser, Noell, Burnett, *Ocular jellyfish stings.*

CASE REPORT   **"Sea Lice" stings**

During a diving doctors' conference in Bonaire, in 1984, most of the doctors and many of their spouses got stung by numerous small broken coelenterate tentacles ("sea lice") and were in considerable discomfort. Heated discussion about the treatment eventuated.

The modern "vinegar" proponents lost converts rapidly as it was totally ineffectual, whereas the old fashioned "alcohol" users retained a small following. The local anaesthetic was winning advocates, but slowly. An old lady offered us the use of her Gebauer's Tannic Acid Spray, and in return received dissertations on the uselessness of tannic acid for any disease known to medicine. She would have received more information on nematocyst pathophysiology, had not one of the victims tried the spray. It worked immediately and fully. Mutual agreement spread as fast as the spray bottle was passed around.

One possible explanation of the effectiveness of the Tannic Acid spray, was that it contained not only tannic acid, but also coolants, local anaesthetic, volatile alcohols and many other chemicals. It taught many of us to be less arrogant about our "scientific" knowledge. Tannic acid has more recently been shown to be an effective therapeutic denaturing agent, inactivating many allergens by replacing water groups with phenols. Medicine has now caught up with the leather tanning industry, which has known about this for many centuries. Will cold tea replace vinegar in the surf life savers thirst aid kit?

Just recently, the same scientists who demonstrated the danger of alcohols and the value of vinegar for some coelenterate stings, have demonstrated that with different species of coelenterate, these substances can have the opposite effects. Life was not meant to be easy for jellyfish victims.

Prevention

1. Avoid waters known to contain stinging coelenterates. This information can be elicited from other swimmers and life-savers, or from local inhabitants who are aware of seasonal dangers, or by inspecting the seashore (where jellyfish may be beached).
2. Protective clothing such as wetsuits, lycra suits, body stockings, gloves, costumes and face masks or swim goggles are all effective.
3. Recent reports suggest that some skin preparations, such as water resistant sunscreens, may give some protection, at least to the less potent jellyfish.

PORTUGESE MAN O'WAR, PHYSALIA

Species	■ *Physalia physalis* (utriculus)
Common names	■ Bluebottle, Seeblase,
Distribution	■ Most tropic, subtropic and temperate waters. In the cooler regions it is more prevalent in summer months.

Physalia, which is really a colony of organisms, is brought onto beaches en masse by the onshore winds. The animal has a pneumatophore (a gas filled transparent sac, usually blue coloured and a few centimetres long) which allows it to float on the surface of the water. The presence of right and left sails ensures it will drift at 45 degree angles to the wind. It trails many short frilled tentacles and one or more long "fishing" ones which may extend for many metres and it is the"fishing" tentacle which, when coming into contact with its prey or victim, contracts and discharges many nematocysts—paralysing small fish and stinging humans.

The nematocysts (40 microns diameter) may remain potent even after being desiccated following the animal's death. There is some suggestion of partial and temporary immunity following mild Physalia stings.

There have been a couple of deaths from Physalia stings, but there are many more close calls. There was one death in Florida, U.S.A. .Many cases have required resuscitation at the coastal hospitals near Sydney beaches, in Australia. For details of toxins, see page 255.

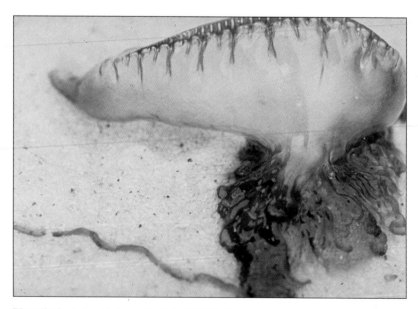

Physalia, body length 8 cm. Photo by K. Gillett

Clinical features

LOCAL. Initially there is a sharp sting. This may be aggravated by pulling on the tentacle, removing it, leaving the water, rubbing the area or by the application of fresh water. The sting rapidly increases to an intense ache which spreads to involve surrounding joints and then moves centrally. The adjacent axilla or groin may be affected and the associated lymph glands become tender. Duration of severe pain may range from a few minutes to many hours. It is followed by a dull ache which lasts a similar period.

The area affected develops a red line with small white pinpoint lesions, often giving a ladder type pattern, and in severe cases a central weal or blister appears after the redness. The weals only last a few hours, looking like a string of beads, and the redness disappears within 24 hours. Ulceration, permanent discolouration and scarring is rare.

GENERAL signs are not uncommon, but rarely last longer than one day. The patient may be in mild shock and develop syncope (fainting on standing). He is often pale, cold and sweaty, with a rapid pulse and hypotension. Generalised chills and muscle cramps may develop. Abdominal symptoms include nausea, pain and vomiting. Neurological signs, with the patient showing irritability and confusion, may be present. Death is not common, but a number of cases have come close to it. If the patient has difficulty breathing or develops a cyanotic (bluish) colour, respiratory depression must be presumed.

Prevention

1. Do not touch these animals.
2. Use protective clothing, face mask, sunscreens, etc.
3. Remain out of the water when they are observed.
4. Beware of the onshore wind.

First aid and **medical treatment.** See pages 96-98.

CHIRONEX, BOX JELLYFISH, SEA WASP

Order   ■ Cubomedusae
Species   ■ *Chironex fleckeri*
Common names ■ Deadly Sea Wasp, Sea Wasp, Fire Medusa, Indringa
Distribution   ■ It is restricted to the warm waters of the Indian and
Pacific Oceans, and the 70 or more box jellyfish fatal-
ities have occurred in the waters off northern Australia from November to April. It, or similar species,
may exist in other months if seasonal conditions permit and in other territories north of Australia, including Papua New Guinea, Indonesia, Philippines,
Malaysia.

This is said to be the most venomous marine animal known. Its box-shaped body
can measure 20 cm along each side with as many as 15 tentacles measuring up to
3 metres in length on each of its four corners (pedalia). If small fish make contact
with the tentacle it contracts and fires nematocysts into the prey. Sudden tension
on the tentacle may also result in nematocysts firing all along its length. The con-
vulsed and the dying fish is slowly drawn into the bell of the *Chironex*.

Development through the egg and polyp stages takes place in estuaries and
mangrove swamps, and terminates in a free swimming medusa which flood
along the coastline waterways, following heavy rains. The animal is usually
small at the beginning of the "hot" season, and increases in size and toxicity as
it matures. It is encountered more frequently after bad weather and on cloudy
days, when it moves into shallower water.

Being pale blue and transparent, it is almost invisible in its natural habitat.
It tends to avoid noises made by speed boats, and turbulence caused by the
surf—but this should not be relied upon. Its swimming speed may reach up to 4
knots, but it more often drifts with the wind and tide when near the surface.

Most authorities discourage the popular use of the name sea wasp, as
tourists tend to look skywards, out to sea, for an air borne threat. "Box jellyfish"
also receives criticism because of the number of box shaped jellyfish which are
not as potent as *Chironex*.

The severity of the sting increases with the size of the animal, the extent of
contact with the victim, and the delicacy of the victim's skin. Deaths have occurred with as little contact as 4 metres of tentacle length and a skin lesion
(weal) width of 4 mm, within minutes. Adjacent swimmers may also be affected
to a variable degree. The tentacles tend to adhere with a sticky jelly-like substance. They can usually be removed by bystanders, due to the protection afforded by the thick skin on the palms of their hands. This protection is not
always enough, and stinging can occur even through surgical gloves. Also,
stinging can result when the nematocysts on the hand touches more sensitive
skin or eyes.

It is especially dangerous to children and patients with asthma or other cardiac or respiratory disorders.

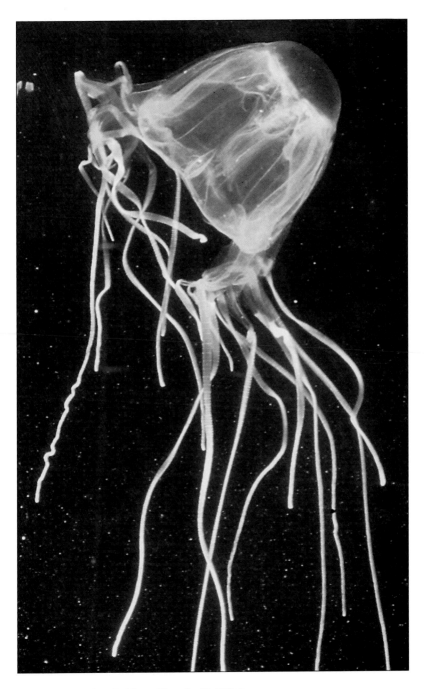

Chironex, body length 18 cm. Photo by K. Gillett

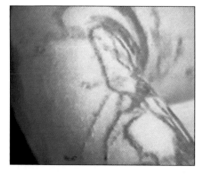

Chironex sting on leg of child. Multiple interlacing "whiplash" injury, with beadlike pattern.

Some cases have received prompt and efficient resuscitation techniques, but still resulted in death. Many others have survived despite the absence of resuscitation.

TOXIN. See appendix (page 256).

Clinical features

See also Antivenoms and Advice, (page 250).

Usually the animal is not seen before the incident. The person usually screams as a result of the excruciating pain, occurring immediately on contact, and then claws at the adherent tentacles (whitish strings surrounded by a transparent jelly). The victim can become confused, act irrationally or lose consciousness, and may drown because of this.

LOCAL. Multiple interlacing whiplash lines—red, purple or brown—0.5 cm wide develop within seconds. The markings are in a "beaded" or "ladder" pattern, and are quite characteristic. These acute changes will last for some hours. If death occurs, the skin markings then fade. If the patient survives, the red, swollen skin may develop large weals, and, after 7-10 days, necrosis and ulceration develop over the area of contact. A whitish frost-like appearance commonly develops.

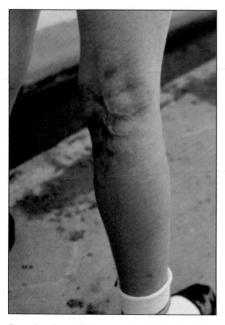

Scarring from Chironex sting. Photo by P. Fenner

The skin lesions may take many months to heal if deep ulceration occurs. Itching may also be troublesome and recurrent. Discolouration and scarring at the site of these injury may be permanent.

GENERAL. Excruciating pain is the dominant feature, while impairment of consciousness may proceed to coma and death. The pain increases in intensity over the first 15 minutes, often coming in waves. It diminishes in 4-12 hours. Amnesia occurs for most of the incident following the sting. If death occurs, it usually does so within the first ten minutes. Survival is likely if unassisted breathing and cardiac activity is maintained during the first hour.

Cardiovascular effects dominate the clinical picture. The patient may develop cardiac shock, appearing cold and clammy with a rapid pulse and frequent loss of consciousness. The cardiac state may oscillate and give a false impression of improvement just prior to the patient's death. Thus hypertension, rapid heart rate and respirations may fluctuate with hypotension, slow heart rate and respirations, and raised venous pressure.

Respiratory distress, congestion and cyanosis (bluish colour) may be due to cardiac or mid-brain depression from the venom.

Paralysis and abdominal pains may occur. Thirst may be noted. Malaise and restlessness may persist, with physical convalescence requiring up to a week. Irritability and difficulty with psychological adjustment may take weeks or months to disappear. Immunity to the sting is said to occur following repeated and recent contacts, although it is likely that the cross immunity between the species is incomplete or absent.

Prevention

In areas where *Chironex* is found, the following advice should be followed. Do not run or dive into the water. Walk in slowly. Overalls, wetsuits, body stockings made of pantyhose, Lycra suits, or any other adequate protective clothing should be worn. Restrict swimming or wading to the safe months of the year, and at patrolled beaches. Care is especially needed on cloudy days towards the end of the hot season.

Dragging a section of a beach with a 2.5 cm mesh has been used, not very successfully, to clear an area for bathing. It is of value when it does catch the animal, as then swimming is definitely contra-indicated. Enclosures of a permanent mesh are now used to allow for restricted swimming in potentially dangerous areas.

Vaccination against *Chironex,* for those likely to be at risk, was under investigation by the Commonwealth Serum Laboratories, Australia, but has now been abandoned. Some divers expose themselves to *Chironex* throughout the whole season—claiming they build up an immunity while the animal is small and less venomous. This approach appears to be unnecessarily heroic.

First aid

1.   Prevent drowning.
2.   Douse the area with vinegar to reduce the likelihood of further discharge of the nematocysts. This may be repeated. Remove the tentacles as rapidly and gently as possible. If vinegar is not available, other preparations (stale wine, coca-cola, local anaesthetic) may be of value.

     Remove the tentacles and undischarged nematocysts immediately. Do this gently but quickly, easing them off the skin in one direction only. Rough handling or rubbing will cause further nematocysts to discharge. Some experienced fishermen use a razor blade to pare the tentacles off the exposed skin. Businessmen can use plastic credit cards. Although it is possible to be stung when removing the jellyfish tentacles, the thickness of the skin of the hands makes it unlikely that this injury would be serious.

     Local remedies, such as lemon or lime juice, onions, strong black tea, mild denaturing agents or volatile fluids, have yet to be evaluated.

3. Mouth to mouth artificial respiration is required if the patient has stopped breathing, together with external cardiac massage when no obvious pulse is detectable (Appendix I). Resuscitation should be continued and reapplied whenever there is any deterioration in the patient's condition. Do not assume that because the patient initially appears to recover, that there will not be a relapse.
4. Local anaesthetics (see Appendix III) may be of value.

MEDICAL TREATMENT

1. Administer first aid. During the first few minutes a repeat of the traditional vinegar dousing may be of some prophylactic value.
2. Box Jellyfish Antivenom (Appendix V), which used to be called Sea Wasp Antivenene, has been developed by the Australian Commonwealth Serum Laboratories, and is derived from the serum of hyper-immunised sheep. 20,000 units may be sufficient to control the effects of a moderate sting on adults. This may need to be increased to 100,000 u. for a child with massive injury. The antivenom effectively counters both the systemic complications and the skin damage produced by the venom.
3. Local anaesthetic sprays or ointment may be of some value in reducing the intensity of the sting, although they are inadequate by themselves in serious cases. Local steroid applications may also be of value. These may assist during the hours of intensive care that is also needed. Analgesics include morphine 15 mg or pethidine (demerol) 100 mg in incremental doses. This may also protect against shock. Pentazocine has also been used with good results.
4. Hydrocortisone 100 mg is administered intravenously every two hours if needed. Local steroid preparations are valuable for treating local manifestations such as swelling, pain and itching, etc.
5. Intermittent positive pressure respiration, possibly with oxygen, replaces mouth to mouth artificial respiration, if needed. This will require constant attention because of the varying degree of respiratory depression (Appendix I). General anaesthesia with endotracheal intubation and controlled respiration is needed if analgesia cannot otherwise be obtained.
6. Chlorpromazine 100 mg intramuscularly, or diazepam 10 mg intravenously, etc, may be of value after the immediate resuscitation, as they will assist in sedating and tranquillising the patient despite causing significant respiratory depression. Other drugs may be used but are unproven in this clinical disorder. These include respiratory and cardiac stimulants, although verapamil has theoretical benefits.
7. Continuous electrocardiogram monitoring is indicated, as are pulse rate, B.P, CVP, respiratory rate, arterial gases and pH levels. External cardiac massage and defibrillation are given if required. Calcium channel antagonists may reduce cardiac arrhythmias.
8. A local steroid ointment such as Ultralan 0.5% usually relieves the severe itching which can follow the acute skin lesion.

SEA WASP VARIANTS

Order	■	Cubomedusae
Species	■	*Chiropsalmus* spp, *Tamoya* spp, *Carybdea* sp, *Morbakka* spp and others.
Distribution	■	Tropical, subtropical or warmer waters.

Other jellyfish belonging to the Order Cubomedusae are capable of inflicting intense pain and even causing death. These are also often referred to as sea wasps, and include species of *Chiropsalmus,* such as *Chiropsalmus quadrigatus, C. quadrumanus, C. buitendijk.* Like *Chironex* they have multiple tentacles on the four corners, although the body is smaller and the tentacles are fewer and smaller than *Chironex,* but they do have a similar tropical distribution. This species have been incriminated in deaths in the Philippines. There is a possibility that the sea wasp antivenom may be effective against stings of this nature.

Tamoya, Carybdea alata, and *Morbakka* are large Cubomedusa with one thick tentacle on each corner, and may be distributed throughout many of the tropical waters, causing severe envenomations. Episodic stingings have also been reported from the Middle East (specifically the Gulf of Oman).

Even though I do not agree with the widespread use of the name sea wasp being given to many jellyfish, it at least serves to accentuate the importance of

Tamoya bell being held. Tentacles are contracted. Photo by C. Tipton

Morbakka, after preservation. Photo by P. Fenner

some of these stings. In the Australasian region, the term sea wasp is often considered synonymous with death, even though most patients do survive. In other areas, the term has unfortunately been used for much less important injuries . Although one cannot restrict the term to stings only from the Order Cubomedusae, it is best limited to cases of similar clinical significance. Such cases may involve either exceptionally large or very numerous jellyfish from any of the families referred to in this text, or to others which are only occasionally encountered and rarely identified.

[For **clinical findings** refes to pages 94-96 and 104.]

First aid and **medical treatment**

Treatment of such stings is based on the same general principles as those described for the *Chironex* and other jellyfish on pages 96-98, 105-106.

BLUBBER JELLYFISH

Dangerous species ■ *Catostylus mosaicus, Rhizostoma pulmo, R.cuvieri*
Common names ■ Man O'War, Blubber, Brown Blubber, German Blubber, Jelly Blubber
Distribution ■ Temperate and tropical waters, and in estuaries, around the Indian and Pacific Oceans.

The colour of the blubber jellyfish varies with season and location. Often they can be handled with impunity, but not always as their stinging ability varies at different times of the year, being worse during the breeding season. The dome-shaped bell may be up to 30 cm in diameter, and has eight trailing tentacles capable of inflicting stings.

Clinical features, first aid and **medical treatment.** See pages 94-98.

Brown blubber, length 25 cm

CYANEA

Dangerous species	■	*Cyanea capillata, C. annaskala, C. artica, C. nozaki* and others
Common names	■	Sea Blubber, Hairy Stinger, Sea Nettle, Hairy Jelly, Lion's Mane, Malonga, Snotty.
Distribution	■	All oceans, from the Arctic to the Antarctic.

This red or yellow umbrella-shaped jellyfish is most numerous during summer and may have tentacles up to 10 metres long. The tentacles are easily damaged and may separate from the body, leaving the animal harmless. The body may be 30 cm or more across, although they grow to even greater sizes in Antarctic waters. When handled, they leave a sticky mucous which has a fishy smell. Dust from these jellyfish, caught and dried in fishermen's nets, is said to cause irritation to skin, eyes and respiratory passages.

Clinical features, first aid and **medical treatment.** See pages 94-98.

Cyanea with bell expanded, diameter 30 cm. Photo by E. Friese

IRUKANDJI

Order	■ Cubomedusea
Dangerous species	■ *Carukia barnes* and others.
Common names	■ Box Jellyfish, Type A Stinging Jellyfish
Distribution	■ Tropical waters along the east and west coasts of Australia, and occasionally in the islands of the Indian and Pacific Oceans (including Indonesia and Fiji). The distribution could be much wider.

The name irukandji was given by Dr. Flecker, after a local aboriginal tribe living near Cairns, Australia, where the disease was first described. Similar clinical syndromes have now been reported from many other warm water areas throughout the world.

> Similar clinical symptoms may accompany stings from other coelenterates mentioned in this book.

This animal is rarely observed by the victim, though the stinging occurs near the surface and in shallow water. It is one of the small box jellyfish with a transparent body about 1-2 cm long and with four tentacles varying from 5 cm to 1 metre in length, depending on the degree of contraction. Nematocysts, appearing as clumps of minute red dots, are distributed over the body and tentacles. The injury is proportional to the duration, extent and location of the sting.

Stingings occur in clusters in the same locality, often in late summer, where clear warm ocean waters approach the land. Others occur well out to sea, in depths of 10-20 metres.

Clinical features

LOCAL. A few seconds after contact a stinging sensation is felt and this increases in intensity for a few minutes and diminishes during the next half hour. It is usually sufficient to cause many children to cry, and adults to leave the water. It may recur at the commencement of the generalised symptoms, but is overshadowed by them.

A red coloured 5-7 cm reaction surrounds the area of contact within 5 minutes. Small papules (pimples) appear and reach their maximum in 20 minutes, before subsiding. "Kissing" lesions occur, where the original skin lesion comes into contact with other skin, for example, near joints. The red colouration can occasionally last up to 3 hours and there is a dyshidrotic reaction (skin dry at first, with excessive sweating later) over the area. Occasionally, in severe cases the area may remain swollen for many hours.

There is usually a latent period of 5-120 minutes between contact and the development of generalised symptoms. The patient may not relate these symptoms to the local reaction, unless specifically questioned about this.

GENERALISED. Abdominal pains (91%), often severe and associated with spasm and board-like rigidity of the abdominal wall, often come in waves. Muscular aches such as cramps and dull boring pains occur, with increased tone and muscle tenderness on examination. This involves the spine, hips, shoulders, limbs and chest. Headache may also be severe. Profuse sweating, anxiety and restlessness may develop, as may nausea and vomiting.

Respiratory distress with coughing, and grunts preceding exhalations may occur. Pulmonary oedema has been reported. There may be increased blood pressure and pulse rate, with possible arrhythmias.

Later symptoms include numbness and tingling, itching, smarting eyes, sneezing, joint and nerve pains, weakness, rigors, dry mouth and headache. Temperature usually remains normal, although there may be an increased pulse rate.

Symptoms diminish or cease within 4-12 hours. Occasionally malaise and distress may persist and convalescence may take up to a week.

Prevention

1   Wear protective clothing.
2. Evidence of discoid medusae ("jelly buttons," "hard water," transparent coin-like animals) in the area, serves as a warning that conditions are suitable for irukandji stingings.
3. Once stingings have been reported, the water should be avoided by other bathers.

First aid. See page 96 and Appendix I.

MEDICAL TREATMENT

1. Administer first aid.
2. During the severe phase with abdominal pains, spasms and coughing, administer pethidine intravenous e.g.50 mg, to be repeated as necessary (often after 30 minutes). Response is impressive within two minutes. Sometimes larger doses or the use of morphine may be necessary.
3. Alpha blockers have been recommended for the control of hypertension, due to catecholamine release. Phentolamine may be given as a bolus dose and subsequent infusion (1-5 mg initially and 5-10 mg / hr). Hydralazine has also been used.
4. Other medications which have been used with dubious effect include antivenom for the box jellyfish, diazepam, antihistamines and Trilene. General anaesthesia with assisted respiration could be used if the conventional techniques prove insufficient.
5. Monitoring of fluid and electrolyte state, together with cardio respiratory parameters, would seem indicated, especially if there are any respiratory symptoms. Pulmonary oedema has been treated with intubation and controlled ventilation, high inspiratory oxygen and positive end expiratory pressure. Echocardiography may verify early cardiac failure.
6. During the latter part of the illness, when only fleeting neuralgic and arthralgic symptoms predominate, simple analgesics may be effective.

JIMBLE

Order	■	Cubomedusea
Dangerous species	■	*Carybdea rastonii* and others
Common names	■	Sea Wasp (U.S.A.), Small Box Jellyfish, Lantern Medusa, Mona.
Distribution	■	Indian and Pacific oceans, in both tropical and temperate areas, especially during late spring and summer.

Jimble tend to rise towards the surface during the early morning and evening, or on cloudy days, and are sometimes difficult to identify in the water. They occur in swarms can cause injury if they touch more sensitive skin of children or areas such as the forearm. The four tentacles can be a few cm long, or up to half a metre. The symptoms are often more severe than those caused by Physalia stings, and can cause permanent scarring. They are equivalent in many cases to the "Sea Wasp Variants" (page 107).

Clinical features, first aid and **medical treatment.** See pages 94-98.

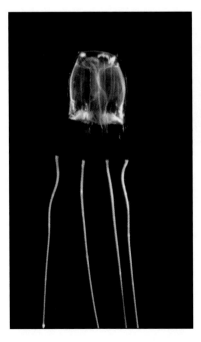

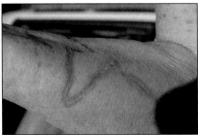

Above: Jimble sting with a few distinct tentacle lines

Left: Jimble, *Carydrea rastonii*, box length a few cm. Photo by R. Southcott

MAUVE STINGER

Dangerous species	■	*Pelagia noctiluca*
Common names	■	Mauve Blubber, Augas Vivas, Quallen.
Distribution	■	Found throughout the warmer parts of the world's oceans during all seasons, but especially prevalent during summer and hot months.

This jellyfish grows to about 13 cm across the bell, and has eight tentacles. Apart from the nematocyst-bearing tentacles, stinging cells are found on the warty upper surface of the bell. Sometimes found in company with Portuguese men o'war.

Clinical features, first aid and **medical treatment.** See pages 94-98.

Mauve stinger, length 10 cm. Photo by D. Henderson

MISCELLANEOUS JELLYFISH, NETTLES & LICE

Order   ■ Coelenterata
Dangerous species   ■ *Aurelia aurita, Chrysaora quinquecirrha, Leuckartiara gardineri, Olindias singularis* and others.
Common names   ■ Saucer Blubber, Stinging nettle, Yaringa, Noko.
Distribution   ■ World wide.

Many jellyfish have nematocysts capable of piercing human skin, especially at certain stages of their development. They often swim near the surface during times of diminished light (on cloudy days and at dusk, for example) and some, like the noko *(Olindias singularis)* are small enough not to be seen.

Sea nettle,
diameter 30 cm.
Photo by J.
Joiner

Their tentacles are often broken up in surf or in areas such as water outlets of power houses, causing small pieces of tentacle with attached nematocysts to be scattered throughout the water. Under these conditions, many swimmers may be stung over wide areas of the body by these so called "sea lice."

As a general rule, the more mature the coelenterate, the more severe the sting. There is much more likelihood of stinging occurring on the soft skin of a child, or the inside of the forearm and thigh than on the tougher palms of hands or soles of feet. Sometimes the nudibranch, *Glaucus,* carries nematocysts and is referred to as sea lice. Free swimming crustaceans such as cymothoids, and cirolanids, are also sometimes known as sea lice, as are some algae.

Clinical features

LOCAL. A minor irritation or sting may increase following trauma, such as rubbing the site, and appear as a blotchy red patch in which there may be a weal formation (blisters) and line markings radiating outwards. The lesions may increase for the first ten minutes and then diminish over the next hour. The pain may precede or parallel the appearance of the lesion.

Pain and tenderness may extend to regional lymph nodes.

GENERALISED. In the event of extensive stingings, there is a possibility of abdominal and back pains, nausea, vomiting and diarrhoea; fever, chills and sweating; increased salivation, coughing and expectoration; shock (pale, cold and clammy appearance, with a rapid pulse and hypotension) due to circulatory failure; apprehension, irritability, restlessness, depression, delirium; respiratory distress with the skin turning blue due to insufficient oxygen.

These symptoms normally clear within an hour or two.

Prevention

  1.   Do not swim when sea lice have been reported.
  2.   Beware of swimming on cloudy days or at dusk.
  3.   Use protective clothing, face mask and gloves.

First aid and **medical treatment.** See pages 94-99.

FIRE CORAL

Dangerous species   ■   *Millepora* spp.

Common names   ■   Stinging Coral, False Coral, Karang Gatal (Itchy Corals)

Distribution   ■   Tropical and subtropical waters, or where the water is warm such as in the outlets of power stations and nuclear reactors.

These animals are called corals because of the similarity in appearance to the true reef building corals. They have a bright yellow-green and brown skeletal covering pitted by many tiny pores (thus "millepora"), through which tentacles

Fire coral. Photo by W. Deas

with nematocysts project. Fire corals grow in different sizes and shapes. *M.com-planata* grows in large upright sheets and blades, *M. alcicornis* is finger-like and branching moose like antlers, and *M. squarrosa* is a squat box-like growth usually found in turbulent waters.

Accidental brushing of the skin against projecting tentacles has caused unexpected pain to many divers. By waving a hand over the fire coral, the pressure wave causes the tentacles to withdraw, allowing the fire coral to be touched without injury.

The sting is more severe on delicate skin, and increases with the area of exposure. The toxin is a water soluble, heat-affected protein.

Clinical features

LOCAL. Varies from a mild prickling sensation to pain in excess of that from a Portuguese man o'war. A burning itch with pinpoint red lesions around the area of contact is common. A red-coloured swelling may develop, along with blisters or weals. These may later fill with pus or may dry and flake off. If severe these reactions may persist beyond 24 hours.

GENERALISED. Nausea and vomiting for 2-3 hours has been reported. The extent of stinging is usually too small to produce these general reactions. However, if extensive contact is made it is presumed that the effects similar to those seen with other coelenterates.

Prevention

1.   Do not handle fire corals.
2.   Wear protective clothing, face masks, gloves.

First aid and **medical treatment.** See pags 94-97.

SEA ANEM

Dangerous species ■ *Actinia* spp, *Actinode.*
spp, *Anemonia* spp, *C*
Physobrachia spp, *Rho*
matactis spp.

Common names ■ Stinging Anemone, Acti
Matalelei.

Distribution ■ Tropical, subtropical and t

This colourful group of coelenterates have similar nematocyst characteristics to
the *Physalia.* Because of their attractive colour and their tendency to remain anchored in one position, they are easy prey for the unwary collector. They often
live at or below the low water mark and have a covering of sticky material
which aids adherence of the nematocysts to the victim.

Some divers claim to develop immunity from these stings, whereas others
develop allergies. In the Admiralty Islands, and elsewhere, anemones have been
used as food—sometimes after scraping off the nematocyst-laden tentacles with
a knife and cooking the animal. Poisoning is possible, and is due to a neurotoxin
producing generalised paralysis. Gastrointestinal symptoms may also occur due

Stinging anemone, *Lebrunea danae.* Up to 30 cm in diameter on Bonaire Island.
Usually found under coral heads, in cracks, inside discarded conch shells and
other cryptic locations. Forked pseudotentacles have blister-like nematocyst
batteries seen as spherical bumps in this photo. Withdraws rapidly when touched.
Photo by G. Lewbell.

it has been stated that anemone were spread on spear
more lethal. It is now thought the toxic substances used
, more than anemones.
the causes of sponge divers' disease is due to the coexistence of cer-
mones with the sponges collected.

Clinical features

LOCAL. The initial symptoms vary from a prickly sensation over the affected
area, to a severe burning pain. This occurs immediately on contact and may increase over the next few minutes. It may then extend up the limb affecting the
regional lymph glands in the armpit or groin. After a few hours the pain lessens,
but a residual ache or itch may persist for weeks.

The area becomes swollen and red—and blisters may develop. In severe
cases necrosis and ulceration of tissue may result. Secondary infection of the ulceration, with a purulent discharge and abscess formation, may follow.

GENERALISED. Malaise, fever, chills and thirst; abdominal pain, nausea and
vomiting; headache, delirium (central nervous system toxicity) and muscular
spasms. In very serious cases there may be shock (pale cold and clammy appearance, with hypotension) and respiratory distress.

Prevention

1. Do not handle or collect these beautifully coloured anemones.
2. Wear protective clothing, gloves and face masks.

First aid and **medical treatment.** See pages 94-97.

Stinging sea anemone.
Photo by K. Gillett

DEE SCARR'S SCUBA DIARY   **Anemones**

All anemones have stinging cells (nematocysts) which they presumably use to stun any prey that might stumble into range. I think the stinging cells also help to keep greedy fish, who might otherwise try to steal the anemone's food, away. The interesting thing about these nematocysts, though, is that in virtually all anemones I've worked with, the nematocysts are not powerful enough to pene-trate through the tough skin on people's palms and the surface of their fingers.

When I introduce divers to anemones, we begin by gently placing a finger in contact with one or more of the tentacles of the common Caribbean anemone, Condylactis gigantea. *The tentacle sticks to the finger, with a sort of scotch tape feel. The strength of the scotch tape is the strength the anemone's nematocysts have. Then we disengage our fingers, and place a small piece of hot dog in con-tact with the tentacle—and watch the anemone stick to the hot dog and draw it, gradually and with more and more tentacles, towards its mouth.*

I found that if I or one of the divers inadvertently thrust our fingers into the anemone too quickly or too roughly, the anemone would seem to swell up—and it would stop sticking. This would logically be a defence mechanism: if the anemone stuck with two much tenacity to prey struggling too hard, the prey would injure the anemone. By avoiding sticking, the anemone saves itself from such injury.

Another interesting Caribbean anemone is Stoichactis helianthus, *commonly known as the sun anemone, but before I knew that I began calling it the "sticky" anemone, and that name, uh, stuck, at least with me. I began showing divers the sticky anemone in the 1970's when I was working in the Bahamas, since those anemones were about the most interesting critters on the shore reef that we used for diver training. We'd place our fingers gently on the tentacles of this anemone, and they'd stick—hard. Years later I read in* Colin's Caribbean Reef Invertebrates and Plants *that "a sharp sting is felt if non callused skin (like a bare stomach) is applied to the anemone." (p.191) Luckily, we never used these anemones for bot-tom cushions or to rub our armpits, and after hundreds of interactions with these animals I can say that I and all my buddies have emerged unscathed.*

In the Caribbean the only critters that reliably live with anemones are in-vertebrates (mostly shrimp), so I was interested in watching the behaviour of the anemone fish I first saw in the Coral Sea. Unlike the shrimp, who tiptoe deli-cately along anemone tentacles, these clownfish seem to bathe among the anemone tentacle. I noticed that sometimes when I placed my finger in contact with the tentacle of an anenome which had clownfish living in it, the tentacle wouldn't stick. Scientists have determined that the clownfish live among the anemones with impunity because they've managed to coat themselves with the same mucus that the anemone uses on its own tentacles, so that it knows not to sting itself—but I still wonder if part of the reason the clownfish stay safe is be-cause their constant disruption of the anemone causes the tentacles to stop sticking, as we found would happen in Caribbean anemones.

Prior to my Coral Sea diving, I had read that in aquarium conditions, clownfish had been observed delivering food to their anemones. When I fed clownfish pieces of fish in the wild, I found that for the first ten minutes or so, they'd faithfully deliver the food to their anemones—but after that time, they'd eat the food themselves. I guess everyone has to pay rent.

STINGING HYDROID

Dangerous species	■	*Aglaophenia* spp, *Lytocarpus* spp.
Common names	■	Stinging Seaweed, Fire Weed, Fire Fern, Feather Hydroid
Distribution	■	Tropical and subtropical regions, and where there are warm waters and shallow reefs.

Although this fern-like hydroid looks like seaweed, it is an animal with a plant-like habit. It is often brownish green in colour, although the range may extend from purple to white. It grows on reefs and in warm waters, such as at power station outlets. It is very variable in its effect and may be handled with impunity on some occasions, yet cause extreme pain at other times.

Some experienced divers are more fearful of this than the sea wasp, being of the opinion that immunity can be developed by periodic exposures to the sea wasp. This exaggerated reputation is most probably due to *L. philippinus,* found around the northern coastlines of Australia and many tropical island resorts of the Pacific, Indian and Atlantic oceans and the Mediterranean.

Clinical features

LOCAL. This may vary from a mild stinging sensation to extreme pain, and usually increases over the first ten minutes. The appearance is that of a patchy area of red skin with raised pinpoint lesions, developing urticarial weals within the first 30 minutes to 2 hours. Over the next 12 hours this may spread to become a generalised blotchy red rash with both flattened and raised areas. The

Stinging hydroid. Photo by K. Gillett

area becomes swollen and vesicles may persist for up to a week, causing local discomfort and itching. Pigmentation and peeling of skin, even ulceration and scarring, may result.

GENERALISED. These reactions are uncommon, but may include abdominal pain, cramps, nausea and diarrhoea; malaise, fever and chills; and a toxi-confusional state; loss of consciousness, probably related to the degree of pain.

Prevention

1. Do not handle or rub against this hydroid.
2. Wear protective clothing.

First aid and **medical treatment.** See pages 94-97.

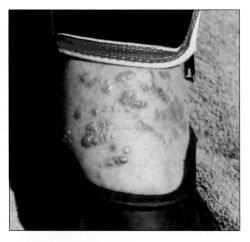

Hydroid sting, showing
vesicles 30 minutes
after injury.

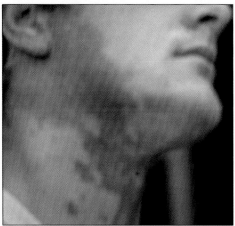

Hydroid sting over neck.
Pigmentation and peel-
ing of skin one day later.
Photo by P. Hamley

Other Venomous Marine Animals

BLUE RINGED OCTOPUS

CONE SHELL

CROWN OF THORNS

GLAUCUS

SEA SNAKE

SEA URCHIN

SPONGE

WORMS, RINGED OR SEGMENTED

NOTES

BLUE-RINGED OCTOPUS

Class	■	Cephalopod
Dangerous species	■	*Hapalochlaena maculosa,* and *H. lunulata*
Common names	■	Common Ringed, Blue-banded or Spotted Octopus
Distribution	■	Indian and Pacific Ocean countries and islands. More common around Australia. Found around New Zealand, Papua New Guinea, Indonesia, Fiji, Japan, etc.

This animal usually weighs from 10-100 g. Its span, with tentacles extended, is from 2-20 cm but usually in the lower range, and the life span is less than a year. It is found at low tide in rock pools and clumps of seaweed. Yellowish brown in colour with ringed markings on the tentacles and ridges on the body, these markings change to a vivid iridescent blue when the animal becomes angry, excited, disturbed or hypoxic. It may also occur when feeding.

The blue-ringed octopus is by far the most dangerous of the octopods, and differs from others in a number of ways. The life cycle takes about seven months, with four months of maturity. As an adult, it has no ability to produce sepia (ink) for its protection. Mating takes place with the male and female embracing tightly. The female carries her 100-200 eggs with her, and dies after they hatch. The characteristic blue rings appear at six weeks, when the animal develops the ability to bite and feed off crustaceans.

If very hungry, the octopus may descend and bite into its prey's (the crustaceans) back, whilst restraining it with its arms. If it had recently eaten, it will

Blue-ringed octopus, outstretched length 20 cm. Photo by K. Gillett

glide over the victim and squirt its toxic saliva into the surrounding water. The prey soon becomes incoordinated and then dies, to be consumed at leisure by the octopus.

The heavier specimens are more dangerous. Handling these attractive creatures has resulted in death within a few minutes. Many such incidents have probably escaped detection by the coroner as autopsy features are non-specific and the bite fades after death.

Venom

See Appendix VI, page 256. It is the same as tetrodotoxin, see page 258.

Clinical features

LOCAL. Initially the bite is almost painless, and may go unnoticed. A whitened area 1 cm in diameter becomes blistered and swollen within 15 minutes.

The signs on the skin vary, sometimes being almost impossible to see, especially if a few hours have elapsed since the time of the bite. At times it may appear as a small bruise, only a few millimetres across, and at others a small "blood blister." There may be bleeding from the wound, and a laceration may be visible—whereas if there is no laceration visible the bleeding may be within the wound. In either case it is minute and sometimes only just visible to the naked eye.

If the patient survives the first hour, he may notice a local stinging sensation for a few hours. A watery or bloody discharge may develop. Local muscular twitching may persist for some weeks.

GENERALISED. A few minutes after the bite, a rapid, painless paralysis dominates the symptoms, which progresses in the next hour or two, in this order:

1. Abnormal sensations (numbness, fullness) around mouth, neck and head.
2. Nausea and/or vomiting may occur.
3. Visual disturbances. Involvement of the eye muscles results in double vision, blurred vision and drooping of the eye lids. Ocular paralysis resulting in a fixed dilated pupil.
4. Difficulty in speech and swallowing.
5. Breathing difficulties with rapid, shallow and noisy respirations which can terminate in suffocation.
6. Generalised weakness and difficulty with co-ordination progresses to complete paralysis.
7. Paralysis can last between 4 and 12 hours, but weakness and incoordination may persist for another day. The patient's conscious state is initially normal, even though the patient may be unable to open his eyes or respond to the environment. The respiratory paralysis finally results in unconsciousness and then death, often within minutes from the commencement of symptoms, unless resuscitation is continued.
8. Low blood pressure and slowing of the heart rate are noted in severe cases.

The symptoms listed above may not progress and so the effects may end in a partial paralysis—or they may proceed to complete paralysis and death. Less severe bites may result in generalised and local muscular contractions (spasms), continuing for six hours or more. Other symptoms noted in mild cases include a light-headed feeling, depersonalisation, numbness in the arms and legs, weakness and exhaustion.

First aid

Before Paralysis

1. Wash the toxin out of the bite, with any fluid available.
2. Apply pressure bandage (see pages 240-242) and immobilisation of the limb.
3. Rest the patient, preferably lying on his side in case of vomiting, and do not leave him unattended.
4. Send for medical assistance.
5. Reassurance.

With Paralysis

1. Mouth to mouth respiration (see page 233) ensuring the patient does not turn a bluish colour. Attention must be paid to the clearing of the airway of vomitus, tongue obstruction and dentures. If an artificial airway is available, this should be inserted—but it is not essential. Artificial respiration may have to be continued for hours, until the patient reaches hospital.
2. If delay has occurred, then external cardiac massage (see page 235) may also be required.
3. Reassure the patient, who can hear but not communicate, that all will be well and you understand this condition.
4. Enlist medical aid, but never leave the patient unattended to obtain this.

Prevention

1. Avoid contact with the octopus, and be suspicious of apparently empty shells.
2. Requests by scientific groups for collection of these specimens should be tempered with caution.
3. A public education program on the dangers of this animal should be directed especially to children, who are attracted by the bright colouration.

MEDICAL TREATMENT

See Tetrodotoxin Poisoning (page 206)

1. Administer first aid. A sphygmomanometer cuff can replace the pressure bandage. When respiratory support is arranged, it can be removed.
2. Respiratory paralysis—administer artificial respiration adequate to maintain normal pO2, pCO2 and pH levels of arterial blood. Endotracheal intubation prevents aspiration of vomitus and facilitates tracheobronchial toilet, when indicated.
3. With total paralysis—no oral foods or fluids. Eye toilets and protection are needed.
4. Respiratory stimulants have been claimed to be of value in borderline cases or during the recovery period. Edrophonium (Tensilon) or neostigmine is of no value during the deeply paralysed state. Tetrahydroaminacrin (T.H.A.) i.v. may be of use, however this has not been subjected to clinical trials on humans.
5. Local anaesthesia (page 243) infiltration to the painful area.
6. For delayed allergic reactions, i.v. hydrocortisone for systemic effects, s.c. adrenalin for bronchospasm, or oral antihistamines for skin lesions, may be of value.

CASE REPORT   **Blue-ringed octopus bite**

Mr. B, age 44, was admitted to ICU on 3.9.81 at 2.50 p.m. He was European born but had spent much of his life in New Zealand before moving to Sydney where he worked as a bus driver, and thus had no previous exposure to the blue ringed octopus. The patient was a member of a group of holiday makers who went on a day trip to South Stradbroke Island. On return to the launch, he picked up two small octopuses from a pool. After discarding the second octopus, he noticed a small drop of blood on the back of his left hand, although he had been unaware of any bite.

On arrival at the launch a few minutes later, he was relating the incident to the skipper when he felt a degree of numbness and tingling around his mouth followed by weakness of his legs, causing him to collapse. Fortunately, there was an off duty customs officer and an ambulance officer standing nearby who were conversing with a seaplane pilot. The ambulance and customs officers were both proficient in cardiopulmonary resuscitation and had recently attended a revision course for this procedure. In addition, the ambulance officer had recently read a headline in the local Gold Coast newspaper which alluded to a plague of the octopus and had read up on the symptoms, signs and treatment of a bite from the octopus. The trio had heard the conversation of the patient with the skipper of the launch and came to the patient's aid. The urgency of the problem was not lost on them and they immediately bundled the patient

continued

into the seaplane, and radioed for an ambulance to meet them on the mainland, which was a few minutes ride away.

Approximately three minutes after take off the patient was noted to twitch mildly, to lose consciousness and then no pulse or respirations were apparent. CPR was commenced. On landing the patient was transferred to the waiting ambulance. CPR was continued but oxygen via a resuscitator replaced mouth to mouth ventilation. The patient was taken to Gold Coast Hospital where he arrived two to three minutes later. Examination showed him to have fixed dilated pupils, no eye opening, no motor or verbal response, no pulse, no respirations and asystole on the life pack monitor. His resuscitation consisted of intubation, ventilation and one ampoule of 1 in 1000 adrenalin IV and 100 ml sodium bicarbonate. His asystole was converted to ventricular fibrillation which was reverted to sinus tachycardia with a DC counter shock of 200 joules and a spontaneous cardiac output was obtained.

His problems appeared to be paralysis from the bite, aspiration pneumonitis, an ischaemic encephalopathy and possibly brain death. His management was continued with transfer to ICU where he was hyperventilated and started on IV steroids in the form of dexamethasone 8 mg IV initially, Mannitol 200 ml 20% and was also given diazepam 5 mg IV. He was started on Amoxyl 1 G eight hourly as it was felt he may have aspirated during his cardiac pulmonary resuscitation. Results of blood tests at this time showed a sodium of 138, potassium 3.5, chloride 105, bicarbonate 19, glucose 12.2, urea 4.5 and creatinine of 0.14, Hb was 13.1, WCC 10.0, prothrombin time 14.5 seconds. His initial blood gas on a ventilator rate of 12x1000 with no PEEP on 50% oxygen showed a PH 7.42, PO_2 of 183, PCO_2 of 31, bicarbonate 20.0, total CO_2 21.4 with a base excess of -2.5. He was continued on dexamethasone 4 mg four hourly and received 5 doses of this in total. He was also given Gastrogel 20 ml four hourly.

The major concern at this stage was the inability to distinguish between brain death and the effects of the octopus venom. However at four hour's post admission the patient was noted to have some reflex withdrawal to painful stimuli of both hands and feet and at 5 1/2 hours post admission his pupils were mid range and reactive. He had cough and gag reflexes and spontaneous movements of all limbs. He was sedated and placed on an IMV circuit and gradually weaned off the ventilator so that at 18 hours post admission the patient was able to be extubated. However, his cerebral status was still giving cause for concern and he had no comprehensible conversation although he did have spontaneous eye opening and no focal neurological signs.

Investigations on the day after admission showed pH 7.48, pO_2 69, pCO_2 34, HCO_3 25.8 and a base excess 102, bicarbonate 24, glucose 12.2, urea 6.9 and a creatinine of 0.12. Over the next few days his mental state gradually improved, and a 24-48 period of confusion and disorientation had given way to a period of sexual harassment of the nursing staff. He had no recollection of the events of the day of the bite during his stay of 10 days, and he was transferred to Sydney on day 11. However, by that stage a certain degree of confabulation had occurred and the patient claimed to remember the incident and wrestling with the octopus which he said had a six foot span.

CONE SHELL

Family	■	Conidae
Dangerous species	■	*Conus catus* (Cat Cone), *Conus geographus* (Geographer Cone), *Conus gloria-maris* (Glory of the Sea), *Conus striatus* (Striated Cone), *Conus tulipa* (Tulip Cone), *Conus magus, Conus marmoreus* (Marbled Cone), *Conus omaria* (Pearled Cone), *Conus textile* (Cloth of Gold, Textile Cone, Woven Cone, *Conus ermineus* (Agate or Tortoise Cone).
Distribution	■	Many of the dangerous species occur in the Indian and Pacific Oceans, and C. textile is also found in the Red Sea, off Florida and in the Caribbean.

Although there are some 400 species of cone shells, all with a well developed venom apparatus, only the small number of the tropical and subtropical species shown above are thought to be dangerous to humans. They inhabit shallow waters, reefs, ponds and tidal rubble, usually growing to 10 cm long. They have a siphon, sometimes ringed with orange, which is used to suck in water for respiration, and may be the only part visible if the cone burrows under the sand. Some are highly valued by shell collectors, with the *C. gloria-maris* selling for hundreds of dollars.

These attractive univalve molluscs have a proboscis able to be extended from the narrow end, and able to reach around to most of the shell. Holding the shell even by the big end may not be entirely safe, and may court a sting with a resultant 25% mortality rate.

If prey enters the area, the proboscis appears from the cone and thrusts a minute venom carrying harpoon, called a radula tooth, which delivers the coup-de-grace. Sometimes the colourful proboscis pokes above the sand and wriggles, attracting the fish and then stinging the fish in the mouth—causing immediate immobilisation. The proboscis has 1 to 20 developing radular teeth, up to 1 cm long, capable of penetrating skin or light clothing and injecting venom. New radula teeth are formed and stored for use. The venom immobilises the prey, which is then engulfed by the snail's distensible stomach. The scales and bones are regurgitated some hours later.

Fish-eating cones are the most dangerous to man but, as these are difficult to distinguish at first sight, discretion on the part of shell collectors is recommended. Children are especially vulnerable.

Venom. See Appendix VI, page 256.

Clinical features

LOCAL. Effects may vary from being painless to an excruciating pain aggravated by salt water. The area may become inflamed and swollen, sometimes white, with a cyanotic (bluish) area surrounding it, and may be numb to touch.

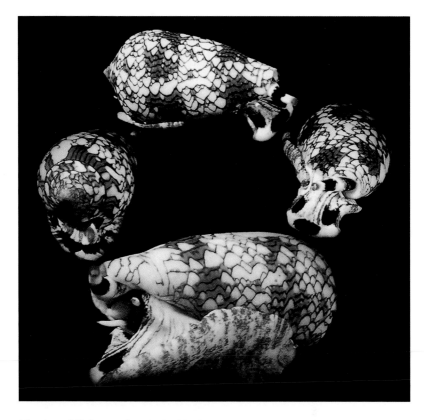

Montage of *C. Geographus.* By R. Chesher

Cone Shells.
Selection of
potenially
dangerous
cones.
Photo by R.
Chesher.

GENERALISED. Numbness and tingling may ascend from the bite to involve the whole body, especially the mouth and lips. This may take about ten minutes to develop.

Skeletal muscular paralysis may spread from the site of injury, and result in anything from mild weariness to complete paralysis. Difficulty with swallowing and speech may occur. Visual disturbances may include double and blurred vision (paralysis of voluntary muscles and pupillary reactions.) These changes are likely within 10-30 minutes of the bite.

Respiratory paralysis may dominate the clinical picture. This results in shallow rapid breathing and cyanotic (bluish) appearance, proceeding to cessation of breathing, unconsciousness and death. Other cases are said to result in cardiac failure, although this is probably secondary to the respiratory paralysis. The full extent of neurotoxic damage in humans is unknown.

The clinical state deteriorates for 1-6 hours, after which improvement is likely. If the patient survives, mobility and activity usually returns within 24 hours. Complete recovery may take a few weeks.

First aid

Without Paralysis

1. Apply pressure bandage (see pages 240-242) and immobilise the limb.
2. Rest the patient, but do not leave him unattended. Give reassurance.
3. Summon medical assistance.

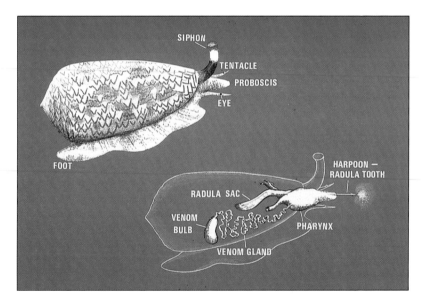

Cone shell. Diagram by C. Lawler

With Respiratory or Generalized Paralysis

1. As above, for those without paralysis, but giving preference to artificial or mouth to mouth respiration (see page 233), ensuring that the patient does not turn a bluish colour. This may have to be continued for hours, until medical assistance is obtained. This artificial respiration is the major contributor to saving the patient's life.
2. Use external cardiac massage (see page 235) as well as artificial respiration if the patient has neither pulse nor heart beat.
3. Reassure the patient, who may hear but not be able to communicate, that everything will be all right and that you understand this condition.
4. Enlist medical aid, but never leave the patient unattended to obtain this.
5. If the patient is shocked (cold, clammy and fainting), ensure the patient is lying down with the head lower than his feet.

Prevention

1. Educate the people at risk, e.g., shell collectors, visitors to the reefs, school children, etc. Many stings occur as the shell collector tries to clean the shell.
2. Avoid contact with the cone shell. Probably no part of it can be touched with complete impunity, unless the animal is dead. Despite advice to the contrary, touching the "big end" is not always safe. If you must collect these shells, use forceps and a tough receptacle. If you must touch the shells, do so with thick gloves.
3. Do not place live cone shells in pockets. The harpoon can penetrate clothing.

MEDICAL TREATMENT

1. Administer first aid and give reassurance.
2. RESPIRATORY PARALYSIS. Administer artificial respiration adequate to maintain normal pO_2 pCO_2 and pH levels of arterial blood. Endotracheal intubation facilitates ventilation and tracheobronchial toilet, and prevents aspiration of vomitus.
3. GENERAL PARALYSIS. No oral foods or fluids. Eye toilets and protection are needed, as is attention to pressure areas.
4. External cardiac massage, defibrillation, vasopressors, etc., as indicated by clinical state and E.K.G. monitor.
5. Local anaesthetic to the wound, if painful.
6. Avoid use of respiratory depressants. Respiratory stimulants and drugs used against neuromuscular blockage are probably not indicated. See also Tetrodotoxin Poisoning, page 203.

CROWN OF THORNS

Phylum   ■ Echinodermata
Dangerous species ■ *Acanthaster planci*
Common names   ■ Crown of Thorns Starfish, Sea Star, Venomous
                           Starfish
Distribution   ■ Throughout the tropics and subtropics, especially in
                           reef areas, and occasionally in temperate zones. They
                           are found in the Indian Ocean and Pacific regions
                           (Polynesia, Philippines, Asia, East Africa and Aus-
                           tralia) and the Red Sea.

This starfish has received considerable notoriety because of its reef destroying properties. It feeds on coral polyps. These animals may completely destroy reefs at the rate of 5 km a month. It is possible that the recent plague of this starfish over the Australian Barrier Reef is due to the removal by tourists of its natural

Crown of thorns, 40 cm across. Photo by R. Chesher

predator, the triton shell *Charonia tritonis,* or from destruction of coral, which is also a predator of the crown of thorns' larvae. This would explain the failure of the starfish to flourish in uninhabited areas. Some authorities now interpret these massive infestations of the reef as being natural cyclic phenomena. The starfish can be destroyed, as can many other marine animals, by divers using formalin injections.

This spiny starfish grows up to 60 cm in diameter and usually with 13-16 arms (range 9-23) compared to the more usual five arms for other starfish. They tend to inhabit shallow sheltered lagoons and leeward reefs. On exposed reefs they tend to inhabit deeper water, away from wave action.

They have many short, sharp spines up to 6 cm long on the dorsal surface, and these are easily capable of piercing skin. Each is made of a single crystal of magnesium calcite, making it strong and light. The tips of the spines may have a variety of colourations; red, orange, yellow or green, with differently coloured arms. It may be difficult to see these colours on the reef and injuries are due to unsuspecting waders treading on the animals, or divers touching them.

Even dead animals, washed up on the beach, are capable of causing severe pain to humans who tread on them with bare feet. The pain is well in excess of that due to penetration of a spine. Contact with the slime covering this starfish may result in a contact dermatitis. The starfish is also said to be poisonous to eat.

One of the worrying aspects of the crown of thorns' epidemic is that in destroying large areas of reef it may promote the circumstances in which phosphates are liberated and *Gambierdiscus toxicus* flourishes. This results in the gradual development of ciguatera toxin (page 194) in the carnivorous reef fish, that were previously safe to eat. The effects of this on tropical island populations and the commercial fishing industry can be very detrimental.

Clinical features

LOCAL. The spines penetrate the skin, and may even remain embedded in the patient. Pain is usually immediate and very severe. This persists for a few hours, then diminishing in intensity. Bleeding may be considerable, or minimal. Signs of inflammation (local swelling, redness, heat, numbness and limitation of movement) may develop. The regional lymph glands (armpit or groin) may be tender and swollen within hours. Weeping of the tissue around the wound is possible. A bluish or black pigmentation may be left where the spines have penetrated.

Continuation of the pain, swelling, weakness and limitation of movement, may continue for many weeks or months, especially if any of the spine is left in the wound. Itching may develop and be severe as the initial acute symptoms diminish.

GENERALISED. In severe cases and those with many spine penetrations, vomiting or retching may commence about an hour after the injury, and may dominate the clinical picture. It can persist for many days, and nausea for much longer. Generalised joint aches and headaches may persist for a couple of days, and cough with expectoration (sometimes with "salty" sputum), may also be noted.

First aid

1. Remove any very loose spines. Spines that are embedded are best left to a medical attendant. They must be pulled straight out, not bent or jiggled out—as they will break off at the tips.
2. Immobilise the limb and allow the patient to rest.
3. Immersing the area in hot water (45°C) may reduce pain. It is not guaranteed. Also immerse unaffected tissues to ensure that scalding does not result. Iced water may also give relief.
4. Obtain medical attention.
5. Local "therapists" suggest collecting the starfish (ensuring no further wounds are inflicted) and turning it over so that the suction pads along the centre of the arms clamp onto the injured area. This allegedly relieves pain and disability. **It does not work, and may result in further injury.** The use of meat tenderiser was in vogue a few years ago, but is not of much value.

Prevention

1. Wear shoes if walking on the reef.
2. Wear gloves if handling the crown of thorns.
3. Wear protective clothing when diving.

MEDICAL TREATMENT

1. Remove spines with forceps. Local anaesthesia (Appendix III) with infiltration into the wound, followed by debridement and cleansing of wound is essential if significant symptoms are present.
2. Soft tissue X-ray or ultrasound may be of value to detect spines that have broken off in the wound.
3. Local antibiotic such as neomycin is applied to the area when it has been cleaned, and should be reapplied q.i.d. until healing is completed.
4. In cases with vomiting, accurate fluid balance sheets should be kept with respect to restoration of fluids and electrolytes by intravenous fluids if needed. Anti-emetics may be effective, for example, prochlorperazine (Stemetil) 12.5 mg i.m. injection.
5. Broad spectrum antibiotics such as doxycycline may be needed if the local area suppurates or if lymphadenopathy persists.
6. If contact dermatitis results from non-penetrating contact with the starfish, local hydrocortisone such as Ultralan 0.5% ointment should be applied regularly until the skin has healed fully. It gives symptomatic relief and is curative in effect. It is also of value in treating the itching which may follow the skin wounds.
7. If local or generalised symptoms persist, the areas penetrated by the spines may need to be excised by a core type excision.

CASE REPORT   Crown of Thorns Sting

L.E. was a 40 year old breathhold diver taking photographs at a depth of 18 metres on the 24/3/86, on an Fijian island. He suddenly noticed a severe pain, and was then aware that he had rested his thigh on a crown of thorns. He then swam back down and picked up the animal, which was a large crown of thorns with spines of a greenish colour with red tips. He felt as though he was going to lose consciousness, but managed to reach the surface. At that stage, he was still able to use his leg, but there was extreme pain. It increased over the next few minutes, and he also lost the ability to move his leg.

It was easy to pull out seven of the exposed spines, but there were others unable to be removed. He felt that there were probably many others still in the wound. It was extremely painful for about three hours, and did not respond to the locals' remedy. This involved the inversion of the crown of thorns, so that the suction pads could be rested on the wound on his thigh. The natives kept pouring sea water over the crown of thorns, so that it would not die. The natives also hosed the patient, probably for the same reason. The local remedy produced no relief of pain "but it may have helped keep me conscious."

There was a complete numbness below the injury, without any sensation of touch or deep pressure, despite his frequent checking. Swelling developed rapidly.

He became aware of painful joints, both elbows and knees especially, and this lasted for three days. He had headaches for two days. Vomiting developed about half an hour after the injury, and this continued in a fairly extreme form for some hours. He was finally bringing up bile stained fluid only. He was still retching and feeling nauseated 5 days after the injury. He was coughing mucus, which tasted salty.

continued

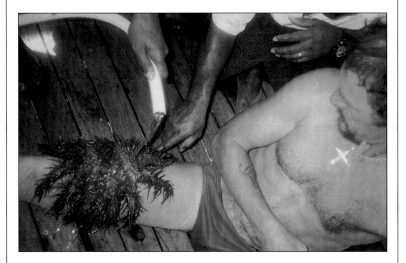

Inappropriate treatment by using the sucker pads of the offending animals. Courtesy of L. Erikson

He felt very giddy and developed a fever ("cold sweats")

He has no memory of the trip back to the local hospital where he was given analgesics, antinauseants and tetanus toxoid injection.

He was flown back to Sydney, probably in a delirious state. He has little memory of that flight. On arriving in Sydney, he was given pethidine, penicillin, erythromycin, etc. No X-rays were performed.

On examination, the thigh was very swollen and there was limited range of movement because of pain. Multiple wounds showed where the spines had penetrated the skin. Routine haematology, with haemoglobin, red cell, platelet, white cell count and blood film examination, was normal. The ESR was raised moderately, 25 mm/h, with an upper limit of normal being 10 mm/h.

Under general anaesthesia, nine of the remaining spines were removed through seven incisions. Pieces of the spine were still lodged in the subcutaneous fat, with pink necrotic tissue surrounding them. This was also removed. Local antibiotic ointment was applied and the wounds were closed.

Immediately after the removal of the spines, the patient's general symptoms ceased. The retching and nausea cleared up and the pain and discomfort was much less.

The histology report was as follows: The skin shows marked necrosis of the epidermis, dermis and subcutis. In some sections a needle shaped zone of necrosis is evident and fragments of foreign material are seen in these zones. The changes are consistent with reaction to a toxin, locally injected.

Previous experience would suggest that this type of case could continue on for months, without surgical excision of the lesions.

Nowadays, ultrasound is used to localise spines in tissues.

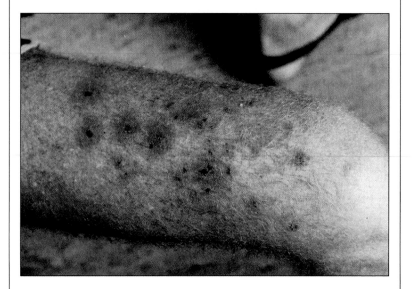

Crown of thorns injury to thigh

GLAUCUS

Class	■ Gastropoda
Dangerous species	■ *Glaucus atlanticus, Glaucilla marginata.*
Common names	■ Lizard Nudibranch, Sea Lizard.
Distribution	■ All major oceans.

This animal is found in surface waters, floating stomach uppermost, because of an air pocket in that organ. Although the colour varies, the upper (ventral) surface is predominantly blue and the lower (dorsal) surface is pearly white. Length is usually 1-3 cm.

Glaucus feeds on planktonic coelenterates, collecting the stinging nematocysts of these animals (of a diameter of 4.5 microns) to use as their own stinging apparatus. The severity of the stings of *Glaucus* therefore depends on the type of coelenterate nematocysts ingested. They have been shown to contain *Physalia* nematocysts, in which case the sting is of comparable severity to that of the *Physalia.*

Clinical features

These vary with the type of coelenterate ingested by the *Glaucus,* and the clinical features will mimic the coelenterates existing in the area at the time. The lesions are, however, scattered over the area of contact, and do not follow tentacle lines.

First aid and **medical treatment.** See pages 96-97.

Prevention

1. Avoid contact.
2. Stay out of water if stingings have occurred.

Glaucus, *Glaucus Atlanticus,* **length 2.5 cm, nibbling on the circular *Porpita pacifica.*
Photo by D. Henderson**

SEA SNAKE

Family	■	Hydrophiidae
Dangerous species	■	*Pelamis platurus* (Yellow-bellied Sea Snake), Laticauda spp (Banded Sea Snake), and others.
Distribution	■	Indian and Pacific Oceans, moving up into the Persian Gulf, throughout Asia, and extending from Africa to America, from Siberia to Tasmania.

They are not found in the Atlantic ocean, not surviving the cold waters around the Cape of South Africa or the Horn of South America. They do not pass through the Panama Canal because of Gatun Lake, the fresh water lake at its centre.

These air breathing reptiles, there being some 87 species, are usually restricted to tropical or temperate zones, being more numerous in the Indian and Pacific Oceans. Although few are dangerous to man, all are equipped with venom glands and fangs to capture prey.

Sea snakes can be subdivided into two major types according to their feeding habits. The bottom feeders have the ability to dive to around 100 metres to locate and devour their prey (eels, fish, etc.). The Laticauda, or banded sea snakes, are characteristic of this type. They are restricted to coastal and relatively shallow waters, often breed and lay their eggs onshore, in crevices or caves, and are capable of existing for long times out of water.

The second group is the pelagic "blue water" type, exemplified by the yellow-bellied sea snake, *Pelamis platurus*. This is a surface feeder that drifts with the warm tides. Mating takes place at sea, where the snake also gives birth to living young. It may be found in packs, far out to sea, but if it is washed up on to beaches or land it is unable to survive. This snake does not tolerate extremes of temperature, and is rarely found when the average sea temperature drops below 20 degrees Centigrade. The lethal limit for the snake's body temperature is 33-36 degrees Centigrade and high temperatures are avoided by the snake diving into cooler water away from the surface when it is travelling in tropical regions. It is for this reason they are more frequently found near the surface during rain or on cloudy days, breathing through their elevated nostrils.

The sea snake is well adapted to the sea water environment, salt excreting glands being present under the tongue, with a flattened paddle-shaped tail and a laterally compressed body which makes it an efficient swimmer. It is capable of remaining submerged for up to 2 hours, possibly by lowering its metabolic rate and thus tolerating lower oxygen levels. Only one breath is needed before it can dive again. Valve-like flaps cover the nostrils. The lung is greatly enlarged, extending all the way to the base of the tail. Parts of this lung may function as a hydrostatic organ, regulating the snake's buoyancy. Gas exchange can take place through the skin, as well as through the lungs, with up to 22% of the oxygen supplied from sea water and all excess carbon dioxide lost into it.

Sea snakes are inquisitive, and sometimes aggressive, especially if handled or trodden upon. They appear to be attracted by fast moving objects, such as divers who are being towed by a boat. They are also caught in trawling nets, especially in the tropics. Land snakes may also take to the water, sometimes causing difficulty with identification. The identification of sea snake is confirmed by the observation of a paddle-shaped tail. No land snake has this flattened tail.

Sea snake venom is approximately 20 times as toxic as that of the cobra, but less is delivered, and therefore only about one quarter of those bitten by sea snakes ever show signs of poisoning, and it appears there is some reluctance to inject venom even when they do bite. Nevertheless, the venom able to be injected by one fresh adult sea snake of certain species is enough to kill three people. In most species the apparatus for delivering the venom is poorly developed even though the mouth can open widely. In a few others the mouth is small and the

Hydrophis species, length 60 cm, showing the paddle-shaped tail

Yellow-bellied sea snake, *Pelamis platurus*, length 1 m. Photo by J. West

snake has difficulty obtaining a wide enough bite to pierce clothing or wet suits worn by divers.

Deaths are usually due to respiratory failure initially, and its cardiac consequences, and renal failure in the delayed cases.

Venom. See Appendix VI, page 257 .

Clinical features. See also Antivenom and Advice, pages 251-253.

LOCAL. An initial puncture at the time of biting is usually noted. There is usually little or no pain associated with sea snake bites, and little swelling or inflammation. Sometimes the fang marks are barely visible.

Occasionally the snake will ravage the victim with many lacerations. Fang and teeth marks may vary from 1 to 20, but usually there are four, and teeth or fangs may remain in the wound.

GENERALISED. The patient is usually without symptoms for 10 minutes to several hours (the latent period) and then other symptoms may develop. these can include a mild psychological reaction of "feeling different," such as euphoria, anxiety, restlessness. The tongue feels "thick." Thirst, dry throat, nausea and vomiting may occasionally occur. So may generalised stiffness and aching, and weakness developing into paralysis. Reddish-brown urine may develop, indicating kidney failure.

Paralysis may be of the ascending Guillain-Barre type, with the legs being involved an hour or so before the trunk, and then arms and neck, or extending centrally from the area of the bite, for example, from a bite on the hand, to the forearm, arm, other arm, body and legs. Usually the proximal muscle groups are the most affected.

Lockjaw (Trismus) and paralysis of the eyelids are characteristic, the latter may be one of the earliest signs and can persist for days. Muscular twitchings, writhings and spasms, difficulty with speech, swallowing, facial and ocular paralysis such as double vision or blurred vision may occur.

Respiratory distress, due to involvement of the diaphragm, may result in death in 5-35% of cases affected by the venom. Death can usually be prevented by efficient artificial respiration—which may have to be continued for up to 24 hours (less if antivenom is employed).

When recovery occurs it is rapid and complete—within 24-48 hours of envenomation.

First aid

1. Use pressure bandage and immobilisation (pages 240-242). Remove surface venom, but retain the material that is used for this, for venom identification.
2. Reduce exertion to a minimum, immobilise the patient and the limb.
3. Reassurance. Remember that the victim may be conscious, although without the ability to respond verbally.
4. Snake retained for identification (it may be harmless, whereas the treatment certainly is not). The venom can also be identified in some cases by biochemical assays and with a snake venom detection kit, if it is a land snake swimming in the water and not a true sea snake.

5. Medical aid should be enlisted, but not if it means leaving the patient unattended.
6. Mouth to mouth or other artificial respiration (see pages 233-238) is required if the patient has difficulty with breathing or stops breathing.

Prevention

1. Do not handle sea snakes.
2. Shuffle feet when walking along a muddy bottom.
3. Wear protective clothing while underwater.

MEDICAL TREATMENT

1. Administer first aid.
2. Ligature, incision and suction may be of value if employed immediately, but are not as valuable as sometimes claimed in land snake bites, and most authorities advise against it.
3. Sea snake antivenom should only be used in serious cases i.e. with signs of envenomation. Care must be taken to administer it strictly in accordance with the directions enclosed in the packet (Appendix V). Antiallergy pretreatment is advised. The antivenom can be dangerous to persons who are allergic to it. Emergency precautions for anaphylactic shock is required. Tiger snake antivenom or even polyvalent land snake antivenom may be tried if sea snake antivenom is unavailable. Their value has not yet been quantified.
4. Ideally the patient should be brought to the intensive care unit with pressure bandage applied and the affected limb immobilised. When resuscitation equipment is ready for use and the antivenom ready to administer, the bandage is then released and subsequent therapy determined by the clinical state.
5. Respiration may require assistance, or even complete control. Cardiovascular shock may need attention. For cardiopulmonary resuscitation, see Appendix I.
6. Acute renal failure is usually obvious from the oliguria, raised blood creatinine and electrolyte changes. A high serum potassium is particularly dangerous and haemodialysis is then required. This may need to be repeated, if the serum creatinine or potassium increase. The haemodialysis may result in a dramatic improvement of the muscular paralysis, and general clinical condition. The acute renal tubular necrosis and the myonecrosis are considered temporary, if life can be maintained.
7. Treat convulsions, if indicated.
8. Sedatives may be required. Paraldehyde and barbiturates have been suggested although it would seem more reasonable to administer diazepam 5-10 mg i.v. as required. This will also assist in sedating the patient while respiration is controlled.
9. Hospitalisation for a minimum of 24 hours.

CASE REPORT   Sea Snake Bite

Mercer HP, McGill JJ, Ibrahim RA. 1981. "Envenomation by sea snake in Queensland." *Med J Aust,* 1, 130-132.

In October, 1979, a two-year-old girl started screaming while playing in the water at a beach, 3 km from the central Queensland resort of Yeppoon at 2.15 p.m. Her mother noticed a snake wrapped around her daughter's left ankle; the snake then swam away towards two teenage boys, who later killed it and took it to Yeppoon Hospital.

Using her hands as a tourniquet around the child's calf, the mother rushed to an ambulance station. At this stage, the child was quite settled and was claiming that a snake had bitten her. After the ambulance officer had cleaned the wound, the mother released her grip on the child's leg, and within 30 seconds the child became drowsy and developed ptosis (droopy eyelids). While being rushed to Yeppoon Hospital, she started to vomit and respiratory distress became obvious.

On arrival at Yeppoon Hospital, 20 minutes after envenomation (four minutes after onset of symptoms), the patient was unconscious, cyanosed, and had tonic movements of the limbs. Her respiratory efforts gradually deteriorated and, approximately 40 minutes after envenomation, she required intubation.

Multiple fang marks and serrated-edge lacerations were present on her foot. The snake 1.6 metres long with a 28 cm girth, was identified by a local herpetologist as *Astrotia stokesii,* and this was subsequently confirmed by the Queensland Museum. After blood samples for coagulation studies, venom identification, and biochemical investigations were taken, the patient was given 1000 units of sea snake antivenom (90 minutes after envenomation).

continued

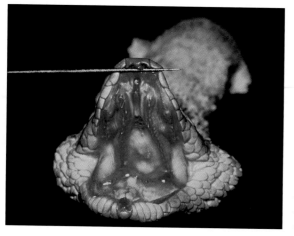

Venom apparatus. Photo by K. Gillett

The child was transferred to the Intensive Care Unit and mechanical venti-lation with 40% oxygen was continued. Further 1000 units doses of antivenom were given 2 $^1/_2$ hours and 3 $^1/_2$ hours after envenomation. General treatment consisted of the insertion of an indwelling bladder catheter, intra-venous infusion of Hartmann's solution and oral administration of an antacid every four hours.

Only slight improvement in the clinical state was noticed before the third aliquot of antivenom was administered; but one hour after this, the child's pupils were reacting normally, she was moving all limbs and some respiratory effort was apparent. Although no further doses of antivenom were given, the clinical improvement continued until, seven hours after envenomation, the child opened her eyes and was able to look about her.

Initial blood tests showed slightly elevated coagulation times. A marked leucocytosis was seen on the first full blood count and the platelet count had fallen considerably by the following day. Serum enzyme levels showed evi-dence of skeletal muscle damage, but no cardiac involvement.

On the following morning, 14 hours after the bite, the child was noted to have spasmodic generalised tonic movements, which resembled the startle re-flex of the neonate, each time she was touched. A further 1000 units of antiven-om was administered.

Improvement continued and the child was successfully extubated at mid-day, 22 hours after envenomation. Two hours later, she was able to sit with support and speak coherently to her mother. However, the spasmodic move-ments continued intermittently when the patient was disturbed. She was also noticed to be hallucinating during this time.

On the following day, the patient was transferred to the children's ward, where she slept most of the time, but still seemed to hallucinate occasionally. At the end of that day (approximately 50 hours after the bite), the patient was able to stand with support, but exhibited gross neuromuscular instability of the lower limbs. The serum level of creatine kinase reached it peak on this day, and myoglobinuria was found for the first and last time.

On the fifth day after envenomation, the patient's condition was much im-proved. The jerky movements returned when she stood, but during the after-noon she took her first steps with support. On the following day, she was running clumsily, and was discharged home to a more friendly environment. There was slight improvement in her gait when she was reviewed two days lat-er, and marked improvement had occurred two weeks after envenomation. One month after the incident, she was functioning normally, except for some return of unstable gait when she was tired.

In their discussion Mercer et al. made a number of important points: Mul-tiple bite marks are suggestive of high-dose envenomation, which would ex-plain the rapid onset of symptoms in our case. The patient's lack of pain at the bite site is typical of sea snake. Our case is unusual in its absence of myoglo-binuria which is normally present within three to six hours. The value of first-aid measures was seen by the rapid onset of symptoms once the mother's grip was released. The correct first-aid measures are immobilisation and pressure bandaging of the affected limb.

CASE REPORT   Sea Snake Bite

Fulde GWO and Smith F. 1984. "Sea snake envenomation at Bondi." *Med J Aust.* 141: 44-45.

On March 30, 1984, at 2.30 p.m. a healthy 19 year old man was bitten on the great toe of his right foot while swimming in water beyond the breakers at Bondi Beach. He experienced pain in the toe, the pain spread up the right leg, and he swam to shore. While walking up the beach, he realised that he was dragging his right leg, and sought help from a lifesaver who noticed two fang marks on the toe and made a provisional diagnosis of a sea snake bite. Firm elastic bandages were immediately applied from the foot to the upper part of the thigh, and the leg was splinted with two boards. At this stage, the patient developed double vision. He was transferred by ambulance to St. Vincent's Hospital, Sydney, arriving at the hospital's Accident and Emergency Centre at 4 p.m.

After triage, he was placed in a resuscitation cubicle, and an intravenous cannula was inserted. The patient now complained of pain in the right leg, and weakness of the right leg and arm. A slight slurring of his speech was noted. Despite these symptoms, he showed no signs of anxiety or distress and, apart from seeming slightly subdued, he seemed inappropriately unconcerned. Intellectual functions appeared unimpaired.

On the tip of the patient's right great toe were two small, clean puncture marks 4 mm apart. The patient could not raise his right leg, had very weak plantar flexion, and marked weakness of the right arm was present in all muscle groups. There was an incomplete motor neurone paresis of the right facial nerve. There was some slight subjective decreased sensation to pinprick on the right arm and on the right side of the face.

The puncture marks were swabbed with a sterile saline-moistened swab for identification of the toxin. Serum was centrifuged and frozen for venom detection.

After a provisional diagnosis of sea snake envenomation was made, the patient, was transferred to the Intensive Care Unit to await the arrival of sea snake antivenom. However, at 5 p.m., about 2 ½ hours after the patient was bitten, it became evident that his motor weakness was increasing. Therefore, after pretreatment with adrenalin (0.5 mg subcutaneously), and promethazine hydrochloride (10 mg intravenously) in accordance with Commonwealth Serum Laboratories' guidelines, he received an intravenous infusion of 3000 units of tiger snake antivenom in Hartmann's solution (500 ml). This was infused slowly at first, and the bandages were removed after the initial infusion.

Over the next 30 minutes, all the patient's symptoms and signs resolved. His affect became more appropriate, and normal power returned to his face and limbs. The blood and urine profiles remained normal. There was no relapse of symptoms and the patient required no other therapy.

The frozen serum was assayed by Dr. S. Sutherland of the Commonwealth Serum Laboratories, Melbourne, who detected a trace of snake venom cross-reacting with king brown snake antivenom. There is no specific sea snake assay available.

The actual species involved in this case remains unidentified. The clinical features, however, permit a positive diagnosis of sea snake bite. The important features were an obvious bite by a two fanged, swimming, sea creature and a progressive myalgia and paresis of lower motor neurone type. Envenomation was later confirmed by serum assay.

SEA URCHIN

Phylum	■	Echinodermata
Family	■	Diadematidae (Centrechinidae)
Dangerous species	■	*Centrostephanus rodgersi, Diadema setosum* (Long Spined or Black Sea Urchin), *D. savignyi* (Needle Spine Urchin), *Echinothrix calamaris, E. diadema.*
Family	■	Echinothuridae
Dangerous species	■	*Araeosoma thetidis* (Tam O'Shanter Urchin), *A. intermediium* .
Family	■	Temnopleuridae.
Dangerous species	■	*Salmacis sphaeroides*
Family	■	Toxopneustidae (Flower Urchin)
Dangerous species	■	*Toxopneustes pileolus, Tripneustes gratilla*
Distribution	■	Found in all oceans, the more venomous urchins are in the tropics, subtropics and even temperate waters.

These animals are named after the hedgehog (echinos) because attached to the rounded body are sharp, brittle spines. A venom gland may be present on the spine tip, and there is considerable variation in the venomous effect, colour and size of each species. They feed on sea weed and kelp and in turn are a choice prey for sea otters, thus their proliferation along the western coastline of North America following the hunting and decimation of the sea otters.

Diadematidae are found in most temperate and tropical waters. Their spines are extremely sharp and 20-25 cm in length. *D. setosum* shows juvenile colouring (purple and white bands) until it reaches a large size,

Sea Urchin. *(T. gratilla).* **Photo by W. Deas**

when it assumes its typical black appearance. The spines tend to break off within the tissues, which they pierce on contact.

After an injury, the embedded spines may become absorbed within a few days by the tissues, but at other times may become encrusted and calcify, and remain for many months—to emerge at sites distant from the original puncture wound.

The Toxopneusidae have only short thick spines poking through an array of flower-like appendages, called pedicellariae. These have hook-like jaws which can deliver a venom which results in severe generalised symptoms. Death has been reported, but is very uncommon.

The roe is considered a delicacy in many areas of the Orient and the Pacific, and sea urchin fisheries exist in Japan, Chile, Canada, Barbados, Peru, Mexico, Korea, France and the U.S.A. In Japan the "uni" or sea urchin roe is used in sushi and sashimi, and is protected by law. In Australia, where the urchins are considered a pest, Samoan and other Polynesian peoples eat their roe, as a delicacy and an aphrodisiac. Symptoms of poisoning including diarrhoea, nausea, vomiting and a migraine-like syndrome may appear, and are more likely when the ovaries rather than testes are eaten.

Clinical features

LOCAL. Severe pain occurs immediately after penetration and is in excess of that due to the injury alone. It lasts for 1/2-4 hours. Attempts to extract the spines usually result in their breaking off within the wound. The area around the puncture may immediately become numb.

Swelling and surrounding inflammation may occur. Black discolouration of the puncture lasts many days, and this can sometimes by mistaken for the spine. If there are no complications, and there is no foreign body or infection in the wound, the lesion heals within a week or two.

The area may become infected and slough in a few days. With this development, the area of inflammation increases, becoming red, swollen, aching and

difficult to move. The ache extends centrally and may involve the whole limb. The lymph glands become tender and swollen. Immediate severe pain merges into a dull ache, which may last many hours. Complications from the foreign body may last much longer. Sea urchin dermatitis is discussed later.

Sea Urchin (*T. pileolus*).
Photo by K. Gillett

Lyn Molzahn could have displayed that long-spined urchin without gloves, since the spines on the ventral surface of the urchin are short and blunt. Bahamas. Dee Scarr in ***Touch the Sea.***

GENERAL Some species including Toxopneustidae are said to have severe effects. They may commence within minutes and last for 6 or more hours. They include malaise, weakness, generalised muscle aching and shock (pale, clammy, fainting and hypotension) . Neurological damage has been reported, and may result in paralysis. Facial paralysis may also occur and result in interference with speech and swallowing. The patient's breathing becomes shallow and difficulty is noted in inhaling enough air. If breathing

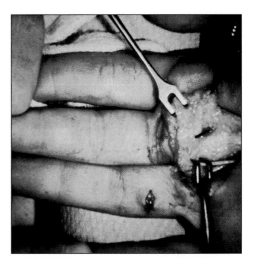

Surgical removal of ***Diadema*** **spine**

Sea Urchin *D. Setosam.* **Photo by W. Deas**

stops, the patient will need assistance from others in order to remain alive. The generalised symptoms may persist for 6 hours or longer

DELAYED REACTIONS: SEA URCHIN DERMATITIS. Delayed reactions may occur up to 3 months after these lesions, and may be of two types.

1. Nodular Granulomatous lesions may appear, consisting of small, firm nodules which may be flesh coloured, or the colour of the dye contained in the spine. Benefit may be achieved by intralesional corticosteriod injection, but this must only be performed if there is no x-ray, ultrasound or clinical evidence of persistence of the spine. In most cases surgical excision is indicated if symptoms persist.
2. Diffuse granulomatous lesions, especially over the fingers and toes, take the form of a cyanotic induration. Fusiform deformity and bone of joint destruction may result. Combined local and systemic corticosteroid therapy may be of benefit. Surgical excision of the presumed spinous trajectory is performed in some cases.

First aid

1. In Nauru it is claimed that urinating on the wound immediately after injury produces excellent results. (Author's note: this will relieve the bladder, if not the pain). Placing the injured limb in thick mud is also advocated by the Nauruans.
2. Immobilise the limb and do not attempt removal of the spines, unless this is done easily, very carefully and without breaking them. If the

spine is irretrievably embedded, it may be crushed by pummelling the area with a fist, and this may relieve pain and aid absorption. Medical assistance should be sought if at all possible.

3. Bathing the wound has been recommended. Both methylated spirits and hot water (45 degrees C) have been suggested.

4. In the case of *Toxopneustes*, immobilisation of both patient and limb may be advisable until preparation has been made to assist with respiratory distress.

5. If general symptoms do supervene, the use of mouth to mouth or artificial respiration (page 233) is indicated if the patient has breathing difficulties, or is bluish in colour. External cardiac massage (page 235) is indicated if artificial respiration has not corrected this colour, or if no pulse or heart beat is detectable. Continue these practices until advised otherwise by a medical practitioner.

Prevention

1. Stay away from these creatures.
2. Wear protective hard shoes when walking on the reef.
3. Some spines will easily penetrate gloves, but these are still of some protective value.

MEDICAL TREATMENT

LOCAL
1. Local anaesthesia (Appendix III) reduces pain rapidly.
2. Perpendicular soft tissue X-ray investigation with a skin tag identifier over the wound site will reveal the foreign body position. Ultrasound may be effective.
3. Complete removal of the spines is then made during surgical exploration of the wound, under local anaesthesia, or with a tourniquet under general anaesthetic.
4. Local antibiotic therapy (e.g., neomycin) applied to the wound following exploration and spine removal, reduces the secondary infection which commonly occurs.
5. Drawing pastes (Magnesium sulphate and glycerine, Magnoplasm, etc.) or poultices may also be of use.
6. Broad spectrum antibiotics (e.g., doxycycline) should be administered if secondary infection occurs.

GENERAL
1. Respiratory or bulbar paralysis. See pages 233-238.
2. Systemic steroids, adrenalin or antihistamines, for the delayed allergic reaction. Hydrocortisone i.v. is of value for generalised symptoms; adrenalin s.c. for bronchospasm and antihistamines for skin lesions.

SPONGE

Phylum	■	Porifera
Dangerous species	■	*Tedania ignis* (Fire Sponge), *Fibula nolitangere* (No-Touch Sponge), *Microciona prolifera* (Red Sponge), *Neofibularia mordens, Lissodendoryx* spp.
Distribution	■	All waters, from the tropics to the polar regions.

Porifera means "pore-bearer," and refers to the surface having small holes which allow sea water to penetrate the sponge. Being sedentary, some defence mechanism is needed.

Although the "sponge fishermen's disease" of the Mediterranean Sea is believed to be due to a symbiotic anemone *Sagartia elegons,* certain sponges cause injury in their own right. The injury may be partly due to silica or glass crystals of the sponge, and partly due to a severe local and systemic toxin. Marine biologists and fishermen who collect specimens are at risk, some individuals seeming to be more sensitive than others.

Fresh water and salt water sponges have been incriminated, some causing severe gastrointestinal symptoms and haemorrhages in experimental animals. Other sponges possess antibacterial properties of possible benefit to mankind.

Sponge *Neofibularia nolitangere*. Direct contact produces almost immediate itching followed by persistent rash. Extremely common sponge on Grand Cayman Island. Often over 1 m across, easily recognized by its rusty brown colour and small white polychaete worms *Syllis spongicola* that are visible on the inner surface of the central cavity. Vinegar, ammonia, meat tenderizer and alcohol are all without effect in reducing the itching. Most hazardous to male divers who handle the sponge, return to the boat and then urinate over the rail, using one or both hands for guidance (unpleasant personal learning experience). Courtesy of G. Lewbell

The potential for both harm and good by this group of marine animals, has not been adequately explored.

Some of the toxins are very resistant to the environment, being able to sustain boiling, freezing, drying and desiccation for many years.

Clinical Features

This is a contact dermatitis affecting only those areas in contact with the sponge.

Initially there may be no reaction. After a variable time (usually 5 minutes to 2 hours) a stinging, prickly or itchy sensation is felt. This may be precipitated or aggravated by wetting or rubbing the contact area.

The stinging sensation may progress over the next day to a burning and distressingly painful condition, with severe itching. The areas may feel as if ground glass has grazed the skin. In some cases this is the first symptom noted, and thus there may be a considerable time delay (one day) between contact and symptoms.

Abnormal sensations may develop over the first 24 hours. The skin may be very sensitive to touch, with a painful reaction or there may be merely a "pins and needles" sensation. The severe symptoms may persist for a week or more, with stiffness and swelling and a throbbing ache in the area. It is aggravated by increased

A "Do-not-touch-me" Sponge, Bahamas. Photo by Dee Scarr in *Touch the Sea*

Sponge injury. The end of the right index finger feels hot and swollen, but with very little to be seen on examination

temperature and with sweating. Although most symptoms clear within 1-4 weeks, recurrences are possible.

The degree of severity is not necessarily related to the clinical signs, and some patients may be incapacitated by the symptoms, without any obvious evidence.

In any site of injury the appearance belies the severity. The initial reaction is likely to commence as a red rash, slightly larger than the area of contact, but of similar shape. Pimples or blisters may develop, as well as weals, giving the appearance of an urticarial rash. Swelling may occur under the area of contact. When the area is small and involves loose skin areas such as the trunk this presents as a generalised swelling; whereas if extensive and over tight areas such as the head, the whole area becomes swollen and tight with greatly impaired movement and circulation.

Thick skinned areas show less response but experience the same degree of pain. The palms of the hands may show little more than a reddish blotchy effect to explain the severe symptoms. Fingers also rarely show the gross signs described above. Occasionally a dermatological disease, cheiropompholyx, is seen.

Peeling or flaking of skin may be seen in the second or third week, giving the appearance of peeling sunburn.

GENERALISED. No systemic manifestations are noted in most cases.

First aid

1. Do not touch any more of the sponge or articles which have been in contact with it.
2. Do not rub the area.
3. Do not rub affected hands across the face or eyes.
4. Local application of cooling packs or lotions, e.g., calamine lotion, methylated spirits, iced water etc., are of value. Local application of very dilute (1:1000) glacial acetic acid has given some relief.
5. Spicules of silicon and calcium can sometimes be removed by applying adhesive tape to the area and stripping it off with the spicules attached.

Prevention

1. Do not touch the sponge—either in the water or on the beach. Use gloves if you must handle it.
2. Do not touch anything that has been in contact with the sponges such as gloves.
3. Harmful properties persist long after the sponge has died.

MEDICAL TREATMENT

1. Administer first aid.
2. Treatment must follow the lines of other forms of contact dermatitis—lotions for gross exudative lesions, creams for exudative lesions, and ointments for dry lesions.
3. The use of specific locally acting preparations, e.g., steriods, zinc, antihistamines, have not usually been very rewarding in the past. Occasional useful results have followed the local application of Benedryl and Histofax. Isopropyl alcohol may help in dissolving some spicules. Ichthammol 10% application may be of value.
4. Topical anaesthesia (e.g., lignocaine in an appropriate base) would be indicated for severe pain. Emlar or other dermatologically active anaesthetics may have a place here.
5. Systemic antihistamines, steriods or antibiotics are not indicated in the uncomplicated cases.
6. Ophthalmological manifestations are best treated by a specialist along general ophthalmological lines.

WORMS, RINGED OR SEGMENTED

Class	■	Polychaeta
Family	■	Amphinomidae
Dangerous species	■	*Chloeia flava* (Beautiful Seamouse, Bristle Worm), *Eurythoe complanata* (Bristle Worm, Saliton Coloured Worm).
Family	■	Glyceridae.
Dangerous species	■	*Glycera dibranchiata* (Bloodworm).
Family	■	Eunicidae.
Dangerous species	■	*Eunice aphroditois* (Biting Reef Worm), *Aphrodite australis* (Seamouse).
Distribution	■	Ringed and segmented worms are found in tropical subtropical and temperate waters, as in the Indian, Pacific and Atlantic oceans, the Caribbean, Gulf of Mexico, etc. Most dangerous species are tropical.

These animals are elongated and subdivided into segments each with a pair of bristles. They often lie under rocks or in corals and may be up to 20 cm in length. Colouration is variable and sometimes most attractive. They cause injury either by

Bristle worm or fireworm, *Hermodice carunculata*. Usual size less than 10 cm long in the Bahamas, although they do sometimes reach 30 cm. It produces an immediate painful reaction and keeps on hurting for several days. I've tried vinegar, ammonia, cortisone cream and alcohol without effect. Some people use adhesive tape to try to pull out the spicules, but this hasn't worked for me. Courtesy of G. Lewbell

penetration of the bristles, or from biting. Its bristles are composed of calcium carbonate which explains their irritant effect, but not the reported generalised symptoms. *E. aphroditois* may grow to 1.5 metres in length and can inflict proportionately more severe biting-type wounds. *Eurythoe complanata* is a nuisance to fishermen when catching certain fish that feed on them.

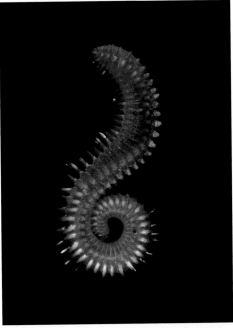

Clinical features

LOCAL. Contact rapidly produces an intense itching or burning sensation lasting up to a week. The appearance is initially that of a white pinpoint rash. This may then become red, swollen and numb over the next 10-30 minutes. Blisters filled either with clear fluid or blood may develop and last for days. The adjacent tissues may become painful and swollen, joints becoming stiff and immobile over the next 24 hours. Regional lymph glands may be swollen and tender. Secondary infection may produce a recurrence of symptoms days later, whereas the overall reaction lasts for 7-10 days, but is maximal in the first to third days. Numbness over the area may persist for many weeks.

Bites are a few millimetres in diameter and rapidly become hot, swollen and inflamed, and may remain so for a day or longer. Secondary infection may occur within hours or days with an increase in the swelling and pain, and with a pus discharge.

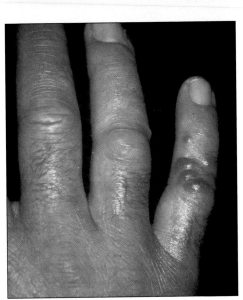

Bristleworm *E. complanata*, demonstrating both the bristles and the skin reaction around the stings. Photo by K. Gillett

GENERALISED. Severe general reactions have been reported, at least with *E. complanata*. These appear to be of a cardiovascular nature, that is, increased pulse rate with palpitations, fainting, chest pain. The patient feels very ill and may be compelled to rest for a day or more. The importance of allergic factors is unknown at this stage.

First aid

1. Bristles may be partly removed by applying the sticky surface of adhesive plaster or adhesive tape to the area and withdrawing it together with the bristles. Individual bristles can be removed with surgical forceps and magnification. Rubbing the area with sand will also remove some bristles.
2. Apply vinegar, alcohols, alkalies or dilute ammonia, calamine or cooling lotions.
3. Apply local anaesthetic ointments, gel or spray (lignocaine), or steroid cream (Ultralan 0.5%), etc., to the area over the first few hours, then as needed.
4. Bites should be washed with salt water, sodium bicarbonate or antiseptic, and apply antibiotic ointment (neomycin)
5. Bed rest may be necessary.
6. Enlist medical aid.
7. Resuscitation (pages 233-238) if required.

Prevention

1. Avoid contact with these worms.
2. Be wary in turning over rocks and corals.
3. Wear protective clothing and gloves (although these may not always suffice).
4. Be especially wary when handling the Barrier Reef yellow sweetlip, or other fish which coexist with these worms.

MEDICAL TREATMENT

1. Administer first aid.
2. The use of systemic antihistamines or steriods should be considered with severe generalised reactions.
3. Tranquillisers and muscle relaxants, e.g., i.v. diazepam 10 mg may be indicated in distressed patients.
4. It is possible that allergy-prone patients may be more susceptible to bristle worm stings. The use of i.v. hydrocortisone (100 mg and repeat p.r.n.) may be indicated in these patients. Adrenalin and related substances may be of value for allergic bronchospasm. Oral antihistamines may be of value with dermatological allergies.
5. Bristles left in a wound may be affected by the bodies own defence mechanism. They may also migrate or become encapsulated by calcarious deposits, when they can then be scraped out.

DEE SCARR'S SCUBA DIARY   **Bristleworms**

Although standard invertebrate books and diving textbooks disagree as to whether the bristleworms's bristles are actually venomous or not, they all agree that the bristleworm is a definite "don't touch" animal—and for years I followed their instructions. I'd point bristleworms out to my diving buddies and signal "no-no" every time we saw one. Sometimes I'd snap my fingers near the bristleworm, so that my buddies could see the bristles bristle.

Then one day I began to wonder: If a bristleworm only bristled when it was stressed, could I safely handle one as long as I didn't stress it? I put my bare hand down in the path of one, and after several attempts to walk around my hand, the worm finally crawled over my hand. It did not bristle, as I'd predicted, and I suffered no ill effects.

After that I began to feed bristleworms. I'd hold a small piece of fish in my fingers, and the worm would climb up and eat the fish as I held it. One time a small greedy grouper grabbed both the fish and the bristleworm from my hand—was that fish ever sorry. It acquired a mouthful of bristles, and was obviously very uncomfortable as it swam frantically along the reef, shaking its head from side to side and hitting its open mouth against rocks in a vain attempt to dislodge the bristles.

More interesting than the behaviour of the grouper, however, was the behaviour of the bristleworms themselves. Instead of moving food into their mouths, as most animals do when they eat, the bristleworm moves its body over the food, engulfing the food in place. The bristleworm's mouth opens almost like the aperture ring in a camera lens, and the worm moves steadily forward as the food is eaten.

One time I must have had a fishy scent on my hand, because a bristleworm readily climbed up on my (I thought) empty palm and, as it moved forward, tested me several times. It was the same rough sensation as being licked by a cat. I guess each time the bristleworm worked its way through the scent and onto my bare skin, it decided my skin was unpalatable and moved on.

The bristleworm is a perfect example of an animal that is totally harmless if it's not threatened, but can cause problems to the person who, deliberately or accidentally, disturbs it.

PART III

Marine Infections
and Dermatitis

NOTES

General
Amoebic Meningoencephalitis/Naegleria
Coral Cut
Creeping Eruption
Bathers' Itch
Bathing Suit Dermatitis
Fish Handlers' Disease
Marine Granuloma
Parasites
Sea Lice
Sea Cucumber

<u>NOTES</u>

General

Cholera outbreaks have occurred in the U.S.A. from eating poorly stored or prepared fish. This can occur with any prepared foodstuffs.

Botulism has been produced from fish products (from *Clostridium botulinium*), usually from poor processing. This would be expected under anaerobic conditions at normal or increased temperatures—such as with smoked fish. It would not be expected with fresh or rapidly frozen fish. Rarer but related organisms can also be hazardous.

Others include *Escherichia coli* gastroenteritis, infective hepatitis, poliomyelitis, *Staphylococcal* gastroenteritis, typhoid and paratyphoid fever, viral gastroenteritis, enteroviruses and adenoviruses.

As these are not specific or characteristic of fish foods, they are not dealt with further, and reference should be made to the established textbooks of medicine.

Marine vibrios may cause local and systemic infections, as well as gastroenteritis from shellfish and crustacean contamination, with a high mortality. *Vibrio vulnificus* has an almost 50% mortality. Severe gangrene and haemolysis (destruction of the red blood cells) may accompany the infections with *V. parahaemolyticus,* entering the skin from wounds—as with fish stings, coral and shellfish cuts. The organism abounds in inshore sediments and shellfish at certain times. Antibiotics of choice are ciprofloxacin or doxycycline, until sensitivity tests are available.

Pharyngoconjunctival fever, from adenoviruses, happens after swimming in poorly chlorinated, fresh water, and has an incubation period is 5-9 days. It is characterised by a sore throat, lassitude, headache, conjunctivitis and fever (39-40°C) lasting for a few days, but contagious for 10 days. Middle ear infections and lymph gland involvement may be complications.

Leptospirosis develops from swimming in fresh water, especially if stagnant. In the New England and Middle Atlantic states, the causative organism is usually *L. icterohaemorrhagica* (from rats) whereas in the West and North-Central U.S.A. it is more often *L. pomona* (from pigs). There is usually an abrupt onset of fever and prostration, 1-2 weeks after infection. It lasts 1-3 weeks and often includes muscular pains, conjunctivitis and headache. Almost all organs of the body can be affected, with a meningitis not uncommon, and the organism can be cultured from the blood.

Algal blooms are now well recognised as a result of disruption of waterways and pollution, as well as a natural phenomenon. Not only may this be associated with fish poisons (see later) but they may also cause dermatological lesions.

Verocytotoxin producing organisms such as *Escherichia coli, Campylobacter jejuni* and *Listeria monocytogenes* have been identified in the 1980s.

Shellfish (see page 213) can carry and concentrate organisms, such as vibrios, hepatitis A, and Norwalk like viruses, which then cause their respective ailments in humans who ingest them.

Many infectious agents can cause disease by contaminating drinking or bathing water, without the necessity of being carried in a marine animal. They include both poisons and infections from a variety of organisms and disease whose description is also beyond the scope of this text—such as hookworm, hydatids, giardiasis, amoebiasis, schistosomiasis, pathogenic algae, angiostrongyliasis, clonorchiasis, opisthorchiasis, paragonimiasis, gnathostomiasis, etc. For descriptions of these disorders, reference must again be made to established medical texts.

The secretions on the skin of many marine animals may cause severe dermatological symptoms, especially if the slime is spread from the hands to more sensitive tissues (eyelids, genitals). For this reason, children and princesses are strongly advised against the kissing of frogs.

For the common infections of divers and swimmers, reference should be made to *Diving and Subaquatic Medicine,* 3rd edition, by Edmonds, Lowry and Pennefather, published by Butterworth/Heinemann. Only common or serious infections, produced specifically by immersion or contact with marine creatures are referred to here.

AMOEBIC MENINGOENCEPHALITIS/NAEGLERIA

Infecting organism   ◆   Naegleria
Distribution   ◆   Warm contaminated fresh water areas, or near sewage
                                        outflows.

A recently discovered and usually fatal illness is caused by amoeba naegleria. This protozoa is found in fresh water, moist soil, septic tank and sewage effluent and other decaying matter. It feeds on faecal bacteria and reproduces by simple binary fission. Infection is only likely to be acquired after diving or swimming in warm contaminated fresh water, as the organism cannot survive in cold water or a marine environment.

The organism probably enters the brain via the nasal mucosa and olfactory nerve. Cases have been reported from Australia, Belgium, Czechoslovakia, Great Britain, New Zealand and the U.S.A. It is likely that many cases have been diagnosed as acute pyogenic meningitis when the infecting organism has not been identified.

Clinical features

The incubation period is probably three to seven days, the patient being in good health prior to the sudden headache and mild fever, sometimes associated with sore throat and rhinitis. The headache and pyrexia progresses over three days with vomiting, neck rigidity, disorientation and coma. A diagnosis of acute pyogenic meningitis is supported by the finding of purulent cerebrospinal fluid, usually under increased pressure. The coma deepens, and death due to cardiorespiratory failure supervenes on the fifth or sixth day of the illness.

Medical Data

The diagnosis should be suspected when the expected pathogenic bacteria are not found in the cerebrospinal fluid, and confirmed by observing the motile amoebae in a plain wet mount of fluid.

Pathological findings at post mortem examination reveal a slightly softened, moderately swollen brain covered by hyperaemic meninges. There is a purulent exudate over the sulci and the basal subarachnoid cisterns. Small, local haemorrhages are seen in the superficial cortex, but the olfactory bulbs are markedly reddened and in some cases haemorrhagic and necrotic. On microscopic examination there is a mild fibrino-purulent meningeal reaction and amoebae may be seen in the exudate. The degree of encephalitis varies from slight amoebic invasion and inflammation to complete purulent, haemorrhagic destruction. The olfactory mucosa is severely ulcerated and the olfactory nerves are inflamed and necrotic. There is no evidence of amoebic invasion elsewhere in the body.

Almost all cases have been fatal. One case survived after treatment with amphotericin B and this was the drug of choice, in high dosage intravenously and small doses intraventricularly. Sulphadiazine has also been shown to be effective in vivo, and should also be used. Combination miconazole and rifampicin has been suggested. A recent literature search, if faced with such a case, would seem warranted—until an established treatment becomes available. Corticosteroids are probably contraindicated because they combine with amphotericin B and reduce the effective tissue concentration. Emetine is effective in vitro, but not in vivo.

Prevention

Control of pollution of waterways by sewage and domestic water must be improved if this disease is to be prevented from increasing in incidence. Swimming and diving should be avoided in potentially contaminated water, especially if the water or environmental temperature is high.

If diving cannot be avoided, a well fitting face mask, with a double seal or positive pressure, should be employed.

CORAL CUT

Other name   ♦ Coral Poisoning
Infecting organism ♦ Stony Corals
Distribution   ♦ Coral reefs of the tropical and subtropical waters

The sharp edges of corals often cause lacerations, and the consequences of coral cuts may well equal the intensity of the more impressive marine animal injuries. Coral is covered by infected slime, and pieces of coral or other foreign bodies often remain in the laceration. Some of the manifestations, especially early ones, are due to the presence of discharging nematocysts.

Erysipelothrix infection can also be obtained from corals (see Fish Handler's Disease, page 179).

Clinical features

LOCAL. A small, often clean looking laceration is usually seen. It causes little inconvenience at the time of injury and may well go unnoticed.

A few hours later there may be a smarting sensation, especially during washing. At that stage a mild inflammatory reaction may be seen around the cut, and this will spread within the next day or two, with local swelling, a red discolouration and tenderness on light pressure and movement. Finally, a festering sore or ulcer may develop with either a pus discharge or abscess formation. Chronic ulceration and even osteomyelitis is possible. Local spreading of the red colour to adjoining skin (cellulitis) is a sign of serious import.

Lymph glands in the groin or armpit may swell and become tender. Pain or aching sensations may be felt in the adjacent joints.

These local symptoms may last for a day or two, if properly treated, or for many months if left unattended. After healing, there may be a small numb area of skin with a fibrous nodule beneath it due to a piece of embedded coral.

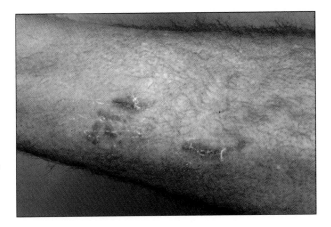

Coral cuts three hours after injury before inflammation has spread

There may also be an extremely itchy lesion which may persist for weeks or months, and may develop into a scratching-induced neurodermatitis.

GENERALISED. Systemic effects of a bacterial infection may involve fever, chills, malaise, prostration and polymorphonoclear leucocytosis.

First aid

1. Thoroughly clean the wound as soon as possible after injury. Use antiseptic lotion (full strength bleach, soaps, Hibitane, Cetavlon, Phisohex, etc.) with removal of all foreign material. Some have argued against the value of iodides or bromides (e.g., Betadine). Hydrogen peroxide, or local applications of alcohols and vinegar also have a good reputation.
2. Apply local antibiotic powder or ointment such as neomycin as soon as this can be arranged.
3. Keep the area dry with a dressing.
4. Enlist medical assistance.

MEDICAL TREATMENT

1. Administer first aid.
2. Thoroughly clean the wound (a soft brush may be used, following the application of a local anaesthetic spray).
3. Local antibiotic powder or ointment (neomycin, bacitracin, etc.) q.i.d.—applied early to prevent infection.
4. Steroid ointment, e.g., Ultralan 0.5% may be used to relieve the itching, which could be troublesome for many weeks.
5. If there are signs of cellulitis, lymphangitis, abscess formation, or other deep infection, broad spectrum antibiotic cover (e.g., doxycycline) should be administered. The affected limb should be elevated to relieve pain.
6. Bacteriological culture and sensitivity tests (cultured in a hypertonic saline medium) may be requested, prior to antibiotic administration.
7. X-rays may be obtained to supply evidence of foreign bodies in soft tissues and/or osteomyelitis in those areas suggestive of this.
8. General medical treatment (bed rest, analgesics, antipyretics, fluid balance, etc.) for those cases with systemic infections.
9. Chironex Box Jellyfish antivenom (page 250) has been suggested for use in the serious cases, although this treatment is very experimental.
10. Tetanus prophylaxis may be indicated.

Prevention

1. Wear thick boots if wading.
2. Wear gloves when handling coral.
3. Be careful when stepping out of boats, onto reefs.
4. Divers should wear fins with full heel protection.
5. Wear clothing that protects against body scratches.

CREEPING ERUPTION

Infecting organisms ◆ *Ancylostoma brasiliense* and other larval hookworms.
Distribution ◆ U.S.A., Central and South America.

This disease is caused by a larval hookworm of the species *Ancylostoma brasiliense* and others, which are natural parasites of dogs and cats. The organisms enter skin from wet infected sand and burrow under the skin causing worm shaped lesions less than 5 mm wide.

Clinical features

Itching, pain, abscesses and pustules may develop.

MEDICAL TREATMENT

Cryotherapy with ethyl chloride may be effective for mild cases. More persistent cases respond to topical or even systemic thiabendazole. Incision and drainage of abscesses and pustules may be needed, and should be accompanied by local antibiotics.

Prevention

In endemic areas, avoid walking or sitting on damp soil or sand, and cover with groundsheets any possibly infested area before using it.

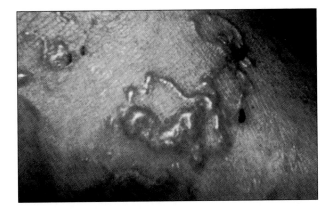

Creeping
eruption.
Courtesy A.A.
Fisher

BATHERS' ITCH

Other names	◆	Schistosome Dermatitis, Cercerial dermatitis, Marine Dermatitis, Paddy Itch, Pelican Itch, Weed Itch, Clam Diggers Itch, Swimmers Itch.
Infecting organisms	◆	Schistosomes (parasitic flatworms).
Distribution	◆	The disease is almost world wide, but is endemic in special areas which are usually well recognised by the locals. Agricultural workers in Asia, Africa and the West Indies are at risk when irrigating crops. Recreational water activities are incriminated in Northern America and Australia. Although fresh water is more commonly involved, salt water infestations from both Southern California and Narragansett Bay, Rhode Island have been well described.

Bathers' Itch is acquired when bathing or wading in tropical, subtropical and temperate regions inhabited by waterfowl and watersnails—infested by parasitic flatworms known as schistosomes. Bathers' itch is only one of a variety of schistosome infestations, and now rivals malaria as a major public health problem. It especially invades waders who are inactive or who are exposed for long periods. It is also present more in surface than deep water. Both factors decrease the frequency of the injury in scuba divers—who are also usually well protected by clothing.

The adult flat worms are blood parasites of birds and some mammals, and attach themselves with one or more suckers to their host. The life cycle therefore involves such animals as the seagull, swan, duck and other waterfowl, passerines, muskrat, voles, mice, acting as the definitive host. The eggs pass into the faeces of these animals and hatch into miracidae, which commonly infest water snails. The intermediate host may be the sea snail, whelk, periwinkle and other rock platform creatures. Inside this intermediate host microscopic immature mobile larvae known as cerceriae are developed and then released into

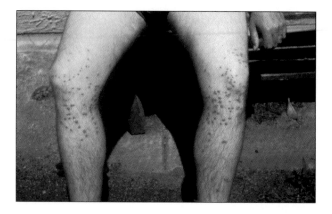

Schistosome dermatitis on exposed legs. Photo by B. McMillan

the surrounding water, where they search for a warm-blooded definitive host. Fresh, brackish or even salt water may be infested with schistosomes.

Although humans are not host mammals, the cerceriae are able to penetrate the skin—but cannot reach the blood vessels. The cerceriae therefore die, but they also produce a foreign body reaction, followed by an antibody reaction, in the surrounding tissues.

The characteristic skin lesions developing after infection are due to the antibody reaction. Further attacks are therefore more severe. Some people, however, do not develop this disease despite contact.

Clinical features

1. A prickly sensation lasts for about 15 minutes, followed by a mild red-coloured rash over the affected area. This disappears within an hour, but may recur over a day or two.
2. In two to ten days, papules (1-2 mm in diameter) appear, often associated with a hair follicle. These may develop into small blisters (vesicles) surrounded by a red halo. Occasionally the vesicles become filled with blood. The whole area becomes inflamed.
3. Itching is a prominent symptom and is aggravated by rubbing, sweating or a hot shower.
4. The vesicles may become secondarily infected with aggravation of the symptoms and signs together with the formation of pustules.
5. After a week or more the reaction subsides rapidly, though rusty brown pigmented marks may remain for a month or more.
6. A generalised anaphylactic shock is possible, especially in those having allergic histories or in those with a previous episode of schistosome dermatitis.

First aid. Apply phenolised calamine lotion.

MEDICAL TREATMENT

1. Antihistamines orally (Phenergan 25 mg t.i.d.) to reduce inflammation and ease pruritus. Antihistamine cream, e.g., Anthisan, is commonly recommended.
2. Anaesthetic cream (lignocaine 1%) may give immediate symptomatic relief, as may steroid ointments (Ultralan 0.5%).
3. Considering the possibility of secondary infection, the use of an antibiotic steroid ointment may be preferable. Neomycin/hydrocortisone or others (e.g., Kenacomb ointment) are applied q.i.d.
4. Broad spectrum antibiotics, e.g., doxycycline may be indicated if pustule or other signs of bacterial infection supervene.

Prevention

1. Dimethylphthallate solutions (25% in anhydrous lanolin) rubbed onto the skin before swimming in infested areas and at 1/2 hourly intervals. This mixture causes damage to the upholstery of vehicles and to plastics. Copper olerate 12.5% in yellow soft paraffin is probably more efficient.

2. Brisk rubbing with a towel immediately after leaving the water may remove some of the cercaria.

3. Eradication of the snail (copper sulphate and lime added to fresh water twice a year in some areas) has been proposed but is usually impractical.

4. Clearing swamps of reeds and weed which harbour the intermediate host.

5. Wear protective gum boots if wading in affected areas.

6. Wear protective clothing impregnated with the materials noted in 1, if there is a need to enter infested waters.

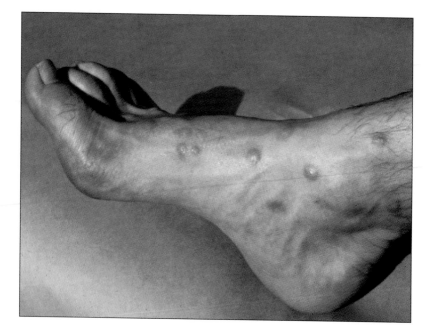

Schistosome dermatitis. Typical skin reaction. Photo by P. Friend

BATHING SUIT DERMATITIS

Other names	♦ Seaweed Dermatitis, Algae Dermatitis, Coelenterate Dermatitis, Seabathers Eruption.
Infecting organisms	♦ Blue green algae, coelenterates and other irritating marine organisms.
Distribution	♦ Worldwide in salt and fresh water.

A number of causes exist for the development of dermatitis underneath the bathing suit. Some are the same infections and irritants associated with any clothing, whether used on land or in water. Marine organisms (plants and animals) can be trapped under the clothing, causing greater damage in the bathing suit area where there is contact with the skin.

Coelenterate dermatitis can develop where small pieces of tentacles, just visible to the naked eye or under a low powered magnifying glass, are trapped and cause skin lesions similar to those of other coelenterate injuries (see page 94). In Florida, the larvae (almost invisible and 0.5 mm long) of the Thimble jelly fish *Linuche unguiculata* have caused extensive injuries when they congregate in the surface layers. The larvae of sea anemone *Edwardsiella lineata* have caused outbreaks of this disorder in swimmers in Nassau County, Long Island, New York.

Algae are among the lowest divisions of the vegetable kingdom, but many have whip-like flagella enabling them to propel themselves through water, similar to some animals. Algae will grow in a variety of water temperatures, varying from zero in the polar regions, to over 70 degrees Centigrade in hot springs. The blue green algae *Lyngbya majuscula,* which looks like hair, sometimes causes dermatitis. Similar irritations can occur with fresh water blue green algae.

Toxicity is variable and unpredictable. Dermatitis occurs after swimming, often in water made turbid by the suspended seaweed fragments, particularly if the wet bathing garment is worn for some time after leaving the water and before showering.

If previous contact has been made with the organism, the reactions may be earlier developing, and may last longer. This reflects sensitisation to foreign protein. Others will develop a resistance or immunity to the organisms—possibly related to the formation of blocking antibodies.

Clinical features

An itching and burning sensation develops within a few minutes to a few hours after leaving the water. Visible dermatitis with redness usually appears after 3-8 hours.

Occasionally it may not develop for some days after exposure, and may recur intermittently for up to a year.

These initial symptoms may be followed by blisters and desquamation, leaving a moist bright red tender and painful area, especially around the genitals. Male patients are most affected in the most dependent part of the scrotum, whereas women may also be affected on the breasts under a close fitting swimming top.

The lesions vary greatly in severity, and may last 1-10 days or longer.

Occasionally, especially in children, generalised features may include fevers, headache, nausea, malaise, vomiting etc. Conjunctivitis and urethritis have also been described.

MEDICAL TREATMENT

1. For coelenterate dermatitis see page 97.
2. For algal dermatitis, treat on the basis of dermatological principles, such as calamine, steroid preparations, etc.

Prevention

The disorder can be prevented by early showering and drying after the exposure, together with washing the bathing suits in soap and water immediately after the swim.

FISH HANDLERS' DISEASE

Other names	◆	Crayfish Poisoning, Coral Poisoning, Erysipeloid of Rosenbach, Swine Erysipelis, Seal Finger, Whale Finger.
Infecting organisms	◆	*Erysipelothrix insidiosa*
Distribution	◆	Throughout the world wherever fish are handled.

Although many organisms may be contaminants, the *E. insidiosa* has been specifically incriminated, and the disease from this organism is described. It is a gram positive, micro-aerophiliac, non-motile bacillus, and may be readily confused with non-toxinogenic bacilli of the genus *Corynebacterium* unless serological differentiation is available. The *Erysipelothrix* can only infect after gaining entry via a break in the skin. Infection is much less likely if bleeding occurs following the skin puncture.

The crayfish (lobster) industry has been greatly hampered by this disorder, which is probably similar to other marine cuts and injuries that become infected.

Clinical features

LOCAL After an injury to the skin, there is a latent period of one to seven days, during which apparent healing may have occurred. The site develops into a sharply defined purplish-red circular area, surrounding the puncture. This spreads outwards at an approximate rate of 1 cm per day.

An itch, pain or burning sensation is felt. Swelling then develops, and the adjacent joints become stiff and painful. Spread is more central than distal. Involvement of the tip of the finger is uncommon, but other parts of the fingers and the hand are frequently involved.

Lymph node enlargement and inflammation is very rare. If the area is exposed to further damage from work, ulceration and secondary infection may result in boil and carbun-

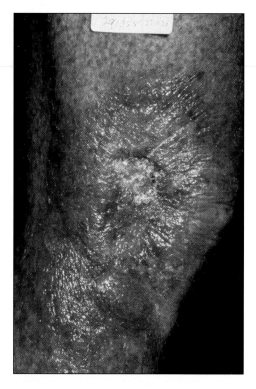

Fish handlers' disease, chronic reaction. Photo by B. Florence

cle formation. If the area is protected against injury, but otherwise untreated, it will heal within three weeks. Relapse is possible.

GENERALISED. Systemic manifestations and complications are rare. Fever may herald a generalised infection. Erysipelothrix endocarditis occurs usually only after the organism has cleared from the skin—but a relevant history will be able to be ascertained. There are no specific features other than possible acute or subacute endocarditis, that is, a severe heart injury diagnosable only by a medical practitioner.

Erysipelothrix arthritis (joint pain) has no specific characteristics, but is suggested by the history of the skin lesion or an *Erysipelothrix* bacteraemia. Laboratory diagnosis of Erysipeloid is best made by a biopsy of the advancing edge of the lesion. Deaths have been reported.

First aid

1. Treat all small marine cuts and injuries seriously.
2. Use antiseptic solution initially, e.g., Hibitane, Phisohex, Cetavlon, and iodine.
3. Apply local antibiotic (e.g., neomycin) powder or ointment four times a day, if it is available.
4. Keep the area clean and dry. Apply a loose dry protective bandage.
5. Avoid further trauma to the area.

Prevention

1. Wear thick and tough gloves, if handling any marine animals.
2. Wear thick boots if wading or fishing.
3. If diving, touch things with your knife, not your fingers.

MEDICAL TREATMENT

1. Administer first aid.
2. Give systemic penicillin. Procaine penicillin 1 mega unit b.d. for one week should be sufficient. If there are doubts about the patient continuing treatment, and if penicillin can be safely given, a depot type of penicillin, e.g., Benzathine Penicillin 1.2 mega units, given in one injection, is of value.
3. Other antibiotics to which this organism is sensitive include tetracycline, erythromycin, chloramphenicol and novabiocin.
4. Local antibiotic powder or ointment (e.g., neomycin) should be used on ulcerations, until cured.
5. Endocarditis and arthritis are treated on their own merits. Massive doses of crystalline penicillin are used in the former.

Other cases of skin disorders in the fish industry

Fish handlers may have many causes for skin diseases. Abrasions, lacerations and fissures, can result from any occupation. Sometimes these are complicated by **secondary infections,** especially from *Staphylococcus*. When the organism is a marine mycobacterium, it produces **marine granuloma** (see page 182). Bites and stings also occur and these are dealt with throughout this book.

Most marine animals have secretions which may produce **allergies** in susceptible people. Sometimes the slimy material which covers the animal is a primary **irritant** (with tuna this is called tuna dermatitis).

Red feed dermatitis is produced from handling mackerel that have fed on a reddish-orange crustacean, and become damaged by this animal, with the resultant liberation of hydrogen sulphide. This "red-feed," plus the digestive juices of the mackerel, burns the hand and is sometimes called "Cayenne" or "red pepper." The hands become very red and swollen, but respond rapidly to mild soaks and cooling lotions.

Skin **cancer** is also common amongst fish workers, possibly associated with sun exposure, use of tar on nets and other factors.

MARINE GRANULOMA

Other names   ◆   Swimming Pool Granuloma; Fish Fanciers' Finger;
                              Swimmers' Elbow.
Infecting organism   ◆   *Mycobacterium marinum*
Distribution   ◆   World wide.

A series of disorders have been described, due to the marine organism *Mycobacterium marinum*. This organism may gain entry to the skin via an abrasion from a swimming pool wall, a ship's hull, a tropical fish tank or its contents, or other marine articles. There is one report of the infection following the bite from a dolphin and another of *M .chelonae* from a turtle bite.

   M. marinum is an acid fast bacillus first described from an outbreak of visceral tuberculosis in fish from a salt water aquarium in Philadelphia.

Clinical features

A granuloma or swelling usually develops over a bony prominence or the site of an obvious abrasion. The onset is noted three to four weeks after the predisposing injury (eight weeks in the case of the dolphin bite). It may develop as a discrete red/purple small swelling or cyst, covered with fine scales and may be large enough to become soft, suggesting fluid or an abscess. The papule or cyst may then become thickened or even ulcerate. Pus may flow from the area, or in some cases, be aspirated. Around the site of the infection there may be swelling, tenderness, other cyst or papule formations, scarring and a gradual spread of the infection and the pathology centrally up the lymphatic system—causing enlargements (nodules along the lymphatic drainage and lymph gland enlargements in the groin or armpit, from lesions of the leg and arm respectively).

   Spontaneous resolution or cure may take up to two years. There is no evidence of systemic or visceral involvement, as the organism does not usually grow at body temperature. It is perhaps for this reason that some of the clinical cases appear worse when they are exposed to cold climates.

Prevention

This includes the use of adequate chlorination of swimming pools, the use of smooth tiles on swimming pools, protective clothing in the case of divers and swimmers, and gloves being used by tropical fish enthusiasts when they are cleaning their tanks.

MEDICAL TREATMENT

Biopsy may demonstrate epitheloid granulomatous lesions, often with caseating areas within them. Acid-fast bacilli may be demonstrated, and may also be grown on culture at 30-33 degrees Centigrade. Sensitivity to antimicrobial agents must be obtained in order to give rational therapy.

It is suggested that the area should be kept as warm as possible, as this is thought to inactivate the organism. Most cases clear spontaneously, in a few months. There is no response to most antibiotics or antituberculous drugs, but usually it does respond to co-trimoxazone or trimethoprim-sulphamethoxazole (Bactrim, Septrin), but this must be continued for a period of up to three months in some cases. It may be sensitive to ethambutol, ciprofloxacin, clarithromycin, rifampicin or cycloserine. If it does not respond to initial therapy, the sensitivity tests must determine further treatment.

Extensive surgical exploration is not usually indicated, as it can aggravate and spread the infection—however each must be assessed on its merits. In one case, extension despite conservative treatment did necessitate surgery.

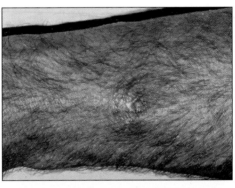

Marine granuloma. Early lesion.

Chronic reaction mimicking tuberculosis verrucosa cutis. Photos by W. Regan

PARASITES

Many fish harbour parasitic infections which could be passed on to humans. For further information about these the reader is referred to the general medical texts, which document them well.

Some parasites are superficial and can be seen on the surface of the fish, and removed. Leeches, anchor worms and fish lice are examples. Others are deep in the flesh or tissues of the fish and may even be encapsulated for their protection. These include flukes (mullet), roundworms (groupers, flounder) and tapeworms (mackerel, sea trout, striped drum). If the fish is not cooked adequately, these parasites can infect man. Adequate cooking, or smoking at 40-70 degrees Centigrade will kill most parasites.

A group of rare tropical infestations are also possible from eating raw crustaceans and fish. Angiostrongyliasis is an eosinophilic meningitis from eating freshwater prawns and snails.

Gnathostomiasis is a skin and organ migration of larvae from raw fish, with a variety of presentations. One Thai lady, for example, presented with exopthalmos and periorbital swelling.

Clonorchiasis is a fluke obtained from eating raw fish, and produces a blockage of the bile ducts and cancer of the liver.

SEA CUCUMBER

Infecting organisms ◆ *Holothuria argus* (Beche-de-Mer, Trepang, Sea Slug, Erico, Hai Shen).

Distribution ◆ Tropical, subtropical and temperate waters, with the larger animals in the tropics.

In order to be injured by this large stationary slug one has the choice of two approaches—neither of which is particularly attractive to most swimmers or divers. One can touch the animal's excreta which may cause a local inflammatory reaction. This toxic material is termed holothurin-A and is a species-specific steroid glycoside which is water soluble and heat stable. Dermatitis is possible where contact is made with skin. Conjunctivitis with ocular damage and blindness is possible if contact is made between the material and the victim's eyes.

The sea cucumber contains a poison (holothurin-B and other saponins) which may act to cause gastointestinal symptoms. Others may cause an irreversible neuromuscular blocking agent. These substances may be ingested by eating this generally unappetising creature without adequate cooking.

**Sea Cucumber,
length 25 cm.
Photo by G. Cameron**

SEA LICE

Other name   ◆   Cymthoidism
Infecting organisms ◆   Coelenterates, Nudibranchs, Algae Cymthoidea.

This general term is usually applied to multiple stingings in the water from various small sources, hence the term sea lice. See pages 99, 115-116.

Some of the crustaceans are free swimming, such as *Cirolana woodjonesi*, or *Excirolana orientalis*. The term cymthoidism comes from the sub-order Cymthoidea, which includes miniscule burrowing crabs such as *Actaecia pallida*. They are especially plentiful during hot weather and at night, and are found along tropical and temperate shorelines, mangrove swamps and estuaries.

They have powerful biting mechanisms, which are used to grip much larger animals. They can attack en masse, and have been seen eating a Port Jackson shark, alive. They can also attack bathers and waders, causing sharp nips, and may have to be picked off the skin. Also, see page 177.

Clinical features

Although an itch and burning sensation may be associated with a red rash and urticaria (weals), a more typical lesion would be isolated or grouped fluid-filled blebs, sometimes haemorrhagic, and with crusts and scabs.

First aid and medical treatment

Treatment includes cleansing and the application of local antibiotics.

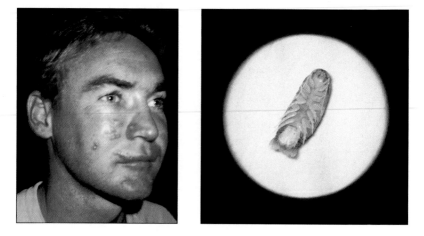

(Left) Sea Lice, *Cirolanidae,* caught inside a diver's face mask, attached themselves to facial skin. (Right) *Cirolanidae,* under low magnification. Length 1 cm. Photo by F. Blackwood

PART IV

Poisonous Marine Animals

NOTES

Introduction
Ciguatera Poisoning
Tetrodotoxin/Fugu Poisoning
Scrombroid Poisoning
Shellfish Poisoning
Clupeoid Poisoning
Crustacean Poisoning
Gastropod Poisoning
Gempylid Poisoning
Hallucinatory Fish Poisoning
Ichthyohaemotoxic (Fish Blood) Poisoning
Ichthyohepatotoxic (Fish Liver) Poisoning
Ichthyootoxic (Fish Roe) Poisoning
Mercury Poisoning
Shark and Ray Poisoning
Turtle and Tortoise Poisoning
Vitamin A (Liver) Poisoning

NOTES

Introduction

There is sometimes an overlap between infections (see pages 167-168) causing toxicity and ingestion of non-infectious toxins (poisons).

The value of seafood is unquestioned, both from nutritional and economic aspects. Fish have less connective tissue than meat and no elastin. For the same biological value as a protein source, halibut has half the calories of steak and one quarter the fat. Shellfish also have good quality protein, are rich in trace elements and low in calories. The low incidence of cardiovascular diseases in fish-consuming Eskimos has been well researched. Fish can be divided into the lean and the oily varieties. It is the oil that is responsible both for the cholesterol lowering properties and the perishability of the food. It oxidises in air to become dark and smelly. Refrigeration reduces, but does not stop, degeneration. The best fish is fresh fish, gastronomically.

Humans consume about 80 million tons of fish and shellfish per year. Japan has the highest per capita ingestion of fish. The U.S.A. commercial harvest is small—3-4 million metric tons of sea food per year over the last decade. Perishability of marine products greatly limits its trading value, but attention to the handling and preservation aspects now permits Iceland and Norway to ship fresh fish daily to the U.S.A. Most of the world wide fish harvest feeds man indirectly, as fish meal fed to poultry and pigs.

For much of the world population, fish is the major source of animal protein—especially in the poorer socio-economic regions, on small islands and in the coastal regions of larger continents. The control over fisheries. including conservation and management, has been extended to 200 nautical miles from the coastlines of countries (under the Magnuson Fishery Conservation and Management Act of 1976), extending another 3.6 million square miles to the U.S.A. marine resources and responsibility.

Food poisoning from ingested marine animals is a serious hazard, especially to those who live in tropical or temperate climates where outbreaks tend to be sporadic and unpredictable. In cold climates, poisoning from marine and polar animals is also of serious concern, but it is more predictable and can therefore be avoided. As a rough approximation, for each million tons of fish food consumed by humans, one death occurs from fish poisoning. There is little doubt about who is the persecutor, and who is the victim—statistically.

Diseases which can destroy whole communities, change the fate of military operations, decimate fishing industries, yet still arise sporadically in a previously safe marine environment, are surely worthy of considerable investigation and research. Such has not been the case. This whole subject is badly neglected, both in medical research and in medical training.

Many traditional communities are compelled to rely heavily on the sea as a source of protein material. This is perhaps less so for the large continents, such as North America and Europe, where the agricultural and grazing areas are proportionately greater than the coastal belts. However, for such island communities as Japan, Indonesia, West Indies, and the Caribbean, the ratio of coastline to agricultural land is high, and therefore, more reliance is placed on seafood.

Even in inland communities, such as most of North America, gastronomic delicacies often have a seafood basis. This fact, together with the speed of air transport, makes it likely that the practising physician will become exposed to the problems of the diagnosis and treatment of marine toxins. To those physicians who are associated with marine medicine, yachting, diving or travel, or those who conduct their general practice near coastlines, a knowledge of seafood poisoning is essential. It is at least as important to those involved in public health, industrial medicine, and the general health of island communities.

One of the most important aspects of public health care is educating those populations at risk from marine food poisons. Tetrodotoxin poisoning can be prevented by avoiding certain species of fish. Scombroid poisoning can be prevented by preservation and refrigeration techniques following the capture of fish. Ciguatera poisoning can develop sporadically throughout temperate and tropical regions, but it is especially associated with reef areas, where fish are abundant and usually safe to eat. Shellfish poisoning can be prevented in some of its forms, but is sporadic in others. Marine pollutants, including mercury and other heavy metals, some organic salts, petroleum and petrochemicals, pesticides, and radioactive material, must all be considered in this very diverse subject.

The commendable aim of providing high quality protein for malnourished people has resulted in tragedies because of ciguatera toxin. Composite fishmeal food is safe only if ciguatera and toxic fish are excluded during its preparation. Ciguatera and hallucinatory fish toxins are not destroyed by heat.

Aquaculture has a venerable history, with China practicing fish farming for over 2000 years. In general it has been often too costly in developed countries, but there are notable exceptions. From Norway to Tasmania, this is a developing industry because it is a controlled and renewable resource. Catfish, salmon, bass, trout and prawns have been successfully grown and harvested, although the localised habitat make them very susceptible to infections, toxins and pollutants.

Space allows the description of only a few of the more significant fish poisonings. Ciguatera, tetrodotoxin and scombroid poisoning will be dealt with in detail because of their commercial implications. In the 15 years up to 1987, the Center for Disease Control in the U.S.A. reported 697 outbreaks of food poisoning by chemical agents. Scombroid and ciguatera were the most common, causing 29 and 34% of the outbreaks and affecting 27 and 24% of the cases respectively.

Shellfish and crustacean poisoning will be summarised. Only brief mention is made of barracouta poisoning, hallucinatory fish poisoning, mercury poisoning and other pollutants, seal liver poisoning, shark and ray poisoning, turtle poisoning, and others. One complicating factor is that there may be more than one type of poison responsible for the clinical manifestations of the fish poisoning in the patient.

Dr Bruce Halstead has highlighted the wide variety of marine food poisonings that are not frequently recognised or reported. There are many potentially poisonous dinoflagellates, quite apart from the common ciguatera and shellfish poisonings. Also, shellfish can accumulate the same toxins (Domoic acid) as are found in ciguatera poisoning. Coelenterates, echinoderms, abalone, cephalopods (squid and octopus), shells (ivory, turban, giant clams), fish roe ,etc. are just some of the less well described causes of marine food poisonings. Some of these are mentioned under the chapters on the specific animal (qv).

First aid

It is worthwhile to promote vomiting if the poisonous food was taken within 6 hours, if the victim has not been vomiting or convulsing, and is fully conscious. It can be achieved by inserting fingers down the back of the throat in some cases. Otherwise the administration of syrup of ipecac, 15-30 ml followed by half a glass of water, is usually successful. The vomitus should be kept for analysis by the public health authorities.

Activated charcoal may be of great value in adsorbing ingested poisons. It is thoroughly mixed with water (10 gram activated charcoal to 100 ml distilled water) to a consistency of thick soup, and taken at a dosage of 5 ml per kg body weight. It can be purchased as a suspension, and this may be a little more palatable.

If the victim is already unconscious, commence resuscitation as needed (Appendix I) and enlist medical attention.

GENERAL MEDICAL TREATMENT

1. Administer first aid. Gastric lavage is indicated and activated charcoal is of value in both early intervention and after lavage, when it can be inserted through the wide bore stomach tube, to reduce poison absorption from the small intestine. Apomorphine 2-8 mg s.c. or other emetics, may be used if the laryngeal reflex is unimpaired and the patient is not already vomiting.

2. If there is a rising arterial CO_2 level or respiratory distress, assistance with respiration is required. The use of an endotracheal tube will prevent the aspiration of vomitus, particularly likely under the conditions of a bulbar paralysis with gastrointestinal symptoms, and make gastric lavage safer.

    When there is a more severe degree of respiratory depression with symptomatic distress and/or cyanosis, an increasing arterial CO_2 and a decreasing arterial O_2, it would be prudent to completely control respiration by the use of endotracheal intubation and mechanical ventilation with 100% oxygen. Monitoring of the serial arterial O_2, CO_2 and pH levels is required, both to monitor respiration and to detect complications—such as aspiration of stomach contents. The patient should be maintained on the regime for at least 6 hours and then gradually weaned from the respirator over the next 12-24 hours.

3. Ensure fluid and electrolyte replacement and administer medication by intravenous means (record vital signs, serial hematocrit, S.G., electrolytes, C.V.P., E.C.G., urinary output and analyses, etc).

4. Treatment of convulsions as in status epilepticus.

5. Sedation should be achieved with non-respiratory depressants, e.g., diazepam 10 mg i.v. repeated as required.

6. On general principles, i.v. steroids (such as hydrocortisone 200 mg repeated as indicated) could be beneficial in the severe cases.

7. General nursing care, with attention to pressure areas, eye and mouth toilets, etc., is axiomatic in these paralysed and debilitated patients.

CIGUATERA POISONING

The term ciguatera is derived from the Cuban word "cigua," referring to poisoning due to the ingestion of a marine snail known by that name to early Spanish
settlers in the Caribbean. On a worldwide basis, ciguatera poisoning is the most
serious and commonest form of the marine intoxications.

Animals involved   ◆   Barracuda, Groper, Snapper, Sea Bass, Surgeonfish,
Coral Trout, Spanish Mackerel, Parrotfish, Wrass,
Jackfish, Red Emperor, Rock Cod, Amberjacks,
Moray Eels and many large reef fish.

                  Of the 400 species implicated, not all are toxic at
any one time or any one place. Ciguatera poisoning
occurs sporadically and unpredictably, and may gradually spread from one area to another.

Ciguatera
poisoning.
Victim holds
cold objects in a
protective cloth
to prevent a
burning sensa-
tion. Courtesy
of S. Edmonds

Around Tahiti, 50% of the cases are due to groupers, parrotfishes and surgeonfishes; 25% due to emperors and snappers; and the rest due to fish such as jacks, mullets, triggerfishes, wrasses, rabbitfishes, moray eels, goatfishes, needlefishes, rudderfishes, barracudas.

In some of the Gambier and Tuamota islands, ciguatera was the main cause of morbidity, with 600 cases from 100,000 inhabitants during 1986.

In the Hawaiian Islands, amberjacks and many other members of the Carangid family are the commonest offenders.

Off the Great Barrier Reef and in Hervey Bay, south of the reef, Spanish mackerel, barracudas, some jacks (trevallies), coral trout, red emperor, rock cods, and snappers are best avoided.

In Puerto Rico, barracudas, hogfishes and groupers are the most frequent offenders.

In other parts of the tropical Western Atlantic, including Florida and the Caribbean, barracudas, groupers and snappers are most often implicated.

Distribution   ◆   It is widespread and is the commonest form of fish poisoning between the latitudes of the Tropics of Cancer and Capricorn, and to a lesser frequency up to 10 degrees north and south of these latitudes.

Outbreaks of ciguatera were recorded in the New Hebrides (now Vanuatu) by de Queiros in 1606, and by Captain Cook in 1774. On one occasion a military campaign—the British attempt to capture Mauritius in 1748—failed because of a ciguatera outbreak, possibly brought about by the destruction of the reefs when sites were prepared for landing of an invasion force.

As many as 50,000 individuals per year are affected by ciguatera poisoning, and the death rate in the Pacific averages 5 cases per 1000. Because of fear of this form of poisoning, fish have to be imported to many Pacific islands, causing great economic hardship to the islanders and their fishermen.

Recent epidemiological surveys have shown an annual incidence of 9 cases per 1000 in Puerto Rico, whereas 3% of the residents of the Virgin Islands may be afflicted annually. From 1960 to 1984 there were 24,000 cases of ciguatera notified from the islands around Tahiti.

About 1300 south Florida residents contact ciguatera each year and Dade county has a 0.5 per 1000 incidence. Cases have been found in Maryland and Massachusetts, from fish shipped in from Florida.

CIGUATERA TOXIN

Ciguatoxin is only one type of ichthyosarcotoxic poisoning. The freshness of the fish has no bearing on its toxicity, nor usually does cooking.

The poisonous fish cannot be identified by their external appearance. They tend to be reef fish, and they may ingest the dinoflagellates, especially *Gambierdiscus toxicus,* which is thought to be the major originator of the toxin, or they may acquire it from eating other fish. The organism lives on dead corals and thrives in a medium rich in bio-detrius, algae, fungi and bacterium. The toxin is harmless to the fish , but it does become more concentrated and lasts longer as it is passes up the food chain to the more active carnivorous predators. It is for this reason that the larger fish of any species tend to be more toxic. These fish retain the toxin for prolonged periods—often for years. The liver and testes are particularly toxic, as are other viscera, while the flesh is less so.

There are at least three separate chemical toxins that contribute to the ciguatera syndromes; ciguatoxin, maitotoxin and scaritoxin (also possibly palytoxin and okadic acid). Each outbreak may be associated with different proportions of these toxins, and thus have somewhat different clinical features. Within each outbreak the clinical features tend to be similar. Also, the symptom complex is somewhat dissimilar for different fish.

Ciguatoxin dominates in most toxic fish and eels, and interferes with sodium channels in nerve, muscle and cardiac cells; maitotoxin is found in surgeon fish and causes noradrenaline release; scaritoxin is found in parrot fish and produces two sets of symptoms, initially like ciguatera and then a disturbance of equilibrium and balance for a week afterwards. Palytoxin is especially found in trigger fish and mackerel, and causes severe tonic contractions of all muscle groups. When the latter occurs in patients with ciguatera poisoning, there will be elevation of the "muscular " enzymes, such as creatine phosphokinase, in the blood.

The demonstrated pharmacological effects of the toxins include: a diminished respiratory rate with increased amplitude, irregular and Cheyne Stokes respiratory patterns prior to cessation. In animal experiments the dose required to produce failure of spontaneous respiration is about half that required to produce cardiovascular collapse, hence the importance of mouth to mouth respiration as a first aid measure and of assisted respiration during medical treatment.

Ecology: It is likely that ciguatera is a consequence of stress to the tropical reef. Outbreaks often follow transitory ecological disturbances that cause reef destruction. These may be natural, such as hurricanes, cyclones, heavy rains, crown of thorns infestation, algal blooms, or man-made disturbances such as urbanisation of a coastal village, pollution, dredging or wharf construction. Naturally occurring outbreaks tend to develop on the windward side of the islands. Outbreaks in Hawaii occurred in fish from the area adjoining the construction of the reef runway at the Honolulu International Airport and the breakwater at Pokai Bay, both in 1978.

That the fish have become poisonous to eat, may not be evident for many months after the disturbance. This may follow an increase in dissolved silicates, lower salinity and temperature, lower sun intensity, the growth of various algae and finally the proliferation of the dinoflagellate *Gambierdiscus toxicus*. This organism produces the poison "ciguatoxin." It is transferred to herbivorous fishes, and thence to carnivorous fishes, where it accumulates.

Gastrointestinal symptoms are more likely in poisoning from herbivorous fish, which are affected first in ciguatera outbreaks. The carnivores are affected later and tend to cause neurological manifestations.

The victims are often anglers or their families, celebrating a particularly large catch. The affected fish is often the largest of the batch caught, and is usually of the carnivorous type. Apparently any large fish is a potential danger, but especially if it inhabits coral reefs. Pelagic school fish are least affected.

Local knowledge regarding areas in which the fish may be poisonous should be seriously considered in all cases. Unfortunately, it is not entirely reliable, as the areas themselves may be constantly changing.

A variety of techniques have been promulgated by folklore to predict which fish will be safe to eat: the presence of worms in the fish, whether ants or flies refuse it, whether a silver coin will turn black, or whether grated coconut will turn green if cooked with the fish. They are all totally irrelevant, despite parochial beliefs. Perhaps the safest method in a survival situation (not recommended in a suburban setting) is to feed a small amount of the fish to a kitten, which is highly sensitive to most fish poisons. If the animal is still alive and unaffected a few hours later, then the fish is probably safe to eat.

A traditional variant to the "cat test" is the rather pragmatic system of feeding the older members of the family first; if they are unaffected, the remainder of the fish is used to feed the children and the more productive members of the society.

Clinical features

The great diversity of symptoms make this a difficult disease to explain or diagnose, but it is the same diversity that points to the diagnosis. In general there are four groups of symptoms, which may occur in any combination:

> **gastrointestinal** (nausea, vomiting, diarrhoea and abdominal cramps), lasts for days. and leads to dehydration and severe debility,

Unicorn fish, length 25 cm.
Photo by D. Brownbill

cardiovascular (irregular, fast or slow pulse, low blood pressure),

neurological (abnormal motor, sensory and cerebral disturbances, causing muscle and joint pains, headaches, delirium, neuropsychological symptoms, insomnia, incoordination, paralysis, coma),

skin sensations (itch, burning, numbness and tingling, temperature variations).

In the case of infants and babies, there is often a distressed, irritable and restless child, who is uninterested in food and fails to thrive. Weight loss is severe and the child may appear to be in considerable pain, especially in the legs. This general ill health may persist for many months.

The gastrointestinal effects tend to be early and of shorter duration, the cardiovascular effects follow soon after, whereas the neurological effects may take a days or more to evolve, but they and their psychological concomitants can last for months or years.

ACUTE SYMPTOMS

1. Symptoms are usually noted from 2 to 12 hours (0-30 range) after ingestion of the fish. Severe cases may occur early and mild cases may be precipitated later by alcohol ingestion.

2. General weakness and dull aches in limbs (especially knees) and head.

3. Paraesthesia, prickling and tingling, then numbness, around the lips, tongue, mouth and throat, face, hands or feet, is noted in 50% of cases, and lasts up to three weeks in severe cases. A painful itching, occurring days after ingestion, may spread from the extremities and be worse at night, leading to insomnia.

4. Metallic taste, dry mouth, thick tongue, aching of teeth or tightness of muscles around the mouth. The teeth may feel loose and taste may be impaired.

5. Muscle pains, weakness and/or cramps. These pains differentiate this disorder clinically from pufferfish poisoning (tetrodotoxin).

6. Lactating mothers notice painful nipples with feeding. Their breast feeding infants may develop diarrhoea. In pregnant women, the toxin can cross the placenta and cause abnormal foetal movements, premature labour and spontaneous abortion. Others are normal. Occasionally a "local" form of toxicity , causing pelvic and vaginal pain can follow 2-3 weeks after sexual intercourse with ejaculation from a ciguatoxic male.

7. Anorexia, nausea, vomiting, diarrhoea and/or abdominal pain, in half the cases. These symptoms may last up to four days. Painful sensations have been reported with urination, defaecation and ejaculation. Sweating is common. Hiccups have been described.

8. Red, itchy rash over palms of hands and soles of feet and sometimes with weals (a punctate erythema with vesicles or urticaria). It is severe for 2-3 days and subsides after 4-5 days. The rash is aggravated by alcohol consumption. Hair and nail loss may occur.

9. Reversal of temperature perception—cold articles feel hot and sometimes vice versa. This may be present for months, with the drinking of chilled beer producing a burning sensation in the throat.

10. Neurological disturbances include insomnia, apprehension, delirium, and visual disorders such as double vision and dilated pupils, incoordi-

nation and ataxia, occasional athetoid movements, convulsions, coma and death. These symptoms usually develop 8-72 hours after the ingestion, and in the Puerto Rican study, were still present in 20% of cases several months later.

11. Respiratory failure, including tightness in chest, laboured breathing, cyanosis (bluish colour).
12. Cold, clammy appearance with hypotension, cardiac arrhythmias, bradycardia or tachycardia, with extra systoles, etc. This usually clears within a few days.
13. Low body temperature.
14. Laboratory tests are inconstant, including blood counts, electrolytes, serum proteins, IgG, cholinesterases. EMG and nerve conduction anomalies may occur.
15. Death rate is around 0.1%, but may be higher in some outbreaks.

Frequency of Certain Signs and Symptoms

From Bagnis, Kuberski and Laugier, 1979: 3009 cases from French Polynesia and New Caledonia) . From Gillespie, Lewis, Pearn *et al*, 1986: 527 cases from Queensland, Australia)

Sign or Symptom	% of Patients with Findings	
	French	Australian
Numbness and tingling	89.2	71.2
Numbness around mouth	89.1	65.8
Burning or pain to skin	87.6	76.1
Joint pains	85.7	76.1
Muscle pains	81.5	83.3
Diarrhoea	70.6	64.2
Weakness	60.0	90.3
Headache	59.2	62.2
Chills	59.0	49.2
Abdominal pain	46.5	52.0
Itchy skin	44.9	76.3
Nausea	42.9	54.9
Dizziness	42.3	44.9
Difficulty walking	37.7	54.9
Vomiting	37.5	35.0
Sweating	36.7	42.6
Shaking	26.8	30.5
Dental pain	24.8	37.2
Neck stiffness	24.2	26.7
Watery eyes	22.4	41.1
Skin rash	20.5	25.9
Pain on urination	18.7	22.0
Salivation	18.7	9.9
Shortness of breath	16.12	8.3
Low blood pressure	12.12	
Inability to move arms of legs	10.5	26.5

In a mild attack, the major symptoms may clear in 24-36 hours, although residual weakness, paraesthesia and the reversal of temperature perception may persist for longer.

In a severe case the serious manifestations usually subside within the week, although total recovery may take many months or years. Recurrent burning or other skin manifestations may also be precipitated by alcohol, nicotinic acid and other vaso active drugs. There may be associated erythema. The body, face and genitals are often affected intermittently for many months. The application of ice packs may cause increased pain for a few minutes, but then relief for many hours.

Insomnia and milder gastrointestinal symptoms may also persist over this period. Symptomatic depression may last for many months, or years in those predisposed to this.

Exacerbation of the illness may follow stress, the eating of certain fish, or some foods such as poultry or pork (especially if the animals have been fed on fishmeal), spices, chocolate, cocoa or coffee. Immunity does not occur, and it is possible that repeated poisonings may be even more serious.

Prevention

1. Do not eat the fish mentioned above. Treat all oversized fish with suspicion
2. Otherwise, one cannot tell from the appearance or smell which fish are poisoned.
3. If there is evidence of an algal bloom (a change in colour of the water, as with a "red tide"), or if sea birds die in unusual numbers, all fish should be treated with caution.
4. In a survival situation, the advice is as follows: do not eat the viscera of the fish such as liver, gonads or intestines. Avoid the exceptionally large reef predators and those species often implicated in ciguatera poisoning. These include barracudas, groupers, snappers, sea basses, surgeonfishes, parrot fishes, wrasses, jacks, and many others. Moray eels are particularly virulent. Boiling the fish many times and discarding the water after each boiling may sometimes be helpful. As an alternative to this last technique, the fish may be sliced and continually soaked in water which should be changed every 30 minutes or so. Eat only small quantities from the same fish.
5. Various "quick check" methods have been used to determine which fish are poisonous. They are not yet suitable for widespread use. See page 257 for details of these.
6. It has been proposed that public health departments legislate and use propaganda to restrict the sale of certain species of fish likely to be toxic. These would vary with the different localities.

In Tahiti, ono (*Syphraena barracuda*), some bass and perch (*Lutjanus* spp), grouper or hapuu (*Epinephelus microdon*) and many other fish have been banned from sale. In Australia, the following species cannot be sold in tropical areas: red bass (*Lutjanus bohar*), chinaman fish (*Symphorus nematophorus*) and paddletail (*Lutjanus gibbus*).

The South Pacific Commission warns of the high risk species in its area, which include spotted trevally (*Caranx melampygus*), one-spotted sea perch

(*Lutjanus monostigma*) coronation trout (*Variola louti*) and a wide range of cods, parrot fishes, surgeonfishes, barracudas, moray eels and trigger fishes.

The Puerto Rican government bans the buying or selling of barracuda, amberjack and blackjack.

When one considers that most common reef species have been incriminated in ciguatera poisoning at one time or another, there is a problem in isolating and then legislating against "risk" species.

First aid. See page 193.

MEDICAL TREATMENT
See poisoning treatment, page 193.

1. Intravenous mannitol has recently been promoted as an effective treatment during the acute stage of ciguatera poisoning. It was tried because of suspected cerebral oedema in two patients who were comatosed. The response was dramatic. In a series of 23 cases it produced rapid improvement in the neurological and muscular manifestations and slower with the gastrointestinal symptoms. None of the patients required more than 250 ml of 20% mannitol intravenously, in a six hour period, with a maximum of 1 g/kg given over 30 minutes, piggybacked with 5% dextrose in Ringers or saline. Infusion was stopped when symptoms and signs disappeared or blood pressure rose more than 15 mm/Hg. (See *JAMA* 1988:259:2740-2742. "Successful Treatment of Ciguatera Fish Poisoning with Intravenous Mannitol," by Palafox NA, Jain LG, Pinano Az *et al.*)

   Subsequent experience with mannitol suggests that acute cases respond rapidly, but those which have lasted more than 14 days will respond incompletely or transitorily. It may also need to be repeated. Some recommend it months after ingestion.

   Also, mannitol is a strong diuretic and can aggravate the dangerous dehydration and electrolyte anomalies, thus these should be corrected first. The therapeutic effect of mannitol may be due to it causing a competitive inhibition of Na, or an osmotic agent at the cellular level, reducing the excessive fluid in the cytoplasm of nerves. It also blocks the passage of Na ions through channels that have been locked open by the ciguatoxin molecule.

2. During the acute stage calcium gluconate has been used to relieve neuromuscular symptoms and increase muscular tone, atropine i.v. to control vomiting, diarrhoea, bradycardia and hypotension. Verapamil has been proposed, and there are many arguments in its favour, especially against maitotoxin. Edrophonium (Tensilon) and neostigmine are successful in some cases, although they had previously been considered as being contraindicated due to the cholinesterase inhibition. Pralodixime has been proposed but is not

continued

yet proven in sufficient clinical or experimental trials to be recommended, despite the theoretical indications. Protamide is used in
the Bahamas and some other areas. Local anaesthetics have some
theoretical support because of their sodium channel blockage effects, and some animal experimentation.

3. Amitriptyline 25-75 mg per night for a few weeks has been said
to suppress many of the symptoms, not just the neuropsychological ones. Confirmation is needed before it can be widely recommended. It is said to affect sodium channels and produce an
anticholinergic effect.

4. Nikethamide, vitamin B, and many other drugs have been suggested
for the long term symptoms, but are best omitted in preference to
general medical care. Nicotinic acid preparations have been observed to prolong clinical manifestations for many months, as have
many other drugs. As a general rule, any drug which has a cardiovascular effect or stimulates autonomic activity, will make the patient worse. Unscientific as this statement is, it is a useful
guideline. An intolerance for medications such as steroids, opiates
and barbituates has been noted, as well as for any which contain
cyclic ethers.

5. Advice may be needed in the convalescent stage, from a neurolo-
gist or an organically orientated psychiatrist. *Small* doses of diazepam, phenothiazides, and tricyclic antidepressants may be of
great short term value in reducing the confusional states, insomnia
and depression that these patients suffer.

6. Joint pains may be partly relieved by non-steroid anti-inflammatory
drugs.

7. Avoid alcohol and all sea foods and foods likely to provoke recurrences such as poultry and pork when the animals have been fed
fish meal. Sometimes coffee, chocolate, spices and other protein
foods will provoke recurrences.

TETRODOTOXIN/FUGU POISONING

Other names   ◆   Puffer Poisoning
Animals involved   ◆   Toadfish, Puffer, Sharp-nosed Puffer, Blowfish,
                            Globefish, Porcupinefish, Swellfish, Toado, Balloon-
                            fish, Sunfish and others may have a similar effect.

> "These ye shall eat of all that are in the waters; all that have
> fins and scales shall ye eat; And whatsoever hath not fins and
> scales ye may not eat it; it is unclean unto you."
> Mosaic sanitary law, Deuteronomy 14:9-10. ca 1451 B.C.

Tetrodotoxin poisoning follows the ingestion of puffer fish (of which there are
hundreds of species), ocean sunfish, or porcupine fish. The name puffer comes
from the fish's ability to inflate itself when alarmed or excited by taking in large
quantities of air or water. This discourages predators and may be used to intimi-
date rivals.

The scales have been modified to form protective plates or spikes. The fish
are recognised as poisonous throughout the world, although they are more common in the tropical and temperate regions. The toxin is concentrated mainly in the
ovaries, liver and intestines. Lesser amounts occur in the skin but the body musculature is often free of poison. The toxicity is related to the reproductive cycle.

In the ancient world, both the Chinese and the Egyptians were aware of the
poisonous nature of these fish. Egyptian tombs of the 5th dynasty (ca 2700
B.C.) have illustrations of *Tetradon stellatus,* labelled as poisonous. It is
claimed that Hawaiians used the toxin on their spears. Haitians used it as a poison fed to victims, who then appeared to die, were buried, and then dug up as
brain-damaged zombies.

Even Ian Fleming's famous spy, James Bond 007, almost succumbed to a
Fugu-tipped shoe-knife in *From Russia With Love.*

With two exceptions, these fish are usually considered inedible. The first exception is the uninformed consumer. Examples range from Captain James Cook
(who on September 7, 1774, sampled this fish in New Caledonia with near fatal
results), to the poor of southern California and Florida looking for a cheap meal.

The other exception is the Asiatic gourmet consuming "Fugu." After a prolonged apprenticeship, specially licensed chefs in Japan are allowed to prepare
this fish, receiving considerable kudos by retaining enough of the toxin to produce a numbing effect in the mouth, but not enough to cause tetrodotoxin poisoning. Nevertheless, accidents do happen, and the rate of poisoning from Fugu
averaged 150 per year, with a death rate of over 50%. Apart from an unintended
gastronomic form of Russian roulette, it is also used as a method of suicide.

A three course Fugu meal could consist of: Hirezake (hot sake with toasted
Fugu fin), Fugu sashimi (raw slices of Fugu) and Fugu-chiri (boiled Fugu with
vegetables). Until recently, no Japanese politician would dare prejudice his political career by proposing to outlaw Fugu, and in fact Prime Ministers Tanaka
and Sato were Fugu devotees. Nowadays there are some limitations in the sale
of Fugu and the preparation of highly toxic liver, at least in theory.

The tetrodotoxin from a medium sized puffer fish could kill 30 people. Last century, in Japan, some paralysed victims recovered while awaiting burial or cremation. They were conscious, but paralysed, and able to remember many comments made by both medical attendants and relatives, which could have influenced future inheritances.

The conflict between epicurean delights and safety is depicted in the traditional Japanese verse:

Those who eat Fugu soup are stupid.

Those who don't eat Fugu soup are also stupid.

Pufferfish are also capable of biting through shells, some fishhooks and the occasional offered finger (see page 42).

Toxin. See page 258.

The Sankyo Pharmaceutical Co. of Tokyo produces the toxin, which is sometimes claimed to be the most potent poison known. Sixty-five milligrams can kill a human, and it costs about $1 million per ounce. It is used as a pain killer in patients with neuralgia, severe joint disease and terminal cancer (although cynics may misconstrue this information). Tetrodon fish are immune to the effects of tetrodotoxin. The toxin is 25 times more powerful than curare.

The toxin is probably identical to that of other animals, such as the blue ringed octopus, some cone shells, Central American frogs and the Californian newt *Taricha torosa*. Apparently one befuddled victim died from drinking half a bottle of whisky and swallowing his pet newt.

Clinical features

GENERAL. The onset and severity of symptoms vary according to the amount of the toxin ingested.

Within 5 to 40 minutes (or as long as three hours) the patient may note weakness, malaise, pallor, dizziness, incoordination and ataxia. During this time numbness and paraesthesia of the lips and tongue (described as tingling or prickling) may extend to the extremities or become generalised.

Increased salivation, sweating, chest pain and headache may also be noted. Gastrointestinal symptoms of nausea, vomiting, diarrhoea and pain are sometimes observed. A decrease in temperature, blood pressure and pulse rate may also be noted.

A haemorrhagic diathesis has been reported, with bleeding into the skin and mucosa, haemorrhagic blister formation and peeling of the skin. Vomiting of blood and other bleeding tendencies are possible.

Untreated, the death rate is 50-60% in some series. Death has occurred as rapidly as 17 minutes after ingestion, but more commonly hours after ingestion.

RESPIRATORY. After the paraesthesia, respiratory symptoms dominate the clinical state. Respiratory distress, with increased rate and decreased depth, proceeds to severe breathlessness and cyanosis (bluish colour of lips). This is due to a paralysis of the respiratory muscles and a depression of the respiratory centre. Death, following respiratory paralysis, may occur within 24 hours after the ingestion of the fish.

Photos of fish causing tetrodotoxin poisoning. Photos by C. Edmonds and D. Brownbill

NEUROLOGICAL. Generalised muscular twitching and incoordination may proceed to a complete muscular paralysis. This may be of the bulbar type involving interference with speech and swallowing (with loss of speech, difficulty in swallowing, and later inability to swallow). The pupils, after initially being constricted, may become fixed and dilated. The bulbar paralysis may then extend to an inability to move the limbs, despite the victim retaining consciousness.

First aid. See page 193 .

Medical treatment. See page 193.

Artificial respiration dominates the treatment for many hours. The presence of fixed dilated pupils in an apnoeic unresponsive patient is expected in this disorder and is not a sign of "cerebral death," merely of temporary paralysis.

Specific pharmacological therapy is not available. Anticholinesterases such as neostigmine or edrophonium may have a beneficial effect, possibly more effective after the paralysis commences to abate. Others are less clearly indicated. Atropine may control vagal tone. Intravenous calcium gluconate (10%) has been recommended to augment the action potential of neurones. Probably none of these have value during the acute phase. Cardiorespiratory stimulants have been suggested, and these have been used. There is little justification for them, although under some animal experiment conditions, both lobeline and pentylenetetrazol have had some value.

Because of the possibility of consciousness being retained in the absence of skeletal or respiratory movement, the periodic administration of a minor tranquilliser such as diazepam would seem humane, and the patient should be given continuous reassurance and explanation. Discussions between the medical personnel should be guarded in the patient's presence.

Prevention

1. Do not eat scaleless fish unless they are known to be harmless.
2. If one is forced to eat Fugu in Japan, it should be purchased at a first class restaurant with a licensed "puffer" chef. All the visceral organs and skin from the fish must be removed. Although the testes are usually non-toxic, it must be realised that these can be confused with the highly toxic ovaries.
3. Cooking by frying, stewing, baking, grilling or boiling, does not inactivate the toxin.
4. If one is forced to eat these fish to survive, they should be eviscerated and only the musculature selected. The meat should then be cut or torn into small bits and soaked in water for at least four hours. The fish should be kneaded during this time and the water changed at frequent intervals. The toxin is partly water soluble, and this soaking may remove it. Do not eat more than is required to maintain life.
5. Exposure to the toxin does not produce immunity.

CASE REPORT   **Puffer poisoning**   Torda *et al.*

A healthy boy of 14 years was on a camping holiday. Fishing off some coastal rocks, the family had caught over 20 small puffer fish, which were cleaned, gutted and left soaking in sea water overnight. The following day they were boiled in sea water and served to the family just before midday. One fish (*Amblyrhunchotes richei*) was eaten by the patient.

As the meal was being prepared, a young, injured crow or magpie, which the family was rearing, was given one fish, and died in a few minutes.

After lunch, the patient complained of numbness in the tongue, a feeling of swelling in the lips and a general feeling of lightness. Perhaps half to three-quarters of an hour after the meal, he vomited. After his recovery, he prepared a written account. "Then I started to lie down feeling weak, tired and miserable with that funny up and down sensation if I moved. It became so critical that I couldn't be bothered with anything and I just lay there trying to expand and contract the diaphragm. My father tried giving me milk... but I couldn't swallow. I could just move my mouth, and I was very, very cold.. I was losing air fast. It was slow and painful. I thought of panic but I became quite paralysed and then unconscious."

On arrival at hospital, he was ventilated and intubated. "The next thing I remember was being in the ambulance receiving air and breathing. I could hear them talking, but I couldn't move or anything. I was completely conscious... and I really heard them. They were laughing and chattering, and they even played with the hooter."

On arrival, he was described as "unreactive, with flaccid paralysis and is areflexic. Pupils fixed and dilated."

"I couldn't feel anybody touching me. I heard nurses later on and they were trying to talk to me, specially one who said good morning and good night. I could also hear surgeons talking mumble jumble. I tried to move and talk but that was impossible. I felt them spraying stuff on me (silicone aerosol) which turned from hot to cold around my legs and body. They usually told me what they were going to do. It was terrible because they opened my eyelids every now and then and I found out I could see but just couldn't open my lids. They always used a torch which was very disturbing. As time passed, I always tried to move. At 6 a.m. I was able to keep my eyes an eighth to a quarter inch open until I could finally open them. It was nice to see, believe me. I was able to communicate a bit. Doctor asked me if I could feel anything, then he pinched my ear, so I closed my eyes which meant yes."

At 8 a.m. he could move his lips and tongue. At 10 a.m. he could move his limbs feebly and a vital capacity of 600 ml was measured. As respiration still resembled that seen after incomplete reversal of neuromuscular block, a test injection of edrophonium, 10 mg was given slowly intravenously. The vital capacity improved to 1000 ml. Tracheal tug, use of accessory respiratory muscles and intercostal recession ceased. A further 10 mg given 15 minutes later resulted in no further increase of vital capacity or other detectable effect.

The patient continued to improve and was seen later in the day to be strolling around the ward, still with fixed dilated pupils. The other members of the patient's family who shared his meal fared better. His father, who did not vomit, developed paraesthesia, weakness of all limbs and neck, weakness of the voice and difficulty in swallowing. He was hospitalised for two days and made an uneventful recovery. The patient's two brothers vomited after eating the fish. They both escaped with paraesthesia only. His mother did not develop symptoms at all.

SCOMBROID POISONING

Other name   ◆   Scombrotoxic Poisoning
Animals involved   ◆   Tuna, Mackerel, Skipjack, Bonito, Albacore, and pos-
                            sibly: Mahi-mahi, Bluefish, Amberjack, Herring,
                            Sardines, Anchovies

There are few problems from this type of fish poisoning in highly civilised areas, because of the tendency to eat well-processed canned tuna or heavily
cooked fish. It is a possible hazard wherever the mackerel-like fishes, tuna,
bonito or albacore, are caught and eaten without adequate preparation, and
wherever unregulated restaurants are frequented. It has also occurred in epidemics due to contaminated canned tuna.

These fish, which are normally safe to eat, become poisonous if handled in-
correctly. If left for several hours on a boat or elsewhere at room temperature, or
in the sun, the histidine in their muscular tissues is able to be changed by bacterial action into saurine—a histamine-like substance. The bacteria involved include *Proteus morganii, Clostridium, Salmonella, Klebsicila, Escherichia.*

Laboratory verification of contaminated fish, is obtained by demonstrating a
histamine content of 100 micromols per 100 g of fish muscle. Urinary histamine
levels are often >10 times normal for the first 4 hours post ingestion, and may
still be excessive for days afterwards. Ingestion of other fish may cause a similar
syndrome, not due to inadequate storage, but to allergy (pages 168, 245-248).

Clinical features

The taste of the fish may be characteristic—sharp, bitter or peppery. A latent period of some 20-60 minutes precedes the other symptoms. Then nausea, vomiting, diarrhoea and upper abdominal distress develop.

Headache is common. It is relieved by venous pressure (obstruction on the
jugular veins by a medical practitioner) and it diminishes later, if hypotension occurs. Throbbing of the cranial arteries is experienced, and is abolished by transitory carotid pressure on that side (to be applied by a medical practitioner only).

Palpitations may be associated with rapid weak pulse. Usually the above
symptoms are noted in the first two hours, and include dry mouth, thirst, burning sensation in throat and inability to swallow.

They may be followed by a generalised red colour of the skin, resembling
sunburn and aggravated by exposure to sun. It may feel burning or painful and can
proceed to itching and blister (urticaria) formation over the whole body; the face
may be flushed and swollen, the eyes inflamed with common cold symptoms;
bronchospasm, respiratory distress, cyanosis; fever, chills, tremors; malaise, muscular weakness, pain, a metallic taste in the mouth; abdominal cramps; cold, clammy appearance with rapid pulse and unconsciousness (syncope) on standing.
Cardiovascular shock with hypotension, and ECG evidence of ST depression.

Usually symptoms disappear within 12-16 hours but severe cases can last
days. Death is possible, but unlikely unless large quantities of contaminated fish
are eaten, compared to the body weight.

First aid. See page 193. In the absence of medical facilities, as often happens on tropical islands, treatment may still have to proceed in order to save lives. It is possible that a pharmacy may be available, or a local inhabitant may possess valuable anti-asthma medications.

An old anti-asthma preparation, Medihaler-Epi, is still available in most parts of the world. This is an adrenalin spray and is absorbed by the mucosa of the mouth and lungs. With a couple of minutes between each puff, this is a very effective way of treating the disorder and tailoring the dose to the symptoms.

Steroid sprays, such as Becotide, are also frequently made available to asthmatics, and can be used safely in such cases. The steroid is absorbed from the lungs. If medical advice is available, the usual dosage limitations of these drugs may be exceeded, depending on the severity of the case.

One may have available, and administer, antihistamine medications (such as used for hay fever, sea sickness, allergies, paediatric sedatives, decongestants, etc.) or anti-ulcer medications such as cimetidine (Tagemet).

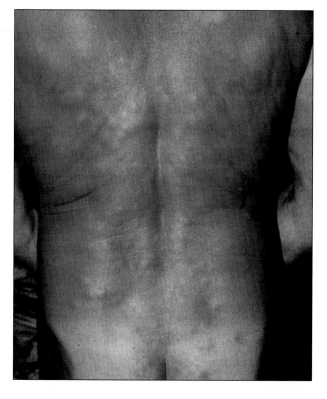

Scromboid poisoning, with blotchy, hive-like lesions. Courtesy of J. Knight. Photo by J. Mannerheim

MEDICAL TREATMENT.
See page 193.

1. Steroids are very effective, hydrocortisone 100 mg i.v. is repeated every few hours as required, for 24-48 hours. This counters most of the harmful effects of the scombroid poisoning and is probably the drug of choice—and it may be used with adrenalin and/or antihistamines.
2. Adrenalin (epinephrine) 1 in 1,000, 0.1 ml per minute s.c. (maximum 1 ml) or other sympathomimetic drugs such as isoprenaline, will counter most of the symptoms if given early. These are of great value for the respiratory manifestation.

    Medihaler-Epi, described above, supplies 0.35 mg of adrenalin acid tartrate per puff, and steroid inhalants may be used. The limitations of these preparations are not so much from the drug itself, as the propellants used to carry it.
3. Salbutamol or other anti-asthma aerosol sprays are of value against the respiratory manifestations.
4. Antihistamines have been proposed and may be of considerable benefit. A H1 receptor antagonist, such as the common antihistamines (e.g., diphenhydramine 50 mg intramuscularly) have been found to be very effective. Cimetidine, a histamine H2 receptor antagonist has been used by some workers with great effect. 100 mg i.v. per minute (or slower) for up to 300 mg, may give an immediate effect. As this may produce hypotension the patient must be recumbent and monitored throughout. 200 mg may be given orally every 6 hours.
5. Ergotamine preparations or the inhalation of 100% oxygen may give symptomatic relief of headaches.
6. After effective treatment, many patients are told that they are "allergic to fish." This is not so in most cases, and the patient can be advised to gradually and slowly return to this food, if they desire it.

Prevention

1. Prepare the fish correctly (refrigeration). Do not leave them in the sun, or exposed to room or boat temperature.
2. If there is any evidence of pallor of the gills, or an odour, or staleness, discard the fish.
3. Do not swallow fish that tastes "peppery."

SHELLFISH POISONING

Acute Yellow Atrophy of Liver

Other names ◆ Asari Poisoning, Venerupin Poisoning.
Animals involved ◆ *Crassostrea gigas, Tapes (Venerupis) semidecussata* and other bivalve molluscs.

Specific situations are known, for example, Lake Hamera in Japan where molluscs concentrate a hepatotoxin. It is only noted between December and April inclusive, because of the presence during those months of a toxic dinoflagellate, *Exuviaella mariae-lebouriae*. The Japanese Government has placed the affected areas under quarantine during the danger season. Ordinary cooking does not destroy the poison.

Clinical features

The major clinical features are those of yellow atrophy of the liver, gastrointestinal symptoms, a generalised haemorrhagic diathesis, jaundice and hepatic coma. These occur within 48 hours of ingestion. The toxic effect is dose dependent, requiring about 50 shellfish to cause symptoms and 100 or so to cause death, in an adult. This will vary with the degree of toxicity of the shellfish.

Medical treatment. As for liver failure.

Allergic (A.S.P.)

Other names ◆ Erythematous Shellfish Poisoning, Mollusc Allergy
Animals involved ◆ Mussels, Clams, Cockles, Scallops, Abalone and other molluscs.

This appears to be an acute hypersensitivity reaction to a protein in the shellfish. It is likely that the victim has previously been exposed to the same or similar protein and has developed an antibody reaction. Symptoms develop after the second and subsequent exposures and are aggravated by exercise, heat and emotion. There may be a history of allergies to other foreign proteins such as hay fever, antitoxins, and horse serum.

Clinical features. See Allergy and Anaphylaxis, pages 245-248.

1. There is usually a delay of 1/2-6 hours following ingestion of the shellfish. Usually only one of the many people eating the shellfish is affected.
2. Diffuse reddening, swelling and itching spreads from the head and neck to the whole of the body.
3. Blisters, weals (urticaria) and generalised swelling (oedema) can be extreme.

4. Generalised shock state, with pale cold, clammy appearance, rapid pulse rate and syncope on standing (fainting), may sometimes occur. Death can occur from this anaphylactic shock.
5. Nausea, vomiting and abdominal pain may develop.
6. Headache, muscular aches, flushing sensation and mild fever are common.
7. Congestion of the respiratory passages may result in laryngeal obstruction, stridor and congestion and swelling of the nasal mucous membrane, tongue, etc.
8. Angioedema is characterised by local oedema (swelling), and usually involves eyelids, lips, sexual organs, mouth, tongue, larynx or gastrointestinal mucosa.
9. Eosinophilia may be present in the blood film.
10. Duration of the disease may extend for weeks.

First aid. See pages 193, 209.

Decongestants or antihistamines may be of benefit.

MEDICAL TREATMENT

See Allergy and Anaphylaxis, pages 245-248.

1. Administer first aid.
2. Hydrocortisone (100 mg i.v. every few hours for 24-48 hours) may be most effective and can be reduced and stopped within a few days. It may be used instead of, or as well as, the regimes noted in 3 and 4 below.
3. Ephedrine 30 mg q.i.d. and antihistamines, e.g., promethazine (Phenergan) 25 mg b.d. or Antistine injection.
4. Adrenalin (epinephrine) 0.1 ml of 1 in 1000 given per minute subcutaneously, to 1.0 ml, may give prompt and dramatic relief of symptoms. Others parenteral sympathomimetics may be used instead of adrenalin, e.g., isoprenaline. They may be needed until the antihistamines and ephedrine become effective.
5. In severe cases of laryngeal or upper respiratory tract obstruction, emergency tracheostomy may prove lifesaving. Severe bronchospasm may require endotracheal intubation and intermittent positive pressure respiration with O_2, with or without nebulised salbutamol.

Prevention

1. If allergic shellfish poisoning has occurred once, it is likely to recur, so avoid future contact with this type of food.
2. As this is an individual reaction to the shellfish protein, the fact that other people eat this food with impunity means nothing to the victim.

Gastrointestinal (D.S.P.)

Animals involved   ◆   Mussels, Clams, Oysters, Cockles, Scallops and other
bivalve molluscs.

This disorder arises following the ingestion of shellfish which are contaminated
by organisms capable of causing gastroenteritis in humans. Oysters are able to
rid themselves of these organisms if allowed to live in purified water before
consumption. The types of infective gastroenteritis vary according to the organisms concerned in each outbreak. A dinoflagellate, *Dinophysis fortii* is one
causal organism, although many others may be incriminated. There have been
cases of typhoid fever and viral hepatitis transmitted by eating contaminated
oysters. Marine vibrios have been incriminated as have viruses and other bacteria. Recently outbreaks have been due to non-01 *Vibrio cholerae*, Norwalk
virus, *Campylobacter* and unidentified viruses.

In one eight-month period, from May to December in 1982, 1017 people
were affected by this disease in New York State. Large outbreaks in Japan,
Spain, the Netherlands and Chile illustrate the widespread nature of the dinoflagellates responsible for most outbreaks of DSP.

Raw shellfish are more frequently implicated. Often the type of cooking
necessary for producing edible shellfish is inadequate to produce sterility. The
prolonged high temperature, high pressure and long duration results in tough
and tasteless food.

Between 7% and 13% of polio viruses survive 8 to 30 minutes when oysters
are cooked in a conventional manner. Clams open their shells after 60 seconds of
cooking, and are then considered ready for eating, whereas it actually takes 4 to 6
minutes of steaming for the internal temperature to reach 100 degrees Centigrade.
Nevertheless, steaming the shellfish halves the attack rate in many outbreaks.

Faecal coli bacterial counts should be regularly performed on oysters intended for human consumption, as an indication of pollution.

Clinical features

There is usually a long delay after eating the shellfish, this may be from 8 to 12
hours with some, about 36 hours with marine vibrios, up to 72 hours with others
(such as the Norwalk virus) and much longer with some other viruses. Presenting
features include anorexia, malaise and weakness; nausea, vomiting; diarrhoea
and abdominal pains, often of a colic type, headache, muscle pains and fever.

Usually the acute gastrointestinal disturbances do not persist for more than
48 hours.

First aid

1. Rest the patient.
2. Encourage high fluid intake, but prohibit spicy foods or foods difficult
   to digest.
3. Obtain medical assistance.
4. Use whatever home remedies are available to reduce the incidence of
   diarrhoea or vomiting.

MEDICAL TREATMENT

1. Administer first aid.
2. Antiemetics if indicated. Prochlorperazine (Stemetil) 12.5 mg i.m. is of value. Other drugs include antacids, antihistamines, hyoscine, phenothiazines, etc.
3. Diarrhoea is controlled by the use of Lomotil (4 tabs initially and 2 after each defaecation. Maximum 12 per day). Morphine and opium derivatives are of value, especially codeine phosphate, mist opii, etc. Kaoline compounds (Kaomagma) may be used.
4. Fluid and electrolyte balance is maintained by intravenous infusions, e.g., i.v. Hartmanns solution is a reliable first choice while waiting for laboratory results. Hypertonic saline may be needed if diarrhoea is severe, as may i.v. caloric fluids, amino acids, etc.
5. Antibiotics may be of value. Neomycin (Neogastrin) 20-40 ml q.i.d. acts locally in the bowel, as does dihydrostreptomycin (Streptomagma) tabs 1 q.i.d. Ciprofloxacin 1000 mg single dose is used.
6. Stool specimens can be tested for enteric pathogens, including salmonella, shigella, campylobacter, yersinia, *Staphylococcus aureus, Bacillus cereus, Clostridium perfringens,* vibrio bacteria, enteroviruses, rotaviruses and adenoviruses. Incriminated shellfish can be cultured for the same organisms and for coliform counts. Antibody testing of serum, using radioimmunoassay techniques may be performed to identify the causative agents for epidemiological studies.

Prevention

1. Avoid the ingestion of shellfish of unknown origin and of raw and lightly cooked shellfish.
2. Regular faecal coliform counts on the shellfish, performed by a responsible public health authority, are a valuable check on organism pollution of the marine environment in which the shells are growing. Marketing and locality identification also needs to be under control to trace outbreaks rapidly and restrict supply.
3. Cleansing the shellfish can often be achieved by keeping them in clean circulating water previously treated with ultraviolet light or ozone, for at least 36 hours to allow the bivalves to "depurge" themselves of the bacterial contamination. Viral reduction may be much less rapid and more dependent on species variation.

Paralytic (P.S.P.)

Other names   ◆   Saxitoxin Poisoning, Gonyaulax Poisoning
Animals involved   ◆   Mussels, Clams, Oysters, Cockles, Scallops and other
                             bivalve molluscs.

This is a natural disorder, usually observed between latitudes 30 degrees north
and 30 degrees south of the equator. Certain areas appear prone to these epidemics. This is probably related to major tidal movements. The coastal areas of
Maine and Alaska are commonly affected in the U.S.A., mid April to mid October, when deep water replaces the surface water moved by the offshore winds.

Observers in Japan, Norway and Balkan states (ex Yugoslavia) have noted
an association between the incidence of this disorder and pollution.

History reveals serious and sometimes large epidemics of poisoning from
eating shellfish. Paralytic shellfish poison is one of the most potent biological
poisons known to man. The poison, however, is not produced by the shellfish,
but from a marine protozoa, of the Order Dinoflagellata. A neurotoxin—P.S.P.
(saxitoxin)—is found in bivalve shellfish, and is often associated with the "red
tide" or "water bloom"—discolouration of the sea due to masses of dinoflagellates. It is concentrated by shellfish such as mussels and clams, which filter
these organisms from the infected water. It usually occurs in epidemics, and affects most of the people consuming shellfish from the affected area.

Other vectors include some starfish and crustaceans, but human poisoning
from these sources needs verification. Other toxins are also produced from contaminated shellfish, sometimes altering the clinical presentations from one epidemic to another. See Appendix VI.

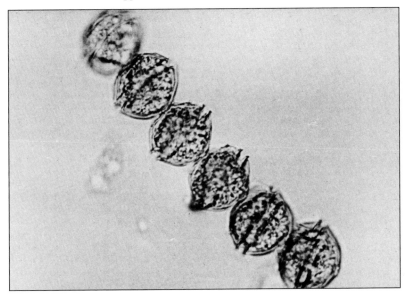

Photomicrograph of *Gonyaulax catanella*, one cause of paralytic shellfish poisoning (PSP)

Many interesting anecdotes regarding this disorder have been described. North American Indians at Port Royal, Nova Scotia, in the 17th century, would not eat mussels even when starving. In preference they would eat their dogs or the bark from trees. On the west coast, some Indian tribes maintained a watch for bioluminescence in the sea, and would not eat shellfish when the sea was "glowing." That many of the natives were aware of the danger was shown by the wilful poisoning of a group of Russian settlers when Indians invited them to a banquet of shellfish in the islands of Baranov and Chichagof. Some extremely toxic shellfish have recently been discovered in this vicinity, and it is of interest that when the U2 pilot Gary Powers was captured by the Russians in 1960, he carried a suicide vial of saxitoxin.

Red tides occur seasonally in some temperate oceans. Usually the dinoflagellates which cause this phenomenon are non toxic, but others such as the genus *Gonyaulax*, are frequently associated with shellfish poisoning. Other blooms which may be associated with this poisoning may be brown, yellow, blue, black and green. The resulting disease is known to have caused at least 300 deaths.

As a general rule, everyone who eats the shellfish is affected, although there is evidence that individuals who habitually eat shellfish containing low levels of toxin can build up a limited immunity. The symptoms are sometimes mistaken for drunkenness, especially when the shellfish are taken in combination with alcohol, as the symptoms summate.

Toxin. See appendix, page 258.

Clinical features

1. There is a latent period which varies from 20 minutes to many hours, following the ingestion of the poison.
2. Paraesthesia (tingling then numbness) is usually the first symptom and occurs around the mouth (88%) and hands (83%) and may spread over the body. There may be a tingling or burning sensation in the gums, tongue, teeth and lips. The circumoral area may become hypersensitive to touch.
3. Weakness of upper (62%) and lower (71%) limbs.
4. Floating sensation (66%).
5. Incoordination and ataxia (57%). Involuntary movements from muscle twitching to convulsions.
6. Difficulty in speech, vision, swallowing, breathing, etc., in serious cases. These may worsen for the next few hours; aches in joints; increased salivation and thirst; nausea, vomiting and diarrhoea are possible associated symptoms; transitory hypertension has been noted. Headache may sometimes be present.

Serum creatine phosphokinase may be increased in those with predominantly muscular symptoms.

Mortality rate varies from 1-10%, and is due to respiratory paralysis, usually within the first 12 hours. If the victim survives 24 hours, the prognosis is good.

First aid. See page 193.

MEDICAL TREATMENT

1. Treat as for Tetrodotoxin poisoning (see page 206).
2. Control of the epidemic. The public must be warned of the danger associated with the ingestion of shellfish. This can be achieved by the communications media (radio, T.V. newspapers) and by direct approaches to the fishing co-operatives and distributors.
3. Tracing the source from the patient to the distributors and the fisherman to prevent further contaminated shellfish being supplied for public consumption.

Prevention

1. The unexplained presence of dead sea creatures (eels, sea birds or mollusc eating fish) is a good indication that something in the sea is poisonous.
2. Red tides (dinoflagellates) and luminescence of the water are also warning signs. Unfortunately, concentrations of 20 000 or more cells per ml of sea water are required to cause the discolouration, whereas only 400-500 are necessary to cause poisoning. However, not all red tides are poisonous.
3. Cooking, and the discarding of cooking fluids afterwards, diminishes the amount of poison ingested, but cannot be relied apon, as often the cooking may be inadequate to remove the toxin.
4. Whenever there is any possibility of poisoning, shellfish should be subject to toxicity tests in the public health laboratories. See Appendix VI, page 258. Often the shellfish purify themselves after a few weeks non-exposure to the offending organism.
5. There is no way in which shellfish can be shown to be safe by visual inspection. Discolouration, folk lore techniques, and smell are unreliable guides. If in doubt, throw it out.

CLUPEOID FISH POISONING

Other names   ◆ Herring-like Fish Poisoning, Clupeotoxic Poisoning.
Animals involved   ◆ Herring-like fish of the Order Clupeiformes.

First described in the West Indies, it causes a strikingly rapid illness, with the victim even dying with the fish still in his mouth. It may be related to ciguatera poisoning.

Symptoms include nausea, abdominal pains, itching, sweating, shock, respiratory failure, coma and death. At autopsy the blood is coagulated and the liver hard. If the victim survives, jaundice and liver failure may supervene.

Plankton feeders such as anchovies and herrings may also feed upon the red tide dinoflagellates, producing similar toxicity and deaths.

CRUSTACEAN POISONING

Animals involved   ◆   Crayfish, Prawns, Shrimp, Lobster, Crabs, Yabbies
and other crustaceans.

These arthropods, so well liked by our gourmets, appear to be able to induce
similar reactions to the shellfish poisonings. Paralytic poisoning (see page 215
and 258) has been reported, and gastrointestinal poisoning (see page 213) may
occur following the ingestion of these crustaceans. Probably the commonest
form of crustacean poisoning is of the allergic type—with a similar clinical picture to that of the allergic shellfish poisoning (see page 211) and requiring the
same first aid and medical treatment.

Poisoning, with severe neurological disease and sometimes death, from eating crab meat have been reported from many Pacific Islands, Asia, Africa, Indian Ocean, West Indies, and elsewhere.

It is not easy to determine which crabs are safe to eat. Local knowledge
must be respected, as a species in one area may be safe whereas in an adjoining
area may be poisonous. Folklore may be based on the ugly appearance of the
crab, distasteful meat, crabs eating toxic food, allergic responses in certain din-
ers, contamination by organisms or pollutants, or species-specific poison.

Many of the reports incriminate the Xanthidae, and Rumphius in 1705 described these poisonous crabs of the Moluccas. "All crabs, the pincers of which
have fingers black or brown, are not fit for consumption, as if they are marked
as such by Nature." Similar poisonings have followed the eating of king crabs
and horseshoe crabs, throughout the tropical Indo-pacific and Atlantic oceans.
The coconut crab of the Pacific Islands is usually eaten with impunity, but has
caused cases of gastrointestinal poisoning.

GASTROPOD POISONING

Animals involved   ◆ *Neptunea arthritica, N. intersculp*ta (snails, whelks and slugs).

The toxins include tetramine from the whelks' salivary glands and possibly saxitoxin (see page 215, 258) from ingested molluscs. It is partly destroyed by cooking. Incidents have been reported in the Pacific, especially Japan, but there is also toxicological evidence of the poison from Norway, Canada and the United Kingdom.

Clinical features

Headache, visual disturbances, dizziness, vomiting and urticaria (hives). Paralytic manifestations have been reported.

First aid and **medical treatment.** As for shellfish poisoning, pages 211-217.

GEMPYLID POISONING

Other name ◆ Gempylotoxic Poisoning, Barracouta Poisoning
Animals involved ◆ Escolars or pelagic Mackerels. *Leonura atun, Lepido-cybium flavobrunneum*

The diarrhoea occasionally produced by eating these fish is probably the result of a direct effect on the bowel. No abdominal cramps or generalised symptoms are found.

MEDICAL TREATMENT

1. Lomotil (diphenoxylate with atropine) 4 tablets immediately, with two after each bowel motion (maximum 12 per day).
2. Other anti-diarrhoea medications, e.g., Mist opii, Kaomagma etc.
3. Attention to fluid and electrolyte status.

HALLUCINATORY FISH POISONING

Animals involved   ◆   Mullet, Goatfish, Unicornfish, Surgeonfish, Rudderf-
                             ish, Damselfish, Drummers, Rockcods, Sea Chub and
                             others.

This rare disorder occurs in scattered localities, either in epidemics or endemi-
cally around some tropical and semitropical islands especially in the Indo-Pacific region. It has been reported around South Africa, Mauritius, Norfolk Island
and Hawaii. At Norfolk Island, off the eastern coast of Australia, the fish are
known as "dreamfish," and cause troublesome nightmares.
    The toxin is not destroyed by cooking.

Clinical features

There is a latent period that varies between a few minutes and two hours. Disturbances of vision and hearing vary from misinterpretations (such as illusions) to hallucinations. The disturbed conscious state waxes and wanes for many hours.
Neurological changes may be transitory and affect coordination, muscle strength, etc.
    Sleep is disturbed, with nightmares and bizarre dreams. The victim may de-
velop paranoid feelings that people are trying to harm him. Sensations may include constriction to breathing, impending death, gastrointestinal and skin
disturbances.The symptoms usually terminate spontaneously with 24 hours, although symptoms of other fish poisoning may be present.

First aid. See page 193.

1.   Reassurance, in a protective, well lit environment, by friends and rela-
     tives whom the patient trusts.
2.   Give tranquillisers if available, but do not give stimulants such as cof-
     fee or tea, or sedatives like alcohol and barbiturates.

MEDICAL TREATMENT. See page 193.

1. Administer first aid.
2. Phenothiazines, e.g., thioridazine (Melleril) 50-200 mg statim and repeat p.r.n. Diazepam 10 mg i.v. may also be of value in quieting the
   patient. As it is not known whether the toxin is related to STP, chlorpromazine is best avoided.
3. Treat other associated fish poisonings on their merits.

Prevention

Take note of the local knowledge, otherwise a planned holiday may result in an
extended "trip."

ICHTHYOHAEMOTOXIC (FISH BLOOD) POISONING

Poisoning from drinking the blood of some fishes, especially eels, is distinct from the ciguatera poisoning from eating some marine eels. It has been described from Europe, Asia and North America. The toxin in the blood is destroyed by heat and is antigenic, being bound to a protein.

Symptoms include nausea, salivation, vomiting, abdominal pain and skin lesions similar to hives. Numbness or tingling around the mouth, muscular weakness, respiratory paralysis and death are possible.

ICHTHYOHEPATOTOXIC (FISH LIVER) POISONING

Eating the liver of certain fish can produce a disease similar to hypervitaminosis A (page 229). Such fish may include scombrids (tuna and mackerel), serranids (sea bass and groupers), sparids (snappers) and trichodontids (Japanese sandfish, hatahata).

ICHTHYOOTOXIC (FISH ROE) POISONING

Following the eating of the eggs of fish (fish roe), a rare illness causing dryness of the mouth, nausea, vomiting, diarrhoea and tinnitus, has been reported. Respiratory distress and coma are seen in severe cases, and recovery may take a few days. The barbel roe poisoning of Europe is the most notable example of this disease, but bacterial contamination can occur in sturgeon roe (caviar).

MERCURY POISONING

Other name   ◆   Minamata Disease
Animals involved   ◆   Tuna, Sharks, Swordfish, other large predators and
                            large crustaceans.

Between 1953-1960, 111 cases of mercury poisoning were reported in people eating contaminated shellfish and fish from Minamata Bay, Japan. Forty-three of these people died. The mercury was originally derived from industrial effluent. In Minamata Bay, values as high 1-10 micrograms per litre were recorded. This was later followed by an outbreak in Sweden, due to ingestion of contaminated fish from fresh water lakes polluted with mercury by paper and pulp mills. Other industries with similar potential hazards include the manufacture of chlorine, caustic soda, electric batteries, fluorescent lamps, plastics, fungicides and seed dressings.

Commercial fishing has been prohibited in parts of the Great Lakes of Canada and some rivers in the United States of America and Sweden, because of mercury contamination. Bass and other fish have been affected from the Everglades in Florida. If the surface water mercury concentration exceeds 0.2 micrograms per litre, significant contamination is present. In the marine environment, the mercury compounds decompose into the inorganic form, and are then converted to methyl mercury, the toxic substance which accumulates in fish. The mercury level is increased in major predators such as tuna, shark and the larger crustaceans. Paradoxically, the mercury levels of tuna and swordfish caught in 1878 and 1946 and preserved in museums are not much different from those detected today.

Mercury poisoning occurs when the blood level reached 50-100 micrograms per 100 ml. The safe limit has been estimated as 10 micrograms per 100 ml. This limit is thought to be reached with a daily consumption of 100 micrograms of mercury, which happens to be the content of one 200 gram can of tuna fish contaminated with 0.5 p.p.m. mercury. The World Health Organisation recommendation for a safe limit is 0.05 p.p.m. The biological half life of mercury in humans is about 70 days. The neuropathological manifestations of mercury poisoning include cellular degeneration of the cerebellum, basal ganglia, hypothalamus, midbrain and cerebral cortex. Methyl mercury, and other mercurial compounds, may be especially hazardous to the foetus because of the tendency to cross the placenta and become concentrated in foetal blood. Probably the maximum safe level of methyl mercury for pregnant females is 30 micrograms per day.

Clinical features

ACUTE. With acute mercury poisoning pain occurs in the ear, throat and larynx. Abdominal cramps with nausea and vomiting develop with 15 minutes.

Mercury is concentrated in the kidneys, where it damages the tubules. This produces an increased urine flow within the first 2 to 3 hours, but then proceeds to total cessation of urine formation. The combination of vomiting, dehydration and tubular damage in the kidneys leads to renal failure and uraemia, the usual cause of death.

Mercury is also excreted in the colon and produces severe enteritis with bloody diarrhoea and pain.

SUB ACUTE. Gradual development of renal failure (oliguria and anuria).

CHRONIC POISONING. The following manifestations may be noted:

1. Salivation, sore mouth, diarrhoea, etc.
2. Numbness in periphery of legs and arms, progressively extending centrally to include the tongue and lips. Visual fields may constrict.
3. Weakness of the muscles, with tremors, jerking, rigidity, etc. In late cases the muscles become wasted.
4. Irritability, agitation, moodiness, depression and sometimes overactivity.
5. Insomnia, confusion, delirium and headaches.
6. Incoordination, Parkinsonian tremor and other extrapyramidal movements, vertigo and disturbances of gait.
7. Difficulty with speech, swallowing, vision and hearing.
8. Neurological evidence of damage to cerebellum, cerebrum, extrapyramidal and midbrain areas.
9. Death may be due to neurological involvement, starvation or secondary infections. The biological significance of small concentrations of mercury are not known, however it has been suggested that general vitality and reproductive capacity may be affected.

MEDICAL TREATMENT

1. Binding of the mercury by the use of parenteral dimercaprol (BAL) or penicillamine is recommended. The latter is effective for both inorganic and phenyl compounds.
2. Symptomatic treatment along customary medical lines for the clinical manifestations.
3. Neurological damage may be permanent.

Prevention

1. Elect only local, regional and national governments which have forward planning and constructive policies on controlling environmental pollution.
2. Regular sampling and chemical analysis of fish from waterways.
3. Rigid control over the release of industrial waste effluents into the sea.

SHARK AND RAY POISONING

Other name   ◆ Elasmobranch Poisoning

Animals involved ◆ *Carcharhinus melanopterus* (Black-tip Reef Shark), *Galeocerdo cuvieri* (Tiger Shark), *Prionace glauca* (Blue Shark, Great Blue Shark, Blue Whaler), *Heptranchias perlo* (Seven-gilled Shark), *Carcharodon carcharias* (White Shark, White Pointer), *Sphyrna zygaena* (Hammerhead), *Aetobatus narinari* (Spotted Duck-bill Ray, Spotted Eagle Ray), and other sharks or rays, particularly in the tropic and temperate zones. A similar syndrome may result from eating the vitamin A enriched livers of other fish, especially large ones such as tuna and sea bass. See later.

The toxin in this case is thought to be a parasympathomimetic substance. The ingestion of livers from tropical sharks, and from an arctic shark, is the commonest cause of this poisoning. The gonads are also toxic, but the musculature is less so and usually causes only a gastrointestinal upset. The symptoms may be aggravated if the victim exercises. Cooking does not destroy the poison, although it does appear soluble in water. Ciguatera poisoning and hypervitaminosis A may also be acquired from eating sharks. Some fishermen develop a shark allergy due to contact with sharks.

Clinical features

There is usually a latent period of 20 minutes or more after ingestion of the flesh. Severe poisonings present more rapidly than minor ones. The following features may be present:

1. Anorexia, nausea, vomiting, abdominal pain and diarrhoea.
2. Headaches, malaise, prostration.
3. Joint pains.
4. Rapid thready pulse.
5. Numbness and tingling around the mouth with burning sensations of the tongue, throat and oesophagus.
6. Skin is itchy and may peel off.
7. Neurological and neuromuscular symptoms may develop, with weakness, incoordination, ataxia, visual disturbances, muscle cramps, lockjaw, paralysis, etc.
8. Respiratory distress including cyanosis or cessation of breathing.
9. Delirium, coma and death may result.
10. Complete recovery may require 5-20 days.

First aid. See page 193.

Medical treatment. See page 193.

Prevention

1. In survival situations, feed a small portion of the flesh or liver to a small test animal.
2. Thorough washing then drying of the flesh over a considerable time.
3. Repeated washing of the flesh, with disposal of the effluent water each time.

TURTLE AND TORTOISE POISONING

Animals involved   ◆   *Caretta caretta* (Loggerhead Turtle), *Eretmochelys imbricata* (Hawksbill Turtle), *Chelonia mydas* (Green Turtle), *Dermochelys coriacea* (Leatherback Turtle), *Pelochelys bibronia* (Soft Shell Turtle).

The marine species of *Chelonia* are termed turtles and the freshwater or land species are called tortoises. Both have been used as food, and some of those in the central Pacific waters weigh over 200 kg. One would have thought that the unpleasant consequences of ingestion would have made them obsolete as foodstuff, but this animal is still consumed by ships crews, and the illness is particularly reported amongst islanders around the Malay Archipelago and New Guinea.

There is no way of determining whether a turtle is poisonous except by trial and error on humans or animals. Some authors believe the poison to be similar or identical to ciguatera. Autopsy findings include hepatocellular damage, to the extent of acute yellow atrophy of the liver, necrosis of the kidney, haemorrhages and ulceration of the bowel.

Clinical features

Symptoms commence a few hours to several days after ingestion of the turtle, they include anorexia, nausea, vomiting, abdominal pain and diarrhoea in many cases; abnormal sensation around the lips, mouth, tongue, throat, etc., may extend to include dryness or increased salivation and difficulty in swallowing, mouth ulcers and inflammation may supervene and become extensive—lasting for weeks or months before healing is completed.

Other symptoms include weakness, sweating, pallor, vertigo, headache; a generalised red itchy rash may later peel; difficulty in breathing or tightness in the chest, may extend to severe respiratory distress, central cyanosis (bluish tinge to lips) and death.

Liver damage may result in jaundice, liver enlargement and tenderness, coma and death.

Other manifestations may mimic ciguatera poisoning (page 194).

Mortality rate is over 25% (this may reflect the remoteness from medical attention).

Renal failure may result in a decreased urinary output and then the development of uraemia over the next few days.

First aid. See page 193.

Medical treatment. See Ciguatera, pages 193, 201.

Monitor renal and hepatic damage, and treat as indicated.

VITAMIN A (LIVER) POISONING

Other name	◆	Hypervitaminosis A
Animals involved	◆	Polar Bear, Seal, Dolphin, Whale, Arctic Fox, Husky, Fish.

The validity of this clinical entity is questioned by some workers. Others claim that it is also seen with ingestion of fish and shark livers, scombroid (tuna and mackerel), serranid (sea bass and groper) and sparid (snapper).

Vitamin A originates in marine algae and passes up the food chain to reach its greatest concentrations in the large carnivorous animals.

This disorder is due to the over ingestion of vitamin A in amounts of 1,000,000 i.u.. At an estimated concentration of 12,000-14,000 i.u./g in bearded seal liver, it is believed that eating 80 g (or 40 g of polar bear liver) can cause this illness, an amount easily exceeded in one meal. Some whales have also been incriminated. Seal livers can be obtained in temperate and cold climates, and they are said to be more toxic in summer than in winter months. The symptoms and signs are reminiscent of arsenic poisoning, and this disorder should always be considered in the differential diagnosis.

Trichinosis has also been reported from eating the flesh of seals, polar bears, white whales and walruses.

Clinical features

The symptoms may occur up to seven days after ingestion of a single dose of vitamin A, but subclinical manifestations from multiple ingestions may lead to delayed hypervitaminosis A.

General symptoms develop within hours and may include headache, drowsiness, malaise, weakness, nausea, vomiting and abdominal pain.

Central nervous system involvement may result in epileptic convulsions, a confusional state, changes of sensation, weakness and paralysis, difficulty in speech and swallowing, blurred or double vision, and signs of raised intracranial pressure including papilloedema, increased reflexes, extensor plantar responses, etc. Peripheral neuritis produces numbness, tingling and weakness of the limbs.

Skin changes may be seen within 24 hours and include excessive perspiration and angular breaks in the skin at the corner of the mouth. Facial swelling has been described. Increased pigmentation and gross peeling of skin is widespread but especially on palms and soles.

In subacute cases, X-ray of bones may show periosteal new bone formation and clinically there may be painful or tender swellings on the bone.

The manifestations of an acute attack may last from a few days to many weeks, and the poisoning has caused death and disability to Antarctic explorers. Serum vitamin A is elevated, in excess of 500 micrograms % (normal = 50-100).

First aid

1. Not applicable. The vitamin A has been absorbed by the time clinical manifestations appear.
2. Enlist medical aid.
3. Rest and reassurance.
4. Stop ingestion of vitamin A foodstuffs.

MEDICAL TREATMENT

1. As above.
2. Treatment as for any other case of raised intracranial pressure and neurological syndromes.
3. Maintenance of fluid balance and electrolyte state, in those cases with vomiting or diarrhoea, along general medical lines.
4. Investigations include E.E.G.s, serial serum vitamin A estimations, X-ray of bones etc.

Prevention

Do not eat livers from the above animals.

Appendices

<u>NOTES</u>

APPENDIX I

Basic Cardiopulmonary Resuscitation

BASIC LIFE SUPPORT

Basic life support (basic cardiopulmonary resuscitation, or C.P.R.) prevents death by supporting the respiratory and cardiac systems when these cease to function. The object is to provide oxygen to the brain, heart and other vital organs until appropriate definitive medical treatment (advanced life support) can replace or restore normal respiratory and cardiovascular function.

When breathing ceases (primary respiratory arrest) the heart can continue to pump blood for several minutes, and the existing oxygen in the lungs and blood will still circulate to the brain and other organs. Respiratory arrest can be due to problems within the lungs, in the muscles needed for breathing, in the nerve supply to these muscles, or in the part of the brain that controls breathing. This may result from drowning, marine venoms or poisons, and is treated by artificial respiration, mainly mouth-to-mouth respiration.

When the heart stops beating (primary cardiac arrest) oxygen is not circulated and the oxygen stored in the vital organs is depleted within a few seconds. Cardiac arrest can be due to disruption of the cardiac muscle contraction, the rhythm of heart contraction, the nerve supply, or the areas of the brain which controls heart activity. It may result from lack of oxygen (with respiratory arrest), marine venoms or poisons. It is treated by external cardiac compression.

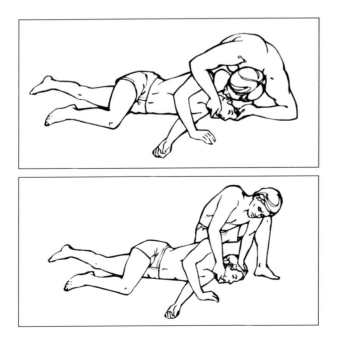

THE A.B.C. OF BASIC CARDIOPULMONARY RESUSCITATION TECHNIQUES

A IS FOR AIRWAY

An effective airway must be established as soon as possible. Not a second must be lost.
1. Quickly examine the patient's mouth and throat, cleaning it out with fingers or cloth.
2. Roll him on to his back and tilt the head backwards by applying firm backward pressure with the palm on the forehand, using the fingers of the other hand under the lower jaw near the chin.
3. Lift the jaw forward, bringing the lower teeth in line with the upper teeth. This will pull the relaxed tongue away from the back of the throat. Sometimes this may be facilitated by a pad of clothing or sand placed under the shoulders.

B IS FOR BREATHING

1. Kneel or lie at the side of the patient's head.
2. With one hand block off the nostrils with the forefinger and thumb, the wrist pressing on the patient's forehead, and place the other hand, palm uppermost under the neck, to maintain a backward tilt of the head.
3. Inhale and fit your lips around the patient's mouth to make an airtight seal, then breathe into him. At the same time look to see if the patient's chest rises. If it does not rise then the airway is not yet cleared. With adults breathe fully; with children breathe shallow and gently.
4. Remove your lips from the patient and inspect his chest, allowing him to exhale. This will be done without assistance.
5. Repeat this cycle rapidly, fully inflating the patient's chest six times, then settle down to a rate of 12 breaths per minute (breathing at five seconds intervals).

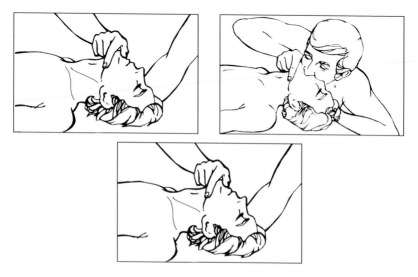

Because of the remote possibility of transmission of infection from the victim to the rescuer (or perhaps in the opposite direction in litigation orientated societies) it may be warranted to use one of the artificial airways to ventilate the victim. The AIDS scare has given greater respectability to this technique, but it has other advantages such as holding the tongue away from the airway.

C IS FOR CIRCULATION

If the heart has stopped beating, there will be no pulse felt at wrist, over the heart or between the "Adam's apple" and neck muscles; the patient will have enlarged pupils which do not react to light; there will be no improvement in colour (bluish) even after artificial respiration has been started. In these circumstances external cardiac massage must be performed immediately, alongside mouth-to-mouth respiration.

1. Place the patient on his back on a hard surface—not a bed or couch.
2. Take a position at his right side near the chest and place the heel of your left hand on the lower half of his breast bone (sternum) with the middle finger across the chest in line with the nipples. In this position it will be found that a ridge across the lower third of the breast bone fits into the groove between the base of the thumb and the base of the hand.
3. Place the other hand over the first, keeping your arms straight with your shoulders directly above the patient, use your own weight to depress the casualty's breast bone 4 to 5 cm in adults. Use one hand and depress 2 to 3 cm for a child; use two fingers depress 1 to 2 cm for an infant. Use a slow bouncing motion producing 80-100 compressions per minute.
4. Mouth to mouth respiration and external cardiac massage may be carried out by two operators—one breath to five heart beats, or by one operator—two breaths to 15 heart beats.

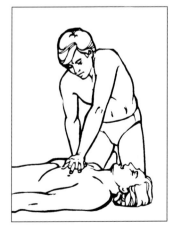 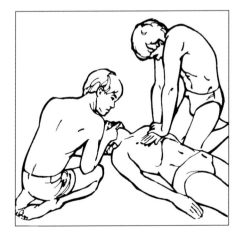

Positioning the Patient

For basic C.P.R to be effective the victim must be lying on his back on a firm flat surface. Even correctly performed external cardiac compression will produce inadequate blood flow to the brain if the head is positioned higher than the chest.

Moving the Patient

The victim should not be moved until effective C.P.R. has been started and the victim has a spontaneous pulse, and unless C.P.R. can be performed without interruption during transit.

When to Stop C.P.R.

In cases of drowning or hypothermia, spectacular successes have be achieved long after C.P.R. would have been considered ineffectual under other circumstances, consequently resuscitation should be more prolonged and enthusiastic.

　　The other feature of hypothermia, when the subject has spent a long time in the water, is that many manipulations and movements are likely to cause cardiac arrest. Nevertheless, when these activities are urgently indicated, they should not be withheld.

ADVANCED LIFE SUPPORT (CARDIOPULMONARY RESUSCITATION)

Artificial Ventilation

Respirations must be maintained. If respiration is shallow, then assisted intermittent positive pressure may be all that is needed. In more severe degrees of respiratory paralysis it would seem prudent to completely control the respirations, with the use of an endotracheal tube and a mechanical ventilator. The type of ventilation depends on the monitoring of serial arterial oxygen, carbon dioxide and pH measurements.

　　A high $PaCO_2$, in excess of 45 mm Hg, may indicate the failure of ventilation because of problems in the airway, muscular activity or neurological dysfunction. The airway must be checked, supplementary inspiratory oxygen should be used, and if this proves to be inadequate, then assisted ventilation or intermittent mandatory ventilation is indicated. If this is insufficient then intermittent positive pressure ventilation is required. In the extreme case this can be used with expiratory retardation to minimise the airway's resistance.

　　If there is a failure of oxygenation, then the arterial oxygen level is usually less than 100mm Hg even with an inspiratory oxygen of 50%. Under these circumstances one must use a higher oxygen inflow, between 50 and 100%—at least for the first few hours. The airway pressure at the end of exhalation can be increased to 5 to 20 cm H_2O.

　　If spontaneous breathing is inadequate to produce a return of normal arterial oxygen levels then continuous positive airway pressure may be required. If that proves inadequate then intermittent mandatory ventilation may be applied, followed by intermittent positive pressure ventilation without positive end expiratory pressure (PEEP).

Positive end expiratory pressure (PEEP) may be required, especially in the case of drowning or aspiration.

Endotracheal Intubation

An endotracheal tube can protect the airway, isolate it from the effects of regurgitation and aspiration, ensure that it is kept patent and facilitate ventilation, oxygenation and suction.

Because vomiting is a common accompaniment of both marine animal venoms and poisons, it is especially important to protect the airway. In the unconscious patient, especially one who has had some respiratory problems, endotracheal intubation is the ideal.

During basic C.P.R. high pharyngeal pressures are often produced which can cause gas passage to the stomach. This can produce regurgitation and aspiration. Thus the trachea should be intubated as soon as possible, but only after adequate preoxygenation and without interrupting cardiac compressions if these are required, for more than 15 seconds at a time.

In the conscious patient endotracheal intubation is indicated when there is inadequate spontaneous clearing of the airways, suspected or potential aspiration, the loss of laryngeal reflexes or the need for prolonged mechanical ventilation.

In the unconscious patient endotracheal intubation is the definitive means of emergency airway control. It is indicated in most comatose patients unless the upper airway reflexes are intact and the coma is expected to be brief in duration and the patient is attended continuously throughout. As a guide, the patient who tolerates an intubation attempt, needs an endotracheal tube.

In many of the marine toxins and poisons there is already a paralysing effect on the respiratory muscles and therefore further relaxation may not be needed to intubate the patient. In most of these venoms and poisons, the respiratory paralysis precedes the significant cardiac effects, and therefore the importance of maintaining ventilation will often prevent the subsequent cardiac complications.

The endotracheal tube, with the improved cuffs and adequate attention, should be satisfactory for more than a week, thereby removing the need for tracheotomy in most marine injury cases.

Gastric Intubation

The insertion of a nasogastric tube, is often of value. In the conscious patient, gastric intubation usually presents very little difficulty if the patient can assist by swallowing.

It is not advisable to attempt gastric intubation if the patient is in coma, prior to the airway being secured with the cuffed endotracheal tube, since the gastric tube can produce vomiting and therefore aspiration.

A large bore tube is usually used if gastric lavage is required, as in the case of fish food poisonings (see page 193).

General

Where there is a possibility of consciousness persisting, despite the absence of skeletal or respiratory movement, and especially with mechanical ventilation, the repeated administration of minor tranquillisers e.g., diazapam 5 mg i.v. would seem humane.

Maintenance of fluid balance could best be performed by intravenous infusions, such as Hartmann's solution and dextrose-saline with or without potassium supplementation—as indicated by serial estimations of the serum electrolytes, together with urine output and specific gravity. It is for this reason that an indwelling urinary catheter is necessary to ensure an adequate urine flow.

Fluid and electrolyte imbalance must be corrected.

In the unconscious hypothermic patient, endotracheal intubation to prevent aspiration should be performed with assisted ventilation to provide effective ventilation and warmed humidified oxygen. In such cases prior ventilation with l00% oxygen may lessen the likelihood of precipitating ventricular fibrillation.

Guidelines for Conscious or Unconscious Critically Ill Patients

Cardiac Investigation and Support

1. Prevent hypoperfusion; restore blood volume and pressure.
2. Central venous and arterial pressure monitoring may be required.
3. Catheterise, monitor and maintain hourly urinary output.
4. Monitor ECG, prevent and control dysrhythmias.

Respiratory Investigation and Support

1. Maintain and optimise arterial PO_2, PCO_2, pH, BE. Start with FIO_2 90-100%; reduce to 50% as soon as possible.
2. Use intermittent positive pressure ventilation (IPPV) and positive end expiratory pressure (PEEP). PEEP, at 5 cm H_2O, may prevent airways closure, but may be increased if needed to achieve normal arterial oxygen levels, with 50% oxygen inhalation.
3. Wean from IPPV, to intermittent mandatory ventilation and spontaneous breathing.
4. Endotracheal tube and cuff, aseptic airway and catheter care is required.
5. Chest X-ray; sputum examination.
6. Noninvasive (pulse) oximetry measures the haemoglobin oxygen saturation, and therefore is a very simple way of monitoring this parameter.

General Investigations and Support

1. Aseptic airway and catheter care.
2. Monitor and restore body temperature.
3. Skin and eye care, as for all unconscious patients.
4. Naso-gastric tube for lavage (see page 237) and suction may be indicated.
5. Monitor and maintain fluid and electrolyte balance.

APPENDIX II

Tourniquets, Ligatures, and Pressure Bandages

Tourniquets are used to stop the arterial blood flow into the limbs. They are therefore tightly fitting and the venous blood flow out of the limb is also stopped. Tourniquets are used to stop haemorrhage from wounds such as shark attacks. They are painful.

Ligatures (venous tourniquets) are used to reduce the venous blood and some lymph flow from the limbs, but are not tight enough to impede the arterial blood flow. They may be used to reduce the speed of venom reaching the general systemic circulation, and also encourage bleeding from the site. They may delay the effects of the venom while action is being taken to obtain medical assistance. It is also likely that the intelligent use of ligatures may result in a more gradual liberation of venom, which is then able to be tolerated by the victim. The limb must be immobilised.

Pressure bandages, with immobilisation, have superseded ligatures in the treatment of most envenomations. The pressure, over a wide area where the venom has infiltrated, probably compresses the lymphatic drainage vessels. This reduces or blocks the venom from reaching the blood stream, until the pressure is removed.

Any long, narrow, flexible piece of material such as a necktie or strong handkerchief may be used for a tourniquet or ligature. Pressure can be applied by wide straps, clothing, air splints and other materials.

Tourniquets (arterial)

Tourniquets are used to stop haemorrhage from a limb, if other methods such as application of pressure are not adequate.

1. Lie the patient down with the limb elevated. Tie a piece of material around the limb, over clothing or padding to avoid pinching the skin.
2. The tourniquet should be placed around the upper part of the limb between the wound and the body. A stick or rod is then passed through the knot.
3. The stick is used as a lever and turned around to tighten the tourniquet until the bleeding stops, after which no further tightening is necessary.
4. Tie a second piece of material around the limb nearby to secure the end of the stick to prevent it further unwinding.
5. Label the patient clearly and prominently, stating the time the tourniquet was applied.
6. The tourniquet must be loosened after 20 minutes. If it is necessary to reapply the tourniquet, it must be loosened every 20 minutes thereafter. If bleeding has stopped after loosening the tourniquet it is probably because of blood clotting around the wound; leave the tourniquet loosely in place ready to be tightened if the need should arise.
7. The injured limb and tourniquet should be left uncovered and kept under continuous observation for recurrence of bleeding. The injured limb may benefit from being exposed to the cold.

Dangers in the use of a tourniquet

There are grave dangers in the use of tourniquets, and they should only be applied as a lifesaving measure—for example, to stop bleeding of a severed main artery or when a limb has been torn off.

The limb beyond the tourniquet is deprived of its blood supply and if the tourniquet is left on too long, the limb will become gangrenous and amputation will then be unavoidable.

Tourniquets can cause damage to underlying tissues such as nerves resulting in impaired sensation of touch, numbness and tingling and paralysis.

Tourniquets are always painful, and local bruising is inevitable. These may both contribute towards the degree of shock.

If the tourniquet is applied too loosely it will act as a ligature and stop the venous blood flow from the limb back to the heart. Arterial blood will still be flowing and because of the ligature effect, blood loss will be increased.

Ligatures (venous tourniquets)

Ligatures are used to reduce the venous blood returning to the heart. They are used in the event of a venomous bite or sting to delay the absorption and transport of the venom into the systemic circulation, and to some extent to assist the removal of venom, by promoting bleeding. A cut across the puncture wound parallel to the long axis of the limb may be of value to facilitate this.

A ligature is of similar material to a tourniquet and is tied tightly around the limb—but not tight enough to cause pain or obliterate the pulse below it. If the ligature is applied almost immediately after the victim has been bitten or stung, it should be placed a few centimetres above the wound. If there has been delay it may be applied to the upper part of the limb.

When a ligature has been applied, check that a pulse can be felt at the wrist or ankle, especially in lightly built people and children. The patient should be made to lie down and all unnecessary movement avoided. The affected limb should be placed in a dependent position (low). In the case of painful stings, immersion of the area in hot water (up to 45 degrees Centigrade) or application of local heat by other means may be beneficial. Reassure the patient and treat for shock. The ligature should be released for 30 seconds every 10-20 minutes and completely discarded after 2 hours. Enlist medical help.

Immobilisation of the limb is essential if the ligature is to be of value.

Pressure bandage and/or pressure pad, with immobilisation

Recent work has been performed at the Commonwealth Serum Laboratories in Australia, and this has a direct bearing on the value of ligatures, tourniquets and other forms of first aid treatment against injected venoms. A radio immuno-assay was developed which could determine the quantity of venom present in the plasma of animals which were injected with this venom. The plasma level was correlated with the symptoms and signs of envenomation, and both these were related to the various first aid manoeuvres.

The application of a broad firm bandage around the bitten area and the adjoining part of the limb, especially the proximal limb, appear to have very sig-

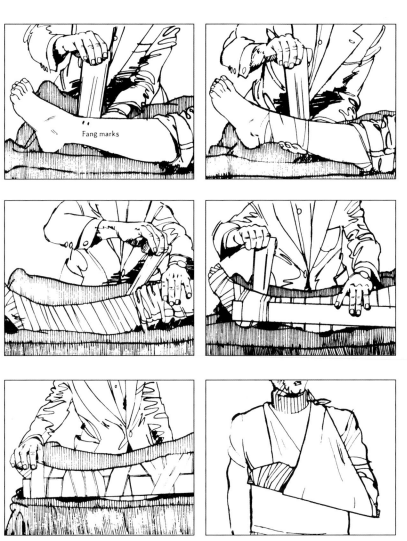

Pressure bandage immobilisation technique. Courtesy of Commonwealth Serum Laboratories, Melbourne

nificant effects both in the prevention of venom being absorbed, delaying its absorption and reducing its clinical effect. The bandage should be as tight as one would bind a sprained ankle (this was estimated at about 50 mmHg). The delay would also allow antivenom to be used when it eventually became available.

After applying the pressure bandage to as much of the limb as possible, it can be supported by other strips of clothing or towels. The limb must be kept as still as possible, preferably bound to some type of splint to ensure that there is no limb movement. Transport should then be brought to the patient, who should not be made to walk or move actively.

The Commonwealth Serum Laboratories' results suggested that the application of a firm crepe bandage (or a localised pressure pad) and splint, is an excellent method of retarding the absorption of venom. The measure seems as effective as an arterial tourniquet in the short term, but far more practical because of the comfort, unlikelihood of ischaemia or gangrene, and the extended duration over which the first aid measure could be applied.

Because there is a delay in the venom absorption, the pressure bandage/immobilisation technique should also be applied even in severely envenomated patients who are seen late, and it should be reapplied if the patient becomes critically ill on removal of the bandage. Application of the bandage allows time for neutralisation of the venom by antivenom, and may also reduce the antivenom requirement.

In comparing the efficiency of pressure bandage to the ligature, it is now believed that the pressure bandage is more effective, but only if combined with immobilisation of the area.

APPENDIX III

Anaesthesia

The principle methods of obtaining effective relief of pain induced by marine animals are:
1. Topical anaesthesia (contact).
2. Local infiltration (injection into tissues).
3. Regional block (injection around nerves).
4. General anaesthesia.

The easier and safer techniques of topical anaesthesia and local infiltration should be employed first, and are often all that is required. Regional block and general anaesthesia require some knowledge and expertise in the field of anaesthesia and therefore should only be undertaken where the above measures are inadequate.

Drugs

There is a wide range of local anaesthetic drugs and preparations available. All may produce central nervous system toxicity (convulsions) if injected intravascularly or if an overdose is administered. Except perhaps in regional block, plain solutions (i.e. containing no adrenaline) should be used, as in many fish stings there are already ischaemic effects from the venom.

Lignocaine (Lidocaine in U.S.A., trade name "Xylocaine"). is the most widely available drug and may be used for topical, infiltration or regional anaesthesia. It has a rapid onset of action and a duration of approximately 60-120 minutes. A 0.5% solution is suitable for infiltration, 1.0-1.5% for regional block. Creams, ointments and jelly preparations usually contain about 4-5% weight for weight. Aerosols deliver approximately 10 mg per puff.

Bupivacaine (trade name "Marcain") is suitable for infiltration (0.25%) or regional block (0.25-0.5%) anaesthesia, because of its much longer duration of action (up to 12 hours for brachial block), It is available in 0.25 and 0.5% solutions with or without adrenaline.

Other Agents. Mepivacaine and prilocaine may be used in similar doses to lignocaine. Cocaine in 4% solution is suitable for stings to the eye where corneal anaesthesia is needed. Care must be taken not to use any substance that will promote further nematocyst discharge.

Administration

Topical Application. Local anaesthetic preparations may be applied to areas permitting penetration of the agent. Such areas are mucous meembranes, open wounds, or areas in which skin has been damaged. Local anaesthetics will not readily penetrate intact skin. Recently a eutectic mixture of local anaesthetic (EMLA) has been made available, and may be of value in marine stings. Local anaesthetics may be useful when superficial skin damage has occurred, for example, with hydroids, Portuguese man-o'-war or jimble.

Local Infiltration. This involves the direct injection of the anaesthetic agent into the tissues involved. Conventional techniques include adequate asepsis, injection of the solution from healthy tissues towards injured tissues, avoidance of significant intravascular injection by keeping the needle moving, and complete encircling of the lesion by the agent. This method is especially valuable with fish spine injuries. Often the injection is made directly into the wound as this is numb and so less painful. Adrenaline should not be added in the treatment of marine stings, as most are already vasoconstrictive in their effect.

Regional Block. This requires a more specialised knowledge of local anaesthesia and neuroanatomy. Examples of blocks that may be useful for marine animal injuries include: brachial plexus block, intercostal nerve block, supra and infraorbital nerve block, femoral and/or sciatic nerve block, lumbar or caudal epidural block, ankle block.

Regional nerve block of a limb by retrograde intravenous perfusion, although technically easier, is probably contra-indicated because it requires emptying of veins draining venom from the affected area. Also pain relief is maintained only as long as the constricting tourniquet remains in place.

General Anaesthesia. One anaesthetic agent, ketamine ("Ketalar") induces a state of dissociative anaesthesia in which essential reflexes are maintained and the cardiovascular system is stimulated instead of depressed. It is of most used in cases involving children, and gives good analgesia over a reasonable time. Intubation is unnecessary unless the respirations are already depressed by the marine toxin. The drug may be given by i.v. injection (1-2 mg/kg) of by i.m. injection (5-10 mg/kg). Repeated injections appear to be non-accumulative.

This drug is best avoided in adults because severe hallucinations sometimes accompany its use. In children with severe pain, however, it may prove to be quite a valuable asset to the attending physician. It also may prove more practical than complete general anaesthesia with muscle relaxants and artificial respiration, when the medical practitioner is compelled to initiate treatment in conditions considerably less than ideal. Diazepam will reduce the hallucination effects.

General anaesthetic techniques with endotracheal intubation and controlled respiration are needed for seriously injured patients requiring extensive surgical techniques (shark attack), or those in extreme agony (box jelly fish sting), or those who have lost control over vital functions such as respiration (blue-ringed octopus, sea snake, cone shell, tetrodotoxin and paralytic shellfish poisoning). All the usual precautions of intensive care regimes should be employed. These include attention to tracheo-bronchial toilet, pressure areas, fluid balance and physiological monitoring. A knowledge of the natural history of the disease allows one to predict the likely duration of anaesthesia required.

APPENDIX IV

Allergy and Anaphylaxis

Allergies associated with the eating of shellfish are widespread and well recognised. Allergic responses can also develop from eating other fish foods, touching, or even smelling fish and fish products. In susceptible individuals they can supervene and seriously complicate any marine animal injury or its treatment.

Allergies, apparently to fish, may be based on associated animals or parasites, preparation methods, contamination (see scrombroid , page 208) or condiments. For example, in Japan one group of patients, thought to be allergic to mackerel, were demonstrated to be allergic not to the fish but to the larvae of parasitic worms, *Anisakis,* that infested it.

Acute Anaphylaxis is a severe, sometimes fatal allergic reaction to an agent to which the subject is hypersensitive. In the most extreme cases, it develops within seconds or minutes of exposure, and death may follow within 10 minutes. Patients frequently experience an aura of mild generalised itchiness, slight chest tightness, tingling of the lips, a tickle in the throat, palate or around the neck, agitation or restlessness.

Allergy is a systemic reaction affecting several target organ systems. The skin is frequently involved and the patient complains of itching, erythema or urticarial reactions. Bronchospasm is common and is usually present in fatal cases. The patient may also complain of cough, stridor, dyspnoea, tightness of the chest and pain, and may be cyanosed from respiratory obstruction as well as bronchospasm. The gastrointestinal tract is involved with cramps, diarrhoea and sometimes vomiting. Women may complain of lower abdominal pain due to uterine cramps. Vascular collapse is a prominent component of this syndrome and may occur alone, without involvement of other systems.

The syndrome may resolve within a few minutes of treatment or may persist for many hours despite treatment. Sometimes symptoms recur about 4-6 hours after apparent resolution of the syndrome, particularly when adrenaline is used as the sole form of treatment. Most deaths outside hospital occur within minutes of exposure but even with treatment the patient may die within the first 2 hours. The longer treatment is delayed, the more refractory becomes the syndrome.

Allergy is due to the release of vaso-active mediators from mast cells which act on many organs, causing contraction of smooth muscle, peripheral vasodilatation and increased capillary permeability. In the typical allergy response, the IgE type 1 hypersensitivity causes chemicals from mast cells which act upon blood vessels and end organs, affecting the involuntary muscle, dilating the vessels and increasing the loss of fluid from the vessels. Management of anaphylaxis demands urgent measures.

Hives (urticaria) is by far the most common allergic reaction, asthma is less common, and serious anaphylaxis relatively uncommon.

In a number of cases both local and general allergies have developed following fish stings. These can be severe, and confusing to the therapist. One incident, which caused a great deal of discomfort, was the injury which was sustained to a fisherman who was stung by the jellyfish Cyanea. The wound rapidly cleared up, but the skin reaction was moderately severe and caused great discomfort for many years whenever he exposed himself to the same ocean conditions at the same time of the year. Local remedies were not particularly efficacious, however, it was found that the reaction could be aborted if steroids were taken very early, for a few days. Old fishermen's stories of wounds recurring at the same time each year for seven years can be explained by this mechanism.

Another case developed severe and generalised dermal lesions approximately one week after being bitten by a blue-ringed octopus, even though he recovered from the initial envenomation.

Many people involved in the fish industry are aware of the allergy reactions after touching fish. It is not so well known, however, that some people develop allergies to the chemical compounds produced during the cooking of fish. In these cases, there will often be an asthmatic type reaction. An abalone diver, with access to unlimited quantities of abalone, and married to a gourmet abalone cook, develops acute asthma whenever he enters the kitchen while abalone is being cooked..

Allergy type responses can also be produced is by eating contaminated fish containing a histamine-like substance (see Scombroid Poisoning). In this case the signs and symptoms may be even more rapidly induced, and the patient having had no previous contact with the foreign protein.

Clinical features

In milder cases of allergy, only the skin may be involved with the development of red, weal-like itchy patches. This is equivalent to hives.

Especially when protein is ingested, there is evidence of abdominal cramps, diarrhoea and sometimes vomiting. Women may complain of low abdominal pain associated with spasms of the uterine muscle.

If the lungs are affected causing increased secretion from the airways and bronchospasm, the patient may develop severe breathlessness, stridor, tightness or pain in the chest, and may have evidence of respiratory obstruction, such as cyanosis.

In the most severe form—"acute anaphylaxis"—the main syndrome develops because the blood vessels are affected, causing a drop in blood pressure, rapid pulse, loss of consciousness, especially when standing, and possibly death. About 40 deaths per year are recorded from this disorder in the U.S.A.

In infants there is a tendency to produce severe respiratory and anaphylaxis symptoms. Acute collapse, syncope, respiratory depression, a stunned drowsy appearance or abdominal distension, with or without bile-stained vomiting, may be the sole manifestation of anaphylactic reactions. Even the milder cases may appear drowsy with abdominal distension and vomiting.

In children many of the features of anaphylaxis are similar to those seen in adults.

Although the syndrome can resolve within a few hours, it is not uncommon for it to last longer—especially if the skin is affected. The respiratory and anaphylaxis presentations tend to be more acute, shorter lasting and dangerous. Death may occur within 10 minutes of exposure, although any patient who survives more than the first few hours should be reasonably safe—assuming adequate treatment has been given. The longer treatment is delayed, the more difficult the syndrome is to treat.

The anaphylactoid reaction from the scrombroid or saurine poisoning is described on page 208.

First aid

1. Use soothing lotions such as calamine lotion on skin lesions.
2. Lay the patient down and relieve symptoms where possible.
3. Give resuscitation when needed (Appendix I)
4. Stop administration of, or exposure to, the causal agent.
5. Some medications used for asthma or hives may be employed, if skilled medical attention is not available. See page 209.

MEDICAL TREATMENT

Administer first aid.

Hives. Antihistamines, orally or systemically, may be of value.

Asthma. Administer adrenaline (epinephrine) as described below. Other anti-asthma medications may be of value, such as salbutamol (e.g., Ventolin) or the steroid sprays (e.g., Becotide), as these may relieve the asthma and also may be absorbed. See page 210.

Anaphylaxis. To restore ventilation and circulation:

1. Consider induction of vomiting or gastric lavage if the allergic material has been recently ingested and if there is full consciousness and laryngeal reflex is present
2. Place patient in recumbent position, elevate lower extremities.
3. Clear airway.
4. Give adrenalin 1/1000, 0.3 to 0.5 ml intramuscularly for adults or 0.01 ml/kg for children. Repeat if necessary in five minutes.
5. Establish intravenous line. Give colloid solution to expand blood volume if the patient is in shock, such as 10% SPPS plus 5% dextrose, or large volumes of electrolyte solutions if colloids are unavailable.
6. If there is no response to intramuscular adrenalin, or if peripheral circulation is poor and shock is severe, give adrenalin intravenously in a dose of 5ml 1:10 000 adrenalin or 0.5 ml 1:1000, diluted in 10ml normal saline over ten minutes. In the presence of venous or arterial stasis, intracardiac injection may be necessary, but can be dangerous. Give external cardiac massage if the patient is pulseless.
7. Give oxygen 100%. Assist ventilation (bag and mask, intubation or even tracheostomy as necessary).

continued

8. Give corticosteroids intravenously, for example, hydrocortisone 200 mg. While steroids are not helpful for the immediate acute situation, they may assist in preventing protracted anaphylaxis, or a relapse.
9. Give antihistamines (promethazine 25 mg or diphenhydramine 50 mg intra-muscularly or intravenously).
10. If there is severe bronchospasm administer aerosol bronchodilators and/or aminophylline.

Supportive Treatment

1. Monitor vital signs frequently and maintain patient under medical observation for at least four hours, and preferable twenty-four hours.
2. Give reassurance. Avoid heat, exercise, alcohol.
3. Avoid hypotensive and vasodilating drugs. Vasopressor drugs are rarely indicated, for example, if there has been no response to adequate colloids and adrenalin.

Follow Up Treatment

1. Determine the cause. Provide identification bracelet (Medic Alert), and advice regarding precautions to prevent recurrence.
2. Provide drug protection if exposure is unavoidable, for example, antihistamines or steroids.

Medical First Aid

Outside the hospital the medical practitioner may find great use in the following:

1. Adrenalin 1/1000 for intramuscular injection; corticosteroids and antihistamines for parenteral administration.
2. Facilities for establishing an intravenous line, such as a drip set and intravenous saline.
3. The capacity to perform artificial ventilation and cardiopulmonary resuscitation.
4. Oxygen.

A major centre would have more sophisticated measures available including colloid solutions for intravenous administration, and facilities for cardiopulmonary resuscitation.

Reference: "Management of Anaphylaxis," *Australian Prescriber 1987,* Vol 9, No 2. Scientific and Therapeutic Subcommittee of the Australian College of Allergy.

APPENDIX V

Antivenoms and Advice
from the Commonwealth Serum Laboratory (Australia)

Stonefish antivenom

This antivenom is prepared by hyperimmunizing horses with the venom of the stonefish *Synanceja trachynis*. The hyperimmune serum is refined, concentrated and standardised, and Phenol 0.25% w/v is added as a preservative.

One unit of stonefish antivenom neutralises 0.01 mg. of stonefish venom (1000 units will neutralise 10 mg of venom). On the average, 5-10 mg of venom is contained in each of the 13 dorsal spines of the stonefish.

Indications for Use. Stonefish antivenom neutralises all the toxic effects of stonefish venom and is indicated in all cases of stonefish sting.

The dominant symptom of stonefish sting is agonising and persisting pain. Oedema, which usually develops rapidly after a sting, may become extreme. Abscess formation, necrosis and gangrene have occurred in untreated cases. In addition to the local effects, muscle weakness and paralysis may develop in the affected limb and varying degrees of shock may occur. The systemic effects are due to the presence of potent myotoxins, which act directly on all types of muscle—skeletal, involuntary and cardiac.

Dosage and Administration. The initial dose will depend on the number of visible punctures:

1 or 2 punctures	-	2000 (contents of 1 ampoule),
3 or 4 punctures	-	4000 (contents of 2 ampoules),
5 or 6 punctures	-	6000 (contents of 3 ampoules), and so on.

The antivenom should be given by intravenous infusion. If symptoms develop or persist and the identity of the stonefish is assured, the initial dose should be repeated.

Precautions. The usual precautions in the administration of heterologous antiserum should be observed.

Supportive Therapy. Local infiltration of the wound with emetine hydrochloride (65 mg/ml), lignocaine or potassium permanganate (5%) may help to alleviate pain. Immersion of the limb in hot water has sometimes brought relief when other measures have failed, but care must be taken to ensure that the patient is not scalded.

Mode of Issue. Stonefish antivenom is issued in containers of 2000 units (approximately 2 ml).

Storage. Antivenoms should be stored, protected from light, at 2-8 degrees Centigrade. They must not be frozen.

Reference: Wiener, S., "Stonefish Sting and its Treatment," *Med.J.Aust.*, 2:218-222 (1958).

Box jellyfish antivenom

Box jellyfish antivenom is prepared by hyperimmunising sheep with the venom of the box jellyfish *Chironex fleckeri,* commonly known as the sea wasp. The preparation contained concentrated immunoglobulins which have the power of neutralising the toxins present in the venoms of *Chironex fleckeri* and *Chiropsalmus quadrigatus.* Phenol 0.25% w.v. is added as a preservative.

The injuries inflicted by the box jellyfish, *Chironex fleckeri,* are unmistakable and have been described by Dr J.H. Barnes as follows:

"During the first 15 minutes pain increases in mounting waves, despite removal of the tentacle. The victim may scream and become irrational. Areas of contact are linear and multiple, showing as purple or brown lines often compared to the marks made by a whip. A pattern of transverse bars is usually visible. Whealing is prompt and massive. Oedema, erythema and vesication soon follow, and when these subside (after some ten days), patches of full-thickness necrosis are revealed. Healing is by granulation and cicatrisation, taking a month or more, and leaving permanent scars perhaps with pigment changes."

First aid measures are of the utmost importance if a severely affected victim is to survive.

1. Apply vinegar to any pieces of tentacle adhering to the skin. Do not use any form of alcohol as this will stimulate discharge of nematocysts. Do not attempt to remove tentacle by rubbing with sand, towel or other means until vinegar has been applied to render the stinging capsules inert.
2. If breathing is impaired, apply artificial respiration, mouth-to-mouth, if necessary.

Indications for Use of Antivenom. The administration of antivenom should be regarded as supplementary to first aid measures; it should be given to any victim of suspected sea wasp stinging who, following the application of the above first aid measures, continues to have difficulty in breathing, swallowing or speaking, or continues to be in severe pain.

Early administration will also prevent the severe scarring usually associated with box jellyfish stinging.

As the object of treatment with antivenom is to neutralise the venom as quickly as possible, the antivenom should be injected intravenously, preferably by infusion. A dilution of one in ten is advisable.

If injected directly into a vein, care must be taken to ensure that the antivenom is given slowly.

The risk of serum reactions normally precludes the use of antivenoms by lay persons, but if remote from medical aid and confronted with an emergency situation, intramuscular injection is justifiable. It is important that any lay person provided with antivenom is fully acquainted with the technique of intramuscular injection and the necessary precautions.

Dosage. The contents of one container of box jellyfish antivenom constitutes the initial dose by the intravenous route. The contents of three containers should be given if the intramuscular route is to be used.

Precautions. As the antivenom is a foreign protein which could cause sensitisation, it should not be given for insignificant lesions.

Mode of Issue. Box jellyfish antivenom is supplied in containers of 20,000 units.

Storage. Store, protected from light, at 2-8 degrees Centigrade. Do not freeze.

References

Barnes, J.H. "Observations on Jellyfish Stingings in North Queensland." *Med.J.Aust.,*2:993-999 (1960).

Baxter, E.H. and Lane, W.R. "Recent Investigations on Sea Wasp Stingings in Australia." *Med.J.Aust.,* 1:508 (1970).

Baxter, E.H., Marr, A.G.M. and Lane, W.R. "Sea Wasp *Chironex fleckeri* Toxin—Experimental Immunity." In DeVries, A. and Kochwa, E., eds. *Toxins of Animal and Plant Origin.* London, Gordon and Breach science Publishers Ltd., 1972, pp.941-945.

Baxter, E.J. and Marr, A.G.M. "Sea Wasp Chironex fleckeri Antivenene: Neutralizing Potency Against the Venom of Three Other Jellyfish Species." *Toxicon,* 12:223-229 (1974).

Sutherland S.K."Response to Chironex antivenom." *Med.J.Aust.* 2:653 (1979).

Williamson, J.A., Callanan, V.I. and Hartwick, R.F. "Serious Envenomation by the Northern Australia Box-Jelly Fish *Chironex fleckeri.*" *Med.J.Aust.,* 1:13 (1980).

Hartwick, R., Callanan, J. and Williamson, J. "Disarming the Box-Jelly Fish: Nematocyst Inhibition of *Chironex fleckeri*" *Med.J.Aust.,* 1:15 (1980).

Sea snake antivenom

Sea snake antivenom is a refined preparation of plasma from appropriately immunised horses. It contains concentrated globulins or their derivatives which have the power of specifically neutralising the toxic substances of the venoms of *Enhydrina schistosa* and several other sea snakes. The contents of one ampoule are sufficient to neutralise 10 mg. of *E. schistosa* venom, the average yield per bite. The lethal dose of this venom for an adult has been estimated at 2-3 mg. The neutralising potency of the antivenom for other sea snake venoms is shown in the table.

Neutralising potency of sea snake antivenom for sea snake species.

Sea snake species	mg of venom neutralised by contents of one ampoule
Enhydrina schistosa	10
Aipysurus laevia	13
Astotia stokesii	18
Hydrophis cyanocinctus	59
Hydrophis elegans	57
Hydrophis major	11
Hydrophis nigrocinctus	64
Hydrophis spiralis	130
Hydrophis stricticollis	11
Laticada semifasciata	17
Lapemis hardwickii	102
Microencephalophis gracilis	53

Tu *et al* have reported that this antivenom also neutralised the venoms of Pelamis platurus, Praescutata viperina and Laticauda laticaudata.

Diagnosis of Sea Snake Bite. Fish stings are much more common than sea snake bites, especially among bathers. Differential diagnosis is usually easy since severe local pain follows a fish sting, whereas a sea snake bite is painless.

Indications for Use. Serious envenomation occurs in approximately 25% of humans bitten by sea snakes. As the bite is a defensive act, the dose of venom injected is usually small. Sea snake antivenom is therefore only indicated in the 25% of victims who shows sings of serious envenomation, viz:
1. Generalised muscle aches, pains and stiffness on movement developing within one-half to one hour of the bite.
2. Moderate or severe pain on passive movement of arm, thigh, neck or trunk muscles developing 1-2 hours after the bite.
3. Myoglobinuria becoming evident on inspection of the urine 3-6 hours after the bite. A dusky yellow colour with positive protein and occult blood tests precedes by an hour or so the red-brown colour of myoglobinuria.
4. Rapid collapse and shock after severe envenomation.

If one hour has elapsed since the bite and distinct muscle groups are not painful on passive movement, serious poisoning can be excluded. Clinical trials have shown that the antivenom is successful in severe poisoning even when given 7-8 hours after the bite. It is, therefore, desirable to wait until there is evidence of systemic poisoning before giving the antivenom.

Administration and Dosage. Skin tests for sensitivity are not recommended. Even patients with no known history of allergy should receive parenteral antihistamine and a small dose of adrenalin subcutaneously. The reasons given for this approach is the relatively high incidence of allergic reactions to the horse anti-venom and the relative innocuous nature of the pre-treatment. Both points have been questioned. Steroid use is less contentious, but may not be as effective as adrenalin. Patients with a known history of allergy should also receive steroids. (Author's note: as should those who need large quantities of antivenom.)

If possible the antivenom should be diluted one in ten in saline or Hartmanns solutions prior to slow infusion. The minimum effective dose is contained in one ampoule. In severe poisoning, as shown by ptosis, weakness of external eye muscles, dilation of pupils with sluggish light reaction and leucocytosis exceeding 20,000 cells/mm^3, the contents of 3-4 ampoules should be administered.

Mode of Issue. Sea snake antivenom is supplied in containers of 1000 units. One unit of antivenom neutralises 0.01 mg of E. schistosa venom.

Storage. Antivenoms should be stored, protected from light at 2-8 degrees Centigrade. They must not be frozen.

References

Reid, H.A., "Sea Snake Antivenene: Successful Trial." *Bri.Med.J.,* 2:576-579 (1962).

Baxter E.H. and Gallichio, H.A. "Protection against Sea-Snake Envenomation: Comparative Potency of Four Antivenenes." *Toxicon,* 14: 347-355 (1976).

Tu, A.T. and Ganthavorn, S. "Immunological Properties and Neutralization of Sea-Snake Venoms from South-East Asia." *Amer.J.Trop.Med.Hyg.* 18:151-154 (1969).

Tu, A.T. and Salagranca, E.S. "Immunological Properties and Neutralization of Sea-Snake Venoms (11)," *Amer.J.Trop.Med.Hyg.* 23:135-138 (1974).

Reid, H.A. "Diagnosis, Prognosis and Treatment of Sea-Snake Bite." *Lancet,* 2:399-402 (1961).

APPENDIX VI

Venoms and Toxins

Stingray venom

Stingray venom is a protein (molecular weight greater than 100,000) heat labile, water soluble, and with an IV LD 50 of 28.0 mg/kg body weight. Low concentrations cause electrocardiographic effects of increased PR intervals associated with bradycardia. A first degree atrioventricular block may occur with mild hypotension. Larger doses produce vasoconstriction, second and third degree antrioventricular block and signs of cardiac ischaemia. Most cardiac changes are reversible within 24 hours. Some degree of respiratory depression is noted with greater amounts of venom. This is probably secondary to the neurotoxic effect of the venom on the medullary centres. Convulsions may also occur.

Stonefish venom

Stonefish venom is an unstable protein, with a pH of 6.0, and a molecular weight of 150,000. It produces an intense vasoconstriction, and therefore tends to localise itself. It is destroyed by heat (two minutes at 50 degrees Centigrade) alkalis and acids (pH greater than 9 or less than 4), potassium permanganate and congo red. The toxin is a myotoxin which acts on skeletal, involuntary and cardiac muscles, blocking conduction in these tissues. This results in a muscular paralysis, respiratory depression, peripheral vasodilatation, shock and cardiac arrest. It is also capable of producing cardiac arrhythmias.

Hot vinegar has been proposed as an alternative to hot water to denature the toxin because of its acidic nature. This awaits confirmation.

Other scorpion fish venom

The venom is a water soluble and heat labile polypeptide. It reduces the rate of inactivation of the sodium channel of the axonal membrane and also interferes with the potassium channel. It produces a fall in arterial pressure, an increase and then a decrease in central venous pressure, respiratory depression and abnormalities in electrocardiogram and electroencephalogram tracings.

Physalia toxin

One toxin is termed physalitoxin and is a glycoprotein. This probably has a molecular weight of 240,000 and readily breaks down into smaller glycoproteins. It is denatured by heating to 60 degrees Centigrade for 15 minutes, or by the addition of ether, alcohol or acetone. It causes neurological depression, affecting motor and sensory areas, and also has oedema producing properties. Respiratory depression occurs in envenomated animals, and has been described in human victims.

Chironex toxin

The venom has three different activities. a *haemolytic* component with a molecular weight of approximately 70,000 is present, but has little clinical significance. The *dermatonecrotic* factor produces rapid skin death, and is antigenic in experimental animals. The toxins are specific antigens and cross immunity does not develop to other species.

The effects of the *lethal* component, with a molecular weight of 150,000, causes death with the heart muscle failing to relax and becoming paralysed in contraction. Other effects on the cardiovascular system include an initial rise in arterial pressure which is followed by hypotensive/hypertensive oscillations. This is probably due to interference with vasomotor reflex feedback systems. The hypotensive states are related to bradycardia, cardiac irregularities (especially a delay in atrioventricular conduction) and apnoea, and these oscillate with hypertensive states. The cardiovascular effects are due to cardiotoxicity, baroreceptor stimulation and/or brain stem depression.

Ventricular fibrillation or asystole will precede death. Autopsy will reveal the typical cigar-shaped nematocysts from skin scrapings without staining and skin biopsy shows the penetration of discharged nematocyst threads into the vascular dermis. The degree of inflammatory response increases with the duration between envenomation and death. Immunological titres can be performed on serum to verify the absence of immunological protection, if considered relevant. Cell membrane disruption affecting calcium transfer is more functional than histologically demonstrable by conventional techniques. The cause of death is direct myocardial damage, possibly with neurological induced respiratory failure.

Blue-ringed octopus venom

Analysis of posterior salivary extracts demonstrates a hyaluronidase, to assist rapid spread of the toxin, and cephalotoxins of low molecular weight. One toxin (maculotoxin) has a molecular weight of 319, is more potent than that of any land animal, and is identical to tetrodotoxin and saxitoxin. The effects demonstrated during animal experiments are of a neurotoxin, interfering with the sodium transport along the nerve, blocking the nerve conduction and producing a neuromuscular paralysis. It is not curare-like, and is not influenced by neostigmine and atropine, at least during the acute phase. Hypotension accompanies respiratory depression. If artificial respiration is commenced before marked cyanosis and hypotension has developed, the victim can be saved.

Cone shell venom

The conotoxins are peptides which inhibit successive physiological targets along the neuromuscular pathways. Presynaptic conotoxins prevent calcium entry into the nerve terminal and release acetylcholine. Postsynaptic conotoxins inhibit acetylcholine receptors. Muscle conotoxins inhibit the sodium channels and directly block muscle contraction.

The conotoxins thus interfere with neuromuscular activity, eliciting a sustained muscular contracture and/or abolishing the excitability of muscle fibre (summating with tubocurare, but influenced by eserine), depending on the mixture of toxins. The major effect appears to be directly on skeletal muscular activity.

Sea snake venom

Sea snake venom is mixture of proteins—29 different toxins have been isolated from 9 different sea snakes. A heat stable non-enzymatic protein appears to block neuromuscular transmission by acting on the post-synaptic membrane, and may thus affect the motor nerve terminals. It has a specific action in blocking the effects of acetylcholine. Presynaptic neurotoxins, cardiotoxins , myotoxins, coagulants and anticoagulants, enzymes and nonenzymes are all present. The damage to cellular membranes is the reason for muscle breakdown and the release of potassium and enzymes into the blood. Autopsy findings include patchy and selective necrosis of skeletal muscles, and tubular damage in the kidneys if the illness lasts longer than 48 hours.

Ciguatera toxin

The main toxin, ciguatoxin, is heat stable and partly water soluble. It is probably a highly oxygenated, white solid lipid (M.W.1112), and $C_{60}H_{86}O_{19}$ has been suggested as the formula. It is a sodium channel agonist and resembles the toxins found in red tide poisonings, some sponges and moray eel viscera. Other toxins are probably also present, producing variable clinical findings.

In experimental animals there may be a cholinomimetic action in which stimulation of autonomic ganglion seems to be the most obvious initial effect. Low doses produce a reduction in heart rate and blood pressure (cholinergic) followed by increases in these (adrenergic), arrhythmias and heart failure.

Ciguatoxin has been reported to cause an opening of the sodium channels. It is lipid soluble and affects the voltage sensitive sodium channels in nerves and muscles , causing pores to open and remain open (partly countered by calcium or tetrodotoxin) resulting in sodium transfer into the cells and a resultant swelling of neuronal tissues (axon and Schwann cells). Nerves then fire in a spontaneous and uncontrolled manner initially, but may later not respond at all. It causes demyelination in peripheral nerves, spinal cord and brain in animals. Direct effects on cardiac, smooth and skeletal muscle are thus possible. Respiratory failure follows a blocking of phrenic nerve conduction.

The mechanism of treatment with mannitol is unknown, but it may inhibit the movement of sodium through the "locked open" sodium channels—related to its competitive inhibition of sodium transfer at the cellular level and reducing the excessive fluid retention in the oedematous Schwann cells and axons.

The presence of ciguatoxin in poisonous fish can be indirectly measured by a variety of bioassays, including feeding the fish to cats or mongooses, injecting extracts into mice, or observing the effects on brine shrimp, mosquitoes or guinea pig heart muscle. A costly and time consuming radioimmunoassay was developed at the University of Hawaii and is now being replaced by a simpler enzyme immunoassay. The preparation of monoclonal antibodies should improve this technique even further, and counterimmunoelectrophoresis is being attempted. A simple poke-stick method of screening fish for ciguatera has been developed by Japanese workers, and the results of field trials are impressive, however reactions also occur with related toxins and some fish species seem more "reactive" than others of similar toxicity.

Tetrodotoxin

The toxin is an amino perhydroquinazoline, slightly soluble in water, and with a molecular weight of 319. It may be represented by the chemical formula $C_{11}H_{17}O_8N_3$ and can be detected by high pressure chromatography. Some in vitro anticholinestrase activity has been demonstrated, but this is not important in vivo. The poison interferes with neuromuscular transmission in motor and sensory nerves and the sympathetic nervous system, because of its effect on sodium transfer mechanism. It also has a direct depressant effect on medullary centres, on skeletal muscle (reducing its excitability) and on intracardiac conduction and the contractile force of the heart. It does not cause depolarisation of nerve and muscle, and does not reduce the sensitivity of the end plate to acetyl choline. Hypotension is due either to the effects on the preganglionic cholinergic fibres or the direct effect on the heart. Respiratory depression may be due to the effect on nerve, neuromuscular function, musculature or a medullary action.

In animal experiments, oral introduction produces lethargy, muscular weakness, incoordination and ataxia. Paralysis is observed first in the hind limbs and later in the fore limbs. Deep reflexes are lost and convulsions may occur. The respiration becomes laboured, and the animal becomes cyanosed. Retching and vomiting are often severe. In cats the oral DL50 of the toxin is in excess of 200 mcg/kg body weight. The minimal lethal dose in mice is approximately 9.0 mcg/kg. Death in mice can be prevented by the injection of sufficient quantities of cysteine to bind the toxin, within 10-30 minutes of ingestion.

P.S.P. toxin (Saxitoxin)

The shellfish toxin can also be found in a variety of shells, especially bivalves, and other marine creatures, including gastropods, crustaceans (crabs) and marine snails. It can affect fin fish and cause their death.

The affected shellfish can be monitored for toxicity, by using a mouse test. The mouse is injected with an acid extract of the affected shellfish, and the toxicity level determines the death time. The material used is a liquid fraction extracted from macerated shellfish meats and injected intraperitoneally. When there is evidence of toxin, there is one of two choices from a public health standpoint. The first is to close the area to shellfish collection and eating, and the other is to continue monitoring until the area is free. The former was chosen following the severe outbreaks of P.S.P. in Alaska, and there has been no official harvesting of clams or mussels since 1947. The mouse test is sensitive to a limit of 58 (expressed as mg per 100g of tissue) toxin level. In the United States, once this has reached 80, no further harvesting of the shellfish is permissible. Once the toxin level has reached 100 there may be moderate symptoms in an adult, with 10,000 producing a lethal limit. In California, the lowest dose causing death, probably from *G. catenella,* is 20 000 MU, whereas from the St Lawrence estuary and the Bay of Fundy, 5 000 MU from *G. tamarensis* was lethal. Obviously the amount of toxin consumed will not only depend on the toxin level in the shellfish tissue, but also the amount of shellfish consumed.

The term "saxitoxin" probably includes many toxins, varying with the geographic locality, the life cycle and species of the dinoflagellate, and modifications carried out by the shellfish. One toxin, identified as P.S.P. or saxitoxin, has a molecular weight of 299 ($C_{10}H_{17}N_7O_4$) and is similar to tetrodotoxin. The protozoa incriminated usually is of the *Gonyaulax* species, also known as *Protogonyaulax, Gessnerium* and *Alexandrium,* and especially incriminated were the *G. catenella* and *G. acatenella* and *G. tamarensis.* In the tropical Pacific, *Pyrodinium bahamense* also contains a similar toxin.

Domoic acid has recently been detected in mussels infected by *Nitzschia pungens.* This chemical affects the same brain receptors as Alzheimers disease and produces an incapacitating headache, short term memory loss, confusion, disorientation, respiratory failure, coma and death.

In some cases, the organism may contaminate at low levels because of various environmental factors, such as the copper content in the form of the cupricion. Along the coast of New England this is of sufficient concentration to suppress the rapid growth and division of *G. tamarensis,* while permitting other phytoplankton to flourish. However, after a heavy rain and flushing of organic material from intertidal seaweeds, as well as estuaries, or a mixing of organic materials from the shallow bottom, the copper would be reduced to non-toxic levels, and then *G. tamarensis* could divide and bloom. Also, with increased organic material there is greater availability of iron compounds, which dinoflagellates require in larger quantities than the amount needed by the other members of the phytoplankton community. Although these hypotheses need testing, it is of interest that along the Maine coast, the area where no toxin has been detected, is associated with igneous rocks, including those from abandoned copper mines. Even the seaweeds in this area have greater levels of copper than elsewhere.

The major effect of P.S.P. is the inhibition of the sodium pump that controls the electrical conductivity of nerves. The major clinical effect of P.S.P. is the respiratory paralysis due to the peripheral action of this toxin, by blocking the conduction in the motor nerves, and also by a direct effect on respiratory muscles. There is a little evidence to incriminate a medullary paralysis, and possibly the poison may not pass the blood brain barrier. P.S.P. also has a vasodepressant action producing hypotension in experimental animals, together with conduction defects in the heart.

References and Recommended Reading

BALDRIDGE H.D. (1974) *Shark Attack.* Berkley, New York.

BAGNIS R. (1973) *Fish Poisoning in the South Pacific.* South Pacific Commission Publications Bureau, Sydney.

BAGNIS R., SCHEUER P.J. (1985) "Ciguatera and other reef seafood poisoning." In *Proceedings of the Fifth International Coral Reef Congress,* Tahiti, Vol 4.

BARNES J.H. (1964) "Cause and effect in Irukandji stingings." *Med J Aust* 1:897-904.

BARSS P.G. (1982) "Injuries caused by garfish in Papua and New Guinea." *The British Medical Journal,* Vol 284 9.10:77-79.

BASLOW M.H. (1969) *Marine Pharmacology.* The Williams and Wilkins No., Baltimore, Maryland.

BULLETIN SUPPLEMENT of the Post Graduate Committee in Medicine, University of Sydney, (1963). Gilbert P Whitley 4.05, Vol 18, No 3.

BURNETT J.W., CALTON G.J. (1987) "Jellyfish envenomation syndromes updated." *Ann Emerg Med* 16:1000-1005.

CLELAND J.B., SOUTHCOTT R.V. (1965). "Injuries to Man from Marine Invertebrates in the Australian Region." *National Health and Medical Research Council, Special Report Series No 12,* Commonwealth of Australia, Canberra, ACT.

COPPLESON V.M. (1958) *Shark Attack.* Angus and Robertson, Sydney.

CHUBB I.W., GEFFEN L.B. (1979) *Neurotoxins, Fundamental & Clinical Advances.* Adelaide University Union Press.

DAVIES D.H. (1964) *About Sharks and Shark Attack.* Shuter and Shooter, Pietermaritzburg.

ELLIS R. (1975) *The Book of Sharks.* Grosset and Dunlap, New York.

FENNER P.J., WILLIAMSON J., CALLANAN V.L., AUDLEY L. (1986) "Further understanding of, and new treatment of 'Irukandji' sting." *Med J Aust* 145:569-574.

FISHER A.A. (1978) *Atlas of Aquatic Dermatology.* Grune & Stratton, New York.

FLACHSENBERGER W., HOLMES N.J.C., LEIGH C., KERR, D.I.B. (1987) Properties of the extract and the spicules of the dermatitis inducing sponge Neofibularia mordens Hartman. *Clin Toxicol.* 25(4): 255-272.

GARNET J. (1968) *Venomous Australian Animals Dangerous to Man.* Commonwealth Serum Laboratories, Parkville, Victoria.

GLASSER D.B., NOELL M.J., BURNETT J.W. et al. (1992) "Ocular jellyfish stings." *Opthalmology* 99:1414-1418.

HABERMEHL G.G. (1981) *Venomous Animals and their Toxins.* Springer-Verlag, New York.

HALSTEAD B.W. (1959) *Dangerous Marine Animals.* Cornell Maritime Press, Cambridge, Maryland.

HALSTEAD B.W. (1959) *Poisonous and Venomous Marine Animals of the World.* US Govt. Printing Office, Washington DC

HELM T. (1976) *Dangerous Sea Creatures.* Funk & Wagnalls, New York.

HERCEG I. (1987) *SPUM Journal* 17(2): 95-96, Re Irukandji Stings.

JOHNSON R.H. (1978) *Sharks of the Tropical and Temperate Seas.* Les Editions Du Pacifique, Singapore.

KIZER K.W., McKINNEY H.E., AUERBACH P.S. (1985) "Scorpenidae envenomation." *JAMA* 258(6): 55-63

KLONTZ K.C., LIEB S., SCHREIBER M. (1988) "Syndromes of Vibrio vulnificus infections." *Ann Intern Med.* 109:318-323.

MARTIN J.C., AUDLEY I. (1990) "Cardiac failure following Irukandji envenomation." *Med J Aust,* 153:164-166.

MORROW J.D., MARGOLIES G.R., ROWLAND J., ROBERTS L.J. (1991) "Evidence that histamine is the causative toxin of scombroid fish poisoning." *New Engl J Med.* 324:716-720, 766-768.

PALAFOX N.A., JAIN, L.G., PINANO, A.Z. et al. (1988) "Successful treatment of ciguatera fish poisoning with intravenous mannitol." *JAMA* 259:2740-2742.

PICKWELL G.V., EVANS W.E. (1972) *Handbook of Dangerous Marine Animals for Field Personnel.* NUC TP 324 (Available from Dr GV Pickwell, Dangerous Animals Research Program, Code 5045, Bldg 149, Naval Undersea Centre, San Diego, California 92132).

RAGELIS E.P. (1993) "Seafood Toxins." In ACS Symposium Series, No 262, *Seafood Toxins,* Ed by Edward P Ragelis, Published by American Chemical Society.

RUSSELL F.E. (1971) *Marine Toxins and Venomous and Poisonous Marine Animals.* T.F.H. Publications, Inc.

SAFAR P., BIRCHER N.G. (1988) *Cardiopulmonary Cerebral Resuscitation.* Saunders, London.

Sharks(1985) Brochure from Natal Anti-Shark Measures Board.

SHARKS: Silent Hunters of the Deep. (1986) *Readers Digest,* Sydney.

SMITH M.M. *Sea and Shore Dangers.* J.L.B. Smith Institute of Ichthyology.

SOUTHCOTT R.V. "The neurological effects of noxious marine creatures." In Contemporary Neurology Series' *Neurological Problems in Oceania.* Ed by R W Hornabrook, F .A. Davis and Co Philadelphia.

SUTHERLAND S. (1983) *Australian Animal Toxins.* Oxford Australia.

SWIFT A.E.B., SWIFT T.R.(1993) "Ciguatera." *Clinical Toxicology,* 31(1), 1-29.

TORDA T.A., SINCLAIR E., ULYATT D.B. (1973) "Puffer fish (Tetrodotoxin) Poisoning." *Med J Aust* 1: 599-602.

TU A.T. (1987. "Biotoxicology of sea snake venoms." *Ann Emerg Med.* 16:1023-1026.

VICK J., PICKWELL G., PHILLIPS S.J. (1990) "Studies on the toxicity and treatment of sea snake venom and sea snake envenomation." *Proceedings of the 15th Meeting of the EUBS,* Eilat.

WILLIAMSON J. (1985) *The Marine Stinger Book.* 3rd Edition, published by Surf Life Saving Association of Australia, Brisbane.

WALLETT T. (1983) *Shark Attack in Southern African Waters.* Struik, Cape Town.

NOTE: Other references are recorded throughout the text and in the appendices.

Acknowledgments

In compiling the information for this book, the most unexpected consequences were the bonds of friendship which were forged. Many marine biologists, fishermen, divers, pharmacologists, physicians and photographers who were once known to me only by reputation, are now old and trusted friends. The co-operation and generosity of this large number of people and organisations can never be adequately acknowledged. An abbreviated and inappropriately unemotional recognition to some of these contributors is now given.

AUSTRALIAN MUSEUM
Dr D. Hoese, Assistant Curator of Fishes, Dr Pat Hutchings, Curator of Worms and Echinoderms, Dr John Paxton, Curator of Fishes, Miss E. Pope, formerly Curator of Worms and Echinoderms, Dr Frank Talbot, Director. Jim Davies, Neil Bruce and Eleanor Williams, Marine Biologists.

OTHER MUSEUMS
Dr R J McKay, W.A. Museum. Dr R.A. Wilson, W.A. Museum. Dr. J.F. Yaldwyn, Dominion Museum, Wellington, N.Z.

MARINE BIOLOGISTS
Dr Gerry Allen, W.A. Museum. Mr Peter Ayres, Chief, Division of Fisheries, NSW Govt. Mr Ralph Collier, Shark Research Committee Inc, California. Mrs Beulah Davis, Natal Anti-Shark Measures Board, South Africa. Mr U. Erich Friese, Sydney Aquarium. Mr Richard H. Johnson, S.E.A. Institute, California. Dr George Lewbel, California. Mr John McCosker, Steinhart Aquarium, San Francisco, California. Dr David Pollard, Fisheries Research Institute, NSW. Dr Julian Pepperell, Fisheries Research Institute, NSW. Dr George Pickwell, U.S.N. Undersea Centre, San Diego, California. Mrs Margaret M. Smith, J.L.B. Smith Institute of Ichthyology, South Africa. Dr Walter Starck, Research Associate, Australian Museum. Mr John West, Taronga Park Zoo, Sydney. Mr Eric Worrell, Director, Australian Reptile Park.

UNIVERSITIES
Dr Joe Baker, James Cook University, Townsville, Queensland. Dr A.H. Banner, University of Hawaii. Dr Cyril Burdon-Jones, James Cook University, Qld. Dr Keith Caincross, Macquarie University, NSW. Dr W.A. Dunson, James Cook University, Qld. Dr Robert Endean, University of Queensland. Dr Robert Hartwick, James Cook University, Qld. Dr Bruce McMillen, University of Sydney, NSW. Dr Martin Rayner, Department of Physiology, University of Hawaii.

GOVERNMENT/OFFICIAL DEPARTMENTS
Dr W.R. Lane, Commonwealth Serum Laboratories, Melbourne. Dr W.A. Langsford, Department of Health, Darwin. Dr Shirley Freeman, Defence Standards Laboratory, Melbourne. Surf Life Saving Association of Australia.

PHYSICIANS
Dr Chris Acott, Royal Adelaide Hospital, South Australia. Dr R. Bagnis, Louis
Malarde Institute of Medical Research, Tahiti. Dr J. Barnes, Cairns. Dr Peter
Barss, Provincial Hospital, Milne Bay, Papua New Guinea. Sir Victor Copple-
son, Sydney. Dr John Clift, Darwin. Dr R.M. Douglas, Queensland. Dr Peter
Fenner, Queensland. Dr Bruce W. Halstead, California. Dr Richard Lee, St Vin-
cents Hospital, Sydney. Dr Christopher Lowry, Diving Physician, Sydney. Dr
William Orris, San Diego. Dr Hans Pacy, Tea Gardens, NSW. Dr A.G. Slark.
Consultant Medical Adviser to R.N.Z.N. Dr R.V. Southcott, Hon. Zoologist to
the South Australian Museum. Dr Straun Sutherland, The Commonwealth
Serum Laboratories, Melbourne. Dr John Williamson, South Australia.

DIVERS
Carl Atkinson, Darwin. Wade Doak, Editor and Publisher of "Dive South Pacific." Clarrie Lawler, Research Associate, Australian Museum. Malcolm McLeod,
of the Diving Company, Sydney. Dee Scarr, Bonaire. Jim Joiner, College of
Oceaneering.

PHOTOGRAPHERS
Gregory S. Boland, Walter Deas. Keith Gillett, Research Associate of the Aus-
tralian Museum. Douglas Henderson. Philip Lane. Steve Parrish. Val and Ron
Taylor.

ROYAL AUSTRALIAN NAVY
Dr Robert Thomas. Keith Gray. John Manley. John Pennefather. Mrs. N. Miller,
Librarian.

Acknowledgment is also given to the publishers and authors of *Diving and Subaquatic Medicine,* 2nd Edition, 1981, for permission to extract both text and diagrams; and the National Heart Foundation for permission to reproduce their
C.P.R. diagrams.

Index

NOTES